WARRIOR MINDSET

FIRST EDITION

LIBRARY OF CONGRESS CATALOGING-IN-PUBLICATION DATA

ASKEN, MICHAEL J. & DAVE GROSSMAN.
WARRIOR MINDSET: MENTAL TOUGHNESS SKILLS FOR A NATION'S DEFENDERS
& PERFORMANCE PSYCHOLOGY APPLIED TO COMBAT / MICHAEL J. ASKEN
& DAVE GROSSMAN.—1ST ED.

10   9   8   7   6   5   4   3   2

PRINTED ON RECYCLED PAPER

PUBLISHED IN THE UNITED STATES OF AMERICA BY WARRIOR SCIENCE PUBLICATIONS

WARRIOR MINDSET

MENTAL TOUGHNESS SKILLS FOR A NATION'S DEFENDERS

PERFORMANCE PSYCHOLOGY APPLIED TO COMBAT

Copyright 2009

by Michael J. Asken, Ph.D. & Lt. Col. Dave Grossman
with
Loren W. Christensen

Acknowledgements

> *Great armies and navies are always tempted to fight the last war...*
> *Truly fearsome militaries*
> *prepare to fight the next war.*
> – Thomas & Barry, 2008

It seems reasonable to conclude that to have a full life one would have to be exposed to people who provided inspiration personally and professionally. I have had that good fortune at each of the three stages of my career. This includes personal acquaintances, as well as individuals who, without having met face-to-face, and most likely without them knowing of their influence, have shaped my professional direction.

Early on, Thomas Hackett, M.D. of Massachusetts General Hospital and Harry Abram, M.D. at Vanderbilt University, through their seminal writings on the psychological aspects of illness and medical care, forged my multi-year pursuit of health psychology. Mid-course, Dr. Jerry May of the University of Nevada at Reno, and at that time, Chair of the United States Olympic Committee's Sports Psychology Committee, sparked an interest in human performance excellence and sport psychology.

This work, which represents a third direction and extension of the earlier applications, is largely due to the pioneering work of my co-author, Army Ranger Lt. Col. (Ret.) Dave Grossman. In a Herculean manner, he has inspired, validated and promulgated the importance of the psychological aspects of military performance. His contribution to the well-being and effectiveness of the military and police communities is incalculable. His efforts are clearly the stimulus for this work, which is a small attempt on my part to contribute in a similar vein. His support, his input and his direction I gratefully acknowledge.

The profound impact of the extensive writings and trainings of Loren W. Christensen continues unabated. It is my honor and personal pleasure to have him as collaborator on this work. Much of its effectiveness is directly due to his expertise. While he is listed as a "with," he is, indeed, a co-author.

Ken Murray is another individual who inhabits my pantheon (and I am sure that of many others) of those who have left an essential and indelible mark on police and military training. He has elevated it to a necessary level by developing and championing reality-based training. Beyond that, he has been in the vanguard of integrating psychological awareness into such training.

A cadre of dedicated individuals, many of whom I cite in this book, have sustained my initial inspiration from Lt. Col. Grossman and Ken Murray's work. My colleagues in law enforcement and the military also are instrumental in providing me with inspiration and creating admiration by their actions. In particular, I wish to thank Major Anthony Manetta, United States Army Reserve, for his constant availability, accessibility and friendship.

As always, untold appreciation goes to my family. To Renie for her patience and support. To Kim, who continues the family tradition of service in cardiac nursing. To Kaitlyn, who also furthers that tradition in nursing, but also, as an officer in the United States Navy. To Tristen, who similarly aspires to service through physical therapy, and who, like his sister, also assumes the responsibility of service to and defense of our nation through Naval ROTC. And to Breton, who has not walked his path, but who gives me daily pleasure and reassurance knowing he will succeed in helping others as he already has done so frequently from loyalty.

Finally, though always insufficient, I express profound gratitude and appreciation to this nation's defenders, military and police, all branches of service, men and women, and their families.

Throughout this book, the pronoun "he" is used predominantly for two reasons: editorial economy or use by the reference source. It is in no way meant to slight female military officers and enlisted personnel or female law enforcement officers and leaders who serve with such distinction. Their considerable contribution to excellence is duly noted and appreciated. Their stories are included in this book. Likewise, the term "military" is used to represent all branches of the armed services. The term "warrior" is respectfully applied to those who serve both in the military and our police forces.

Foreword
by Brad Thor

As the son of a Marine, I was encouraged to make my own way early in life. My father had attended college on the G.I. Bill and had built his company from the ground up. His only "spoken" advice to me regarding success was to pick an underutilized niche somewhere in the world of men and dominate it completely. While that pearl has served me well, it was the "unspoken" advice, or more importantly what I learned from studying him, as well as the other warriors in my life, that proved to be the most valuable.

I quickly learned that success in any area of life, be it in the boardroom or on the battlefield, is overwhelmingly dependant upon a person's mastery of their own mind. General Patton once said:

> *"If you are going to win any battle, you have to do one thing.*
> *You have to make the mind run the body. Never let the body*
> *tell the mind what to do..."*

I couldn't agree more and most of the commanders and trainers I know in the military and law enforcement arenas feel the same way.

Yet, we need to ask ourselves, *are we doing all we can to develop a winning mindset in each and every one of our men and women in uniform- and are we doing it consistently?* The answer is quite surprising.

"Mental toughness," "grace under fire," and "nerves of steel" are just a few of the many commendable attributes we attach to human beings who have performed "heroically" when placed under stress. What if we could equip all of our warriors with these attributes?

These days, members of the military and law enforcement communities are being placed in harm's way more often and in more dangerous life-or-death situations than ever before. Psychological counseling after traumatic events has come out of the shadows into the light and, rightly so, is becoming less and less something of which to be ashamed. But have we been too preoccupied with hiding the horse behind the cart? What about pre-event counseling? What if we could help inoculate our warriors and make them more resilient to stress? What if by doing so we made them even more effective, more efficient warriors? What if it not only made them better at their jobs, but resulted in them being less likely to develop conditions that required extensive post event counseling? Wouldn't that kind of training be worth enacting?

High-level, professional athletes receive training on how to deal with pressure, get it under control, and focus on doing what they need to do to win. It's now time we start doing the same thing for our men and women in law enforcement and the military.

Mastery of their minds <u>can</u> and <u>will</u> make the difference between life and death for our warriors. This mastery will not come as a byproduct of physical training, but rather through training explicitly designed to develop, hone and expand the mental toughness of every single man and woman in uniform. As these men and women better develop their warrior minds, three vital things will happen: self-confidence will increase, mission performance (be it on the beat or the battlefield) will increase, and the damaging aftereffects of traumatic experiences will hold less sway.

The mental and physical — psyche and soma — are two faces of the same coin and cannot be separated. To train the world's greatest military and law enforcement warriors, we must realign our focus and esteem their minds every bit as much as we esteem their physical capabilities and skill sets. No longer can we simply train the way we fight and fight the way we train. We need to rethink the way we train and retrain the way we fight.

This exceptional book teaches how to do exactly that and will be the foundation upon which tomorrow's warriors will begin being built today.

New York Times bestselling author, Brad Thor has served as a member of the Department of Homeland Security's Analytic Red Cell Program and has appeared on FOX News Channel, CNN, ABC, CBS, NBC, and PBS as a National Security Expert to discuss terrorism, as well as how closely his novels of international intrigue parallel the real threats facing the world today.

WARRIOR MINDSET

**MENTAL TOUGHNESS SKILLS FOR
A NATION's DEFENDERS**

**PERFORMANCE PSYCHOLOGY
APPLIED TO COMBAT**

INTRODUCTION

Introduction

> The *mind* is *not* a
> *vessel to be filled*, but a
> ## fire to be kindled.
> – Plutrach

There are probably as many different definitions of leadership as there are roles for leaders. There are civic leaders, political, religious and academic leaders. There are "captains" of industry and "skippers" of sports teams. There are leaders by achievement, assignment or necessity. Some leaders are official, others just emerge. Some lead by insignia, some by action, some by both. Some lead in public and some, like the head of a family, lead in private. There are at least ten different theories of leadership and ten times ten books on how to lead.

Despite this complexity of characterizing leadership, or more precisely *effective* leadership, there is one indisputable reality, a requirement common to all those who would effect successful action. They have the ability to handle crisis because they possess the necessary skills to remain calm and functional when others are rendered confused or overwhelmed by difficult circumstances.

Rudyard Kipling, in his famous poetic description of what makes for mature and effective adulthood, wrote in part:

> If you can keep your head
> When all about you
> Are losing theirs
> And blaming it on you ...
> If you can trust yourself
> When all men doubt you ...

This famous 1909 poem "If" was inspired in Kipling after observing one military leader's actions during the Boer Wars (Lt. Colonel Eduardo Jany, personal communication, October, 2007).

Of all the possible opportunities for leadership, however, nowhere is excellence in leadership more necessary, crucial, developed, or honorable than for those who defend our nation in the United States Armed Forces and our country's police forces. Nowhere will a leader be more likely to have to display leadership under perilous circumstances than in the military arena or police operations. Nowhere will the stakes be higher for the leader, his troops or officers, or his country and way of life, than in military service and in protecting our streets. As Major General William Cohen, USAFR, Ret., notes in his book *The Stuff of Heroes: The Eight Universal Laws of Leadership*, decisions may not be as simple as right and wrong, but rather in taking "the harder right."

Thus, those who lead the military and police need to possess not only the concrete skills of leadership, but also the ability to use those skills in times of extreme challenge. Consider the following question: What percentage of success in a military mission or a police encounter is due to physical skills and what percentage is due to psychological skills? (Physical skills refer to such abilities as shooting, physical conditioning, rappelling, and even weaponry. Psychological skills refer to staying focused, making decisions under stress, not getting angry, and not "freaking out").

While, perhaps somewhat surprising, experience shows that up to 90 percent of successful performance is attributed to psychological skills. Rarely is that number reported to be less than 40 percent. This comes from talking with military personnel, police officers, including SWAT Tactical Team members, and other emergency responders who engage in life and death situations

Quite some time ago, Remsberg (1986) addressed this issue in a slightly different way but with the same conclusion in working with police officers. When considering factors that decided the outcome of a critical encounter, factors that decided an officer's "destiny," he suggested the following: In the mentally *unprepared* officer, physical factors accounted for 5 percent, psychological factors accounted for 5 percent, shooting skills accounted for 15 percent, and LUCK accounted for 75 percent of the outcome. In the mentally *prepared* officer, mental factors accounted for 75 percent of the outcome, luck fell to 5 percent and other factors remained the same.

Judy McDonald (2006) conducted an extensive study of the use of psychological performance techniques by Canadian police officers. When asked about the relative importance of factors in front-line policing excellence, the officers indicated that physical readiness contributed 28 percent, technical readiness contributed 32 percent and mental readiness contributed 40 percent.

Officers were also asked to compare the contribution of these factors when contrasting successful versus disappointing performance and response. There was no difference reported in physical readiness (88 percent vs. 88 percent), there was a 10 percent decrease in technical readiness (88 percent vs. 78 percent), but there was a 24 percent decrease in mental readiness (88 percent vs. 64 percent), again suggesting the importance of the mental aspect of police work.

Beckett (2008) citing the work of Marcus Wynne gives advice to:

> **Train with the understanding that firearms practice is 75% physical and 25% mental; however a gunfight is 25% physical and 75% mental.**

On a closer look, perhaps these estimations are not so surprising. The importance of psychological skills in other areas of human performance is well recognized. An obvious example is sport competition. Yogi Berra said:

> **Baseball is 90 percent mental, and the other half is physical.**

While probably a better player and manager than mathematician, he was trying to emphasize the importance of the "mental game." Many athletes and other high-level performers echo his view. The great basketball coach Bobby Knight has said:

> **Mental toughness is to physical as four is to one.**

Major-General F.M. Richardson (1978) casts some doubt on Coach Knight's originality (and also his math), but again underscores the importance of psychological skill in saying that this was Napoleon's dictum and that the ratio was actually that the mental is to the physical as three is to one. He further suggests, however, that Napoleon's words have been "constantly chanted like a magic mantra in military circles."

More to the point are the observations of those who train police and military personnel. Wes Doss (1994) in his book *Train to Win* writes:

> **What I find amazing is that the best edge up on the other guy is in our very head.**

Cole and Seaman (2009) write that as a Plebe at the U.S. Naval Academy, there is a requirement to memorize the poem "All in the State of Mind." One verse particularly reinforces and guides the importance of mindset for the future warriors:

> **If you think you'll lose, you're lost**
> **For out in the world you'll find**
> **Success begins with a fellow's will**
> **It's all in the state of mind.**

John Giduck, anti-terrorism expert and author of *Terror at Beslan: A Russian Tragedy with Lessons for America's Schools* (2005), has written (2008) the following about elite close-quarters combat:

> **Everything else is just technique. If someone has great technique but lacks these essential mental weapons, he will be defeated by an unskilled fighter who has them. This is why many black belts get wiped out by street punks in alleyways.**

John Maxwell (2001) in his book *The 17 Indisputable Laws of Teamwork* wrote about the Navy SEALs:

> **The key to the success of the SEALs is their training – the real emphasis of which is not learning about weapons or gaining technical skills; it's about strengthening people ...**

Maxwell's comments are reinforced by the Lieutenant Commander, Executive Officer, SEAL Team 10 (Drury, 2008):

> **When I first came into the community, our operations were far simpler. Big boat to little boat, little boat to beach, recon or direct action, back in little boat, reach big boat. Today our primary weapons systems are our people's heads. You want to excel in all the physical areas, but the physical is just a prerequisite to be a SEAL. Mental weakness is what actually screens you out."**

The Department of the Army's Field Manual 3-05.70 states about survival:

> **A key ingredient in any survival situation is the mental attitude of the individual involved.**

There is no doubt that the modern military marches on its technology. However, whether it was an ivory-handled Colt .45, à la General George Patton, or is today's Blue Force Tracker, there is a soldier and, hopefully, fully trained warrior who needs to make skillful use of its capability. While technology clearly is essential in modern warfare and law enforcement, the officer and soldier remain paramount. A statement from the U.S. Joint Chiefs of Staff (1997) underscores this:

The purpose of technology is to equip the man. We must not fall prey to the mistaken notion that technology can reduce warfare to simply manning equipment.

Co-author Lt. Col. Dave Grossman characterized the importance of mental readiness this way:

In the end, it is not about the "hardware," it is about the "software." Amateurs talk about hardware or equipment, professionals talk about software or training and mental readiness.

Moin Rahman is a human factors psychologist and proponent of High-Velocity Human Factors engineering and psychology, which is a field that studies man-machine and man-technology interfaces, especially for performance in high stress situations. He has echoed the above observation by stating (2007a):

I learnt a great deal … on the limitations of technology and the limitlessness of human ingenuity.

The importance of psychological skills in what have been called Mission Critical Domains (military, law enforcement, firefighting, emergency medical care) has been gaining increasing attention. Efforts are underway to promote greater application in the field of Human Factors Engineering and Psychology (Rahman, 2007a,b). While the focus of human factors research has traditionally been on human-machine and human-technology fit, and use and interaction, there is now more awareness of what is called *High Velocity Human Factors (HVHF)* that looks at performance and decision-making under stress.

High Velocity Human Factors is defined through its mission statement as "a focus on those instances when the human agent has to perform in an environment where the stakes are high, physical danger is imminent, and the future is unpredictable and the information is incomplete."

The human factors terms for these conditions are states of Equilibrium (non-stress) and Non-equilibrium (stress-filled). The old saying about police work and other mission critical domain responders spending hours of boredom interrupted by moments of intense action and stress has been translated into the term "punctuated equilibrium" by HVHF.

The fact that psychological skills become more difficult and more essential in high-stress situations should not be surprising. Personal protection expert Gavin DeBecker (2008) wrote:

> **Warriors might experience impairments to vision,**
> **judgment and hearing, or they might experience reduced**
> **motor skills – and they will likely experience all of these**
> **during violence – unless the mind and body are integrated.**

Perhaps even more surprising (and of concern) than the importance attributed to psychological skills in effective performance is the lack of or inconsistency of training psychological skills to maximize performance. While there is time allotted (importantly) for training in psychological areas like dealing with post-traumatic stress, domestic violence and even depression/suicide in the military and law enforcement, it appears that there is less time spent training warriors in psychological performance skills. Remsberg (1986) some time ago observed that:

> **... the orphan child of survival training is mental preparedness**

Doss (2003) commented:

> **Without a doubt, one of the most overlooked areas of training,**
> **that probably comes with the greatest amount of limitations,**
> **is that of the development of the winning mindset.**

Ken Murray, an expert, a strong proponent and the voice of reality-based training notes in his book, *Training at the Speed of Life* (2004), an observation about police training by Lt. James Como of the Ocoee (Florida) Police Department:

> **Unlike the committed martial artist or soldier, the average**
> **police officer doesn't spend much time practicing the**
> **physical skills learned in departmental training, much less**
> **the emotional and psychological conditioning exercises**
> **needed to mentally place one "in the zone" when necessary.**

Lt. Colonel Eduardo Jany has served overseas with the United States Marine Corps. He has an extensive military special operations background and he is a police sergeant and tactical team supervisor in Washington State. He has commented (personal communication, 2007) that:

For years, so many of us involved in military or law enforcement tactical training opted for the "sexier side" of our skill sets, working on deadly force, discriminative marksmanship, or defensive tactics, but rarely, if ever, factoring in the mental side and its importance to our success.

Even where the importance of psychological skills is recognized, it's often true that training on how to succeed psychologically, as well as physically, is not taught consistently. Unfortunately, this is often to the detriment of the important contribution that psychological skills and training can have in maximizing the execution of physical skills. Consider this a form of "training tunnel vision" that slows the development of physical and psychological readiness (mental toughness) for many military personnel and officers.

For example, Appendix A of the Military's manual *Survival, Evasion, Recovery: Multi-Service Procedures for Survival, Evasion and Recovery – Army, Marine Corps, Navy Air Force* is entitled "The Will to Survive." It states that survival is by choice not by chance. It suggests that keeping a positive attitude, anticipating fears, combating psychological stress and identifying signals of distress aid survival.

While excellent advice and valuable goals, nowhere (other than suggesting distraction such as focusing on the Code of Conduct, the Pledge of Allegiance, and patriotic songs) is described the *process* of accomplishing, or the psychological steps needed to achieve the ultimate goal of enhancing survival.

This is much like a coach telling players to "put the ball in the basket," without training the skills on how to pass, shoot, or dribble; that is, training *how* to put the ball in the basket. Loren W. Christensen, who has written extensively on the subject of speed development in the martial arts and starred in a training DVD on the subject, says that too many instructors shout at their students to "punch faster" and "block quicker" without ever teaching the physical and psychological elements needed to do so.

Unfortunately, this type of vague instruction is all too frequent in sport, military training, and other areas of human performance, especially regarding psychological skills. This is seen in Richard Machowicz's (2002) *Unleash the Warrior Within*, an adaptation of his ten years of SEAL experience to personal development. Despite Maxwell's comments (cited earlier) about SEAL training strengthening people, Machowicz says:

No one really teaches how to focus, other than to say 'focus.'

He goes on to say:

> **Where did I get the mental ability to make it through the toughest situations? SEAL training doesn't bestow this quality: they want to see who already possesses it. That surprised me when I realized it. I went into the military looking for masters, the people who would deliver all the secrets of the universe.**

From a different cultural perspective, Hasnain in his 1967 book on *Psychology for the Fighting Man* writes of the importance of psychological preparation of soldiers. He suggests that the goals of "man management" are:

> **1) to make men mentally and physically fit for battle.**
> **2) to keep men mentally and physically fit in battle.**
> **3) to restore men mentally and physically after battle.**

Like others, though, his suggestions are of a general nature, such as ensuring standards of discipline, standards of saluting or recovering one's own wounded from the battlefield.

Why psychological skills in military and police training and performance should at once be so valued and yet ignored is a difficult question to answer. There is the narrow view (though not incorrect) that simulation training, live-fire training and various stress challenges create psychological strength. (See Ken Murray's *Training at the Speed of Life* for an excellent argument for the need and description on how to do simulation training). To the degree that such training techniques help to develop mental toughness, consider this *indirect* training and development of psychological skill. Direct training to succeed and excel in these situations is left to chance or is simply assumed.

Thompson & McCreary (2006), in discussing the enhancement of mental readiness in military personnel, note that there are several problems with the indirect or "implicit" training of psychological skills; that is, expecting mental toughness to develop as a result or side effect of physical training and drills. This indirect approach can:

(1) make mental toughness skills harder to learn.
(2) delay the learning of physical and technical skills because of a lack of mental toughness to master difficult tasks.
(3) undermine operational effectiveness because of sub-optimal mental toughness.
(4) result in a sub-group of individuals who never develop sufficient mental toughness.

Thus, physical, scenario-based and even live training does not eliminate the need for direct or explicit psychological skills training. Just as the elite competitive swimmer makes gains in strength and performance by swimming thousands of laps, even more gains are possible by going to the weight room, cross-training and pursuing high-performance nutrition. Explicit and designed training of mental toughness is more likely to be successful.

One thing that is clear, however, is that failure to emphasize direct training in mental toughness skills in military and police training is different from other areas where human performance occurs under pressure. Firefighters, EMT's/paramedics, and athletes can all experience significant demands on their performance. While at one time these professionals were also told to simply manage their stress (or consider that they didn't have the "right stuff"), there has been movement to directly train athletes and responders to develop the psychological skills to engage in maximum performance during high-stress responses. "Get over it" or "Deal with it" has been replaced with training on *how* to get over it or how to deal with it (Asken, 1993, Murphy, 2005).

Many instructors are still unsure about how to train mental toughness skills, despite recognizing their importance. For example, at one SWAT basic training school, trainees were engaged in bus assault drills. On one entry, the armed driver unexpectedly confronted the point man and shot him (using simunitions). The shot officer then stopped in the doorway to examine his wounds, disrupting the assault and bunching the team in the doorway. The instructor, after holding his temper and tongue while he explained why freezing like this was not a good idea, turned to the other instructors, and mused (and cursed), "I know this is so important [mental toughness to continue to fight on], I just don't know how you teach it."

Holmstedt (2007) describes a scene from the war in Iraq: a young marine, pale and wounded from IED shrapnel, being transported by medics on a litter, crying out, "It hurts! It hurts." The author wrote that the medics kept quiet while they ran. "They didn't know what to say. There wasn't anything to say." Much like the SWAT instructor above, rather than being at a loss at to what to do, an enhanced understanding and direct training in the nature of mental toughness may well have given the medics the psychological tools to aid that marine in coping emotionally. (Contrast this example with those described later in this book of military surgeon Dr. Matt Hing who used relaxation techniques to aid in his care of wounded soldiers).

The U.S. Military Academy at West Point has made a major step in this direction by developing a Performance Enhancement Program that uses psychological skills training not only to maximize the performance of their athletic teams, but also to train military skills. Cadets receive individual training, as well as the

U.S. Army Marksmanship Team at Fort Bragg, and the FBI Physical Training Unit (Zinsser, 2004). And U.S. Navy SEAL trainees in the BUD/S (Basic Underwater Demolition/ Seals) phase of training now receive training in and monitoring of their psychological performance maximization skills.

Executive and personal protection experts Gavin DeBecker and his colleagues, in their engrossing and essential book, *Just Two Seconds: Using Time and Space to Defeat Assassins* (2008), make the critical observation that:

> **Professional protectors already know a lot about maintaining physical readiness, but it's the mind that must be first properly prepared, the mind that controls the hands, arms, eyes and ears. There are strategies available to help prepare warriors, based upon knowing how the body responds to lethal combat, what happens to your blood flow, your muscles, judgment, memory, vision, and your hearing when someone is trying to kill you. Police officers, soldiers, and protectors can learn how to keep going even if shot, and how to prepare the mind and body for survival rather than defeat.**

Thus, the psychological factor is recognized in many areas of human performance. It is, in fact, the understanding and use of psychological performance skills that promotes mental toughness. While aggressiveness and the survival (winning) mindset are part of this, there is more to it. Consider our definition:

> **Mental toughness is possessing, understanding, and being able to utilize a set of psychological skills that allow the effective, and even maximal execution or adaptation, *and persistence* of decision-making and physical and tactical skills learned in training and by experience. Mental toughness expresses itself everyday, as well as in high stress, critical situations.**

In a similar vein, Navy SEAL Machowicz (2002) provides important insight about being a warrior (See the Epilogue, as well):

> **Being a warrior is not about the act of fighting. It's about being so prepared to face a challenge and believing so strongly in the cause you are fighting for that you refuse to quit.**

This is echoed by Strozzi-Heckler (2007) who writes that historical and mythical warriors "found their strength and integrity by defeating their own inner demons, living in harmony with nature, and serving their fellow man."

He goes on to describe the merging of the psychological and physical (as well as philosophical and religious) aspects of the warrior:

> There is a certain legacy that distinguishes the warrior
> from war. The sacred path of the warrior is part of an
> ancient moral tradition. It includes…Homer's hero Odysseus
> who outwitted his opponents rather than slaying them;
> the post sixteenth century Samurai who, in his finest hour,
> administered a peaceful government while still maintaining
> a personal discipline and integrity not only through the
> martial arts but the fine arts of calligraphy, flower arranging,
> and poetry. It includes the American Indians who lived in harmony
> with the land and whose ritual wars were exercises in bravery
> rather than slaughter; the Shambhala Warrior of ancient Tibet
> who applied power virtues to spiritual development…

Focused a bit more directly on combat, Russian military psychologists (Shelyag, et al., 1972) echo a similar theme when they discuss "combat mastery":

> Combat mastery is the name given to that professional skill of
> personnel which makes it possible in the best manner to use the
> capabilities and equipment available to personnel for achieving
> victory in combat.

Richardson (1978) reports that Russian officers have written about the need for psychological hardening or tempering of the will, called *psikologicheskaia zakalka*.

No longer can we ignore this aspect of training, no longer can it be an afterthought, and no longer can it be done inconsistently. Kavanagh (2005) stresses the importance of understanding the relationship of stress and performance in the military "given the nature of today's security environment and the challenges faced by military personnel in frequent and long deployments."

As her review further illuminates, the general stressors of duty are considerable, such as separation from family, uncertainty as to when they are returning home, lack of sanitation, lack of privacy, and other similar aspects. Even more significant are the stresses of urban combat: close-quarter fighting, intense firefights, tall buildings obstructing visibility, and an unidentifiable and ever-changing enemy. Cited are reports from Afghanistan and Iraq showing that the rates of ambush/attack or the rates of being shot at/exposed to small arms fire are between 58 and 66 percent for soldiers in Afghanistan, between 89 and 93 percent for soldiers in Iraq and between 95 and 97 percent for Marines in Iraq.

In a parallel comparison, Murray (2005) has eloquently argued that police work is much more dangerous today than in the past. One reason is that criminals are more vicious, deadly, and have a much different (more lethal) mindset than in the past and, indeed, live a different experience from police officers. It's clear that at least certain criminals are better educated in crime and even better practiced in aggressive skills. This comes from learning in jail or from co-criminals who have learned and now teach such skills as close-quarter combat and ground fighting techniques.

Many criminals grow up with a greater exposure to violence; some have been shot and some have killed. All of this is often fueled by drug or alcohol abuse, and a "nothing to lose" attitude. The contrast and implications to police officers who typically have a much different upbringing – close to family, invested in a career, impacted by public expectations, and legal constraints - should be obvious.

Co-author Lt. Col. Dave Grossman's book *On Killing* made the point that killing another person can be quite difficult. Proper training — emphasis on *proper* — is necessary to assure transfer to live combat situations and effectiveness of response. The failure of many American soldiers to fire, even when directly confronted by the enemy in World War II, led to significant changes in training (discontinuation of "bullseye" targets and institution of silhouettes or mannequins and scenario training). The result was seen in changed combat behavior and responses during the Vietnam War (Grossman, 2004).

Being a warrior and a leader of warriors requires the mental toughness to execute your decisions and tactical skills, no matter what the circumstances. Williams (2006) in his article on the psychology of combat says that the Chinese character for 'bu" in the word "bushi" or warrior means "to stay the spear." Mental toughness training can help you do exactly that.

Perhaps one reason for the inconsistency in training psychological performance skills for military, military officers, police officers and police command has been the lack of a comprehensive and structured training program. The psychological impact of high-stress situations on performance — including such responses as high heart rates, tunnel vision, auditory exclusion, etc. — is decribed excellently and importantly in the pioneering work of such authors as Grossman (2004), Murray (2004), Artwohl & Christensen (1997), Siddle (1995), Doss (1993) and others. They have also acknowledged the presence of psychological techniques to help manage the negative impact of stress on performance.

The Army's Jedi Project in the 1980's demonstrated an awareness of the potential of such training by importing a specific form called Neurolinguistic Programming (Alexander et al., 1990). In 1985, the army and marines supported the Trojan Warrior Project, an innovative experiment to assess the impact of the warrior philosophies and disciplines on performance; an attempt to demonstrate the ways "awareness disciplines" could positively influence the military (Strozzi-Heckler, 2007).

Beginning with Remsberg (1986), Anderson, Swenson, and Clay (1995), and Blum (2000) have described in detail some of the *broader* effective psychological training techniques as applied to general stress management and performance for law enforcement officers. Co-author Loren W. Christensen (1999) described psychological performance enhancement techniques for many areas of life in his book, *The Mental Edge-Revised.*

Nowicki (1994) in his book on mental training for maximal performance in combat sports lists requirements for elite performance. These include self-regulation of arousal, intense focus of concentration, a positive focus on the event, being in control without forcing it and possessing determination and commitment. Martial arts expert Scott Sonnon (2001) has also addressed aspects of the psychology of combat sports in a system he describes as combining stress physiology, sport psychology and combat reality. A technique called Stress Inoculation Training (discussed in some detail later) has formed the basis for psychological performance skills training for military personnel (Thompson & McCreary, 2006).

Yet, no one has fully addressed a synthesis of current work in a comprehensive and structured manner; specifically, direction on how to use such techniques for performance enhancement in a variety of military and police skills (including high-stress situations) to manage the performance skewing effects of stress. My (MA) book *MindSighting: Mental Toughness Skills for Police Officers in High Stress Situations* (2005) was the first attempt at a comprehensive description of psychological performance enhancement techniques for police officers.

Thus, the overriding goal of *Warrior Mindset* is to extend this initial work to provide military, police and their leaders with a foundation in the psychological skills of mental toughness that promotes optimal response, and especially in high stress missions and operations. Individual officers and personnel will vary in their need for this training. As in all areas of high-level human performance, some officers and individuals are already highly adept at such skills. We usually want to study these individuals to learn what makes them so effective. But it has also been our experience that even these war-riors can refine their skills, or come to a better understanding of what they are doing, which will result in even more flexibility and effectiveness in fulfilling their duty.

Ideally, we should integrate training in psychological performance skills with training in other specific military, combat and police skills. While I (MA) am always grateful for time to present psychological skills training, my preference is that they are not taught by a psychologist in a separate block, but by the skills instructor (or in tandem with him) as part of the physical training of combat or other skills. Just as the mind and body are not separate and distinct, neither should be so-called "mental" and physical skills training.

Toney Blauer is acknowledged as one of the world's foremost authorities and trainers on combatives, fear management and personal safety. In an interview with co-author Loren Christensen (2004), Blauer emphasized the importance of integrated training:

> **The premise is quite simple: all training should be three-dimensional, i.e., it should blend the emotional, psychological and physical arsenals; anything you work on should connect to some sort of scenario so that, irrespective of the drill, there's an emotional and psychological rationale for the exercise. This way the training triggers and creates connections between all three arsenals.**

Here are just a few other benefits that can occur from implementing the psychological skills training described in this manual. The first is to help maximize the quality of individual skills and overall response of military and police officers and personnel in all situations, not just high-stress ones. A second goal is to enhance the confidence of officers and personnel in handling the many different types of situations and decisions they face. Experience and success are perhaps the best factors in the development of confidence, but psychological training can accelerate the process and provide support, especially early in a military or police career.

A further important application of the psychological skills presented in *Warrior Mindset* is to keep skills fresh. Trainers and trainees in many aspects of military and police skills are well aware of the "stale beer effect": the degrading of skill quality with non-use over time. The fortunate or unfortunate reality is that the need for some (critical) skills can be infrequent and far between use. While there are specific training approaches that help keep skills fresh (Asken, 2005), psychological skills training can also prevent "rust," that is, promote retention of skills.

Solid preparation can reduce the stress of any situation. Therefore, the integration of a mental toughness psychological skills component with military and police skills training in all areas can enhance missions and reduce response stress. With this comes the possibility of reducing post-traumatic stress. Evidence for this has been found in parallel critical incident stress reactions among police officers. Honig & Sultan in a 2004 issue of *The Police Chief* have written:

> **Positive self-talk, and visualization or mental rehearsal, trained to a level of confidence and competence, may be critical to both improved performance under stress and increased resilience after a traumatic incident.**

Finally, the concepts and techniques presented here have application beyond military skills and police work. They are the foundation for excellence in performance in any area of human endeavor and achievement.

Warrior Mindset will provide the concepts and psychological skills for performance enhancement in a practical manner. Therefore, while we provide references to the sources of the content, it's done to a much lesser degree than a typical academic work. The sources are contained in the bibliography. We have used material from these individuals with respect and appreciation for the contributions they provide.

The concepts and techniques described in *Warrior Mindset* provide a basis for psychological skills for enhanced performance. Our understanding of what leads to optimal performance is ever changing, and unique situations and circumstance call for unique adaptations of these concepts and techniques. As this book goes to press, the journal *Military Psychology* just released a special issue (Fiore & Salas, 2008) on "cognition, competition and coordination: understanding expertise in sports and its relevance to learning and performance in the military." The updating of relevant knowledge and the creative adaptation of the material presented here is fully encouraged, as is empirical input.

Psychological skills training is not a substitute for practice, experience and other military, police, and leadership skills training. In their research on the essence of performance expertise, Williams et al. (2008) emphasize the critical role of practice.

They report the following data during one 10-year period: the best violinists accumulated 7410 hours of practice; good violinist practiced for 5301; and music teachers practiced only 3420 hours. Internationally competitive wrestlers accumulated 5881 hours of practice during their careers compared to 3571 hours for club wrestlers.

Especially crucial is practice of *both* physical and psychological skills. Psychological skills, just as with physical skills, need consistent practice to be optimal. There is often a misconception that because something is "psychological," simply hearing about it or talking about it is sufficient for mastery. Nothing can be further from the truth. We are reminded of the words of a piano virtuoso who said:

> **If I do not practice one day, I know it.**
> **If I do not practice the next, the orchestra knows it.**
> **If I do not practice the third day, the whole world knows it.**

Put another way, Maxwell (2001) said:

> **Champions do not become champions in the ring.**
> **They are only recognized there.**

From *On Combat* (2004)

> **Do not expect the combat fairy to come bonk you with the combat wand and suddenly make you capable of doing things that you never rehearsed before. It will not happen.**

Kavanagh (2005) in her report on stress and performance as applied to the military emphasizes that the "most important moderator" for stress for individuals or groups is training. Practice is essential. The concepts and techniques of *Warrior Mindset* are meant to be integrated with other training such as stress exposure training or scenario-based training (Thompson & McCreary, 2006; Salas, Priest, Wilson & Burke, 2006) to provide a truly comprehensive approach to the preparation and performance of leaders and warriors. This can range from recruit training to specialized applications such as Survival, Evasion, Resistance, Escape (SERE) training (Thompson & McCreary, 2006; Steffan, Bluestein, Ogrisseg, Doran & Morgan, 2006).

Also well recognized is that each leader, police officer, soldier, and individual, and each assignment or mission, despite some common characteristics, is unique. Therefore, evaluate and adapt the information in this book for each situation as may be appropriate and comfortable.

Finally, we close the Introduction with two comments. The first is a challenge to be open to trying new ideas. Secondly, while we use the term "leader" throughout this book, we do not restrict this meaning to only commissioned officers in the military and law enforcement command staff. It is critical to emphasize the fundamental necessity for NCO's to be familiar with the concepts of mental toughness. There can be little argument with generalizing from the statement of General Jim Jones, former commandant and NATO commander, that: "Sergeants run the Marine Corps (Brady, 2007)." The same is true for police agencies. Further, this information is for all "leaders," for we recognize that within any military or police unit, there are the appointed leaders and then there are the "emergent" leaders, those who lead by their actions and inspiration, whether or not wearing the official insignia.

We like to think of leadership as used by Iraqi war veteran, Army Lt. Colonel/Chaplain and Pennsylvania State Police Chaplain, Douglas A. Etter. He sees LDERSHIP (personal communication, 2007) as comprised of:

L oyalty
D uty
R espect
S elfless Service
H onor
I ntegrity
P ersonal Courage

This leadership is obviously more a matter of what is in a warrior's heart and head than what insignia are on the uniform.

The information in this book has application for all military and police. When mastered, share it with those under your command, those you influence and with those you inspire. It's not meant to be hoarded for rank or for isolated benefit. A core attribute of the effective leader is the act of inspiring and developing others. Leaders model by their actions. They teach their values and skills. Openness to learning and inspiring others as leadership attributes is summed up in a philosophy espoused by Newt Gingrich when he was Speaker of the U.S. House of Representatives (Zakaria, 2005). Known for anything but being "weak-kneed and soft," he often spoke of the need to:

Listen, learn, help and lead.

The great statesman Benjamin Disraeli said:

> **The secret of success in life is for a man to be ready for his time when it comes.**

It is our hope that this book will help you and those you depend upon to be fully prepared at your moment, whether it arrives by choice or circumstance.

Inspection, Qualification and Review:
Screening Procedures

chapter

There is **no darkness**
but **ignorance.**

– **Shakespeare**

Both military and police leaders are well aware that a fundamental requirement for success on a mission is to acquire accurate and useful intelligence. Knowing — "What you got," in police and military parlance — information on the background of a situation gives direction as to where to start and where to go. In the 4th Century B.C., Seneca observed:

If a man does not know to what port he is steering, no wind is favorable.

The same is true for successfully learning the psychological skills for maximizing your physical skills. Knowing "what *you* got" in terms of personal mental toughness and psychological abilities allows you to efficiently use your time and energy to enhance your military and police skills.

MENTAL TOUGHNESS PSYCHOLOGICAL SKILLS PROFILE

Given your position, you already have considerable psychological skills. However, completing the Mental Toughness Psychological Skills Profile (MTPSP) helps you better understand the skills you're already using, as well as how to enhance them even further. It will also introduce you to new skills and highlight areas that you need to strengthen.

Please indicate how often each statement on the MTPSP is true for you or how often it applies to you. There are no trick questions so there is no benefit in trying to make yourself look good or make yourself look more skillful than you are. You would not attempt a snow job with physical skills or leadership training so you should not do it here. It's most helpful when you're open and honest in responding to the statements.

Here is how to complete the MTPSP. For each statement, circle or place an X on the number and descriptor that corresponds best with how often the statement is true for you. The choices are:

Almost Always (True)
Often (True)
Sometimes (True)
Seldom (True)
Almost Never (True).

For example, responses from a warrior who feels that question 1 is "often" true and feels that question 2 is "sometimes" true would look like this:

1. I can stay steady when things go badly.

5	**X** 4	3	2	1
almost always	often	sometimes	seldom	almost never

2 I can become stressed or scared on a mission.

1	2	**X** 3	4	5
almost always	often	sometimes	seldom	almost never

Now do the same with the full Mental Toughness Psychological Skills Profile.

MTPSP

1. I can stay steady when things go badly.

5	4	3	2	1
almost always	often	sometimes	seldom	almost never

2. I can become stressed or scared on a mission.

1	2	3	4	5
almost always	often	sometimes	seldom	never

3. I can become distracted and lose my focus when on a mission.

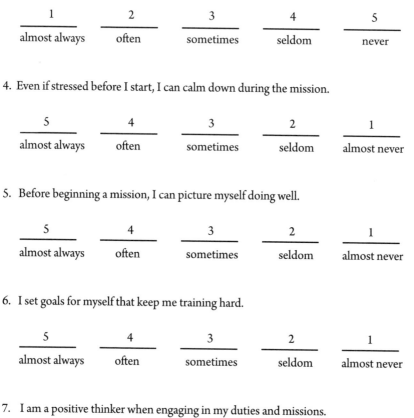

1	2	3	4	5
almost always	often	sometimes	seldom	never

4. Even if stressed before I start, I can calm down during the mission.

5	4	3	2	1
almost always	often	sometimes	seldom	almost never

5. Before beginning a mission, I can picture myself doing well.

5	4	3	2	1
almost always	often	sometimes	seldom	almost never

6. I set goals for myself that keep me training hard.

5	4	3	2	1
almost always	often	sometimes	seldom	almost never

7. I am a positive thinker when engaging in my duties and missions.

5	4	3	2	1
almost always	often	sometimes	seldom	almost never

8. I eat at least two good balanced meals per day.

5	4	3	2	1
almost always	often	sometimes	seldom	almost never

9. I can lose my confidence very quickly.

1	2	3	4	5
almost always	often	sometimes	seldom	never

10. My body feels good, "pumped," and ready to go when on a mission.

5	4	3	2	1
almost always	often	sometimes	seldom	almost never

11. My thinking can get "foggy" during a mission.

1	2	3	4	5
almost always	often	sometimes	seldom	never

12. Even if I am not motivated for a mission, I can "psych" myself up.

5	4	3	2	1
almost always	often	sometimes	seldom	almost never

13. I mentally practice my tactical and leadership skills.

5	4	3	2	1
almost always	often	sometimes	seldom	almost never

14. I need to be told or pushed to train more.

1	2	3	4	5
almost always	often	sometimes	seldom	never

15. I can become excessively self-critical of myself during a mission.

1	2	3	4	5
almost always	often	sometimes	seldom	never

16. I sleep at least seven hours every night.

5	4	3	2	1
almost always	often	sometimes	seldom	almost never

17. I'm mentally tough in my skill performance and leadership.

5	4	3	2	1
almost always	often	sometimes	seldom	almost never

18. I get angry or frustrated easily by problems during a mission.

1	2	3	4	5
almost always	often	sometimes	seldom	never

19. I find myself thinking of past errors and mistakes during a mission.

1	2	3	4	5
almost always	often	sometimes	seldom	never

20. I can keep my emotions positive and in control when on a mission.

5	4	3	2	1
almost always	often	sometimes	seldom	almost never

21. Picturing myself performing my tactical military/police skills is easy for me.

5	4	3	2	1
almost always	often	sometimes	seldom	almost never

22. At my level of expertise, I know all I need to know.

1	2	3	4	5
almost always	often	sometimes	seldom	never

23. I can change negative moods into positive ones by controlling my thinking.

5	4	3	2	1
almost always	often	sometimes	seldom	almost never

24. I smoke cigarettes or cigars.

1	2	3	4	5
almost always	often	sometimes	seldom	never

25. I fully trust my ability.

5	4	3	2	1
almost always	often	sometimes	seldom	almost never

26. I wish my body wouldn't get so "revved" up during a mission.

1	2	3	4	5
almost always	often	sometimes	seldom	never

27. My concentration is rock solid and hard to shake.

5	4	3	2	1
almost always	often	sometimes	seldom	almost never

28. I can clear any interfering emotions quickly and refocus on my skills.

5	4	3	2	1
almost always	often	sometimes	seldom	almost never

29. I mentally rehearse my actions for difficult situations as a way to practice my skills.

5	4	3	2	1
almost always	often	sometimes	seldom	almost never

30. I get bored, burned out and easily demotivated.

1	2	3	4	5
almost always	often	sometimes	seldom	never

31. My superiors and team members would say I have a good attitude.

5	4	3	2	1
almost always	often	sometimes	seldom	almost never

32. I use fewer than five alcoholic drinks per week.

5	4	3	2	1
almost always	often	sometimes	seldom	almost never

33. My expectation is to always succeed in my duty assignments and missions.

5	4	3	2	1
almost always	often	sometimes	seldom	almost never

34. I worry that I might lose it under pressure.

1	2	3	4	5
almost always	often	sometimes	seldom	never

35. My main focus during a mission is using my skills for achieving the goal.

5	4	3	2	1
almost always	often	sometimes	seldom	almost never

36. If I am too "juiced" or too "wired," I can calm myself down.

5	4	3	2	1
almost always	often	sometimes	seldom	almost never

37. It's hard to get a clear image in my mind of myself performing on a mission.

1	2	3	4	5
almost always	often	sometimes	seldom	never

38. Doing my duty gives me a strong sense of pride and honor.

5	4	3	2	1
almost always	often	sometimes	seldom	almost never

39. I worry a lot before or during a mission.

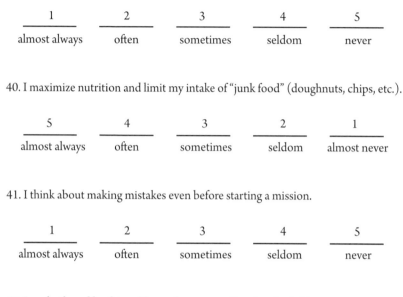

1	2	3	4	5
almost always	often	sometimes	seldom	never

40. I maximize nutrition and limit my intake of "junk food" (doughnuts, chips, etc.).

5	4	3	2	1
almost always	often	sometimes	seldom	almost never

41. I think about making mistakes even before starting a mission.

1	2	3	4	5
almost always	often	sometimes	seldom	never

42. I am bothered by things like my heart pounding, hands shaking or "butterflies" in my stomach during a mission.

1	2	3	4	5
almost always	often	sometimes	seldom	never

43. I find myself "hoping" to do well rather than being confident about doing well on a mission.

1	2	3	4	5
almost always	often	sometimes	seldom	never

44. I worry about "Choking" or "Freezing" at a critical time.

1	2	3	4	5
almost always	often	sometimes	seldom	never

45. When I mentally rehearse my skills, I can really feel all my senses rather than just "seeing myself" respond. (I can see, hear, feel, taste & smell the situation).

5	4	3	2	1
almost always	often	sometimes	seldom	almost never

46. The greater and more difficult the challenge, the better I like it.

5	4	3	2	1
almost always	often	sometimes	seldom	almost never

47. It's hard to clear negative thoughts if they enter my mind.

1	2	3	4	5
almost always	often	sometimes	seldom	never

48. I do regular aerobic exercise at least 30 minutes at a time at least three days per week.

5	4	3	2	1
almost always	often	sometimes	seldom	almost never

49. I worry I will face a situation I cannot handle.

1	2	3	4	5
almost always	often	sometimes	seldom	never

50. If there was a safe and legal substance I could "take" to keep myself calm during missions, it would really help me.

1	2	3	4	5
almost always	often	sometimes	seldom	never

51. Dring a mission, my attention is more on my body's feelings than on my skills.

1	2	3	4	5
almost always	often	sometimes	seldom	never

52. Just thinking about going on or leading a mission makes me nervous.

1	2	3	4	5
almost always	often	sometimes	seldom	never

53. When I mentally rehearse my mission skills, I can actually feel the movements.

5	4	3	2	1
almost always	often	sometimes	seldom	almost never

54. I doubt if I really want to do this type of assignment.

1	2	3	4	5
almost always	often	sometimes	seldom	never

55. Making a mistake distracts me from going on to complete the mission confidently or effectively.

1	2	3	4	5
almost always	often	sometimes	seldom	never

56. I drink more than three cups or glasses of caffeinated beverages (coffee, iced tea, coke, etc.) per day.

1	2	3	4	5
almost always	often	sometimes	seldom	never

When you have completed the MTPSP, score your results on the Mental Toughness Psychological Skills Profile Scoring Sheet. Notice that there are eight categories on the scoring sheet with numbers below them. These numbers correspond with the statements you just completed. Transfer the number that indicates your level of agreement with a specific statement and enter it in the space next to the same number on the scoring sheet.

For example, if for Question 1, you circled or placed an X on "Often," you should write the number 4 in the space for question 1 under the category, Confidence. If you circled or placed an X on "Sometimes" for Question 2, you should write the number "3" in the space for question 2 under the category, Physical Arousal. Continue to do this for all of the statements, transferring the number representing your level of agreement with the statement to the corresponding space on the scoring sheet.

When you have finished, add up the numbers to get your total score for each category. You can now graph these scores on the Mental Toughness Psychological Skills Profile to get a visual representation of your skill profile.

MENTAL TOUGHNESS
PSYCHOLOGICAL SKILLS PROFILE
SCORING SHEET

Confidence	Physical Arousal	Attention Control	Arousal Control	Imagery Use	Commitment	Self-Talk Use	Physical Condition
1. ___	2. ___	3. ___	4. ___	5. ___	6. ___	7. ___	8. ___
9. ___	10. ___	11. ___	12. ___	13. ___	14. ___	15. ___	16. ___
17. ___	18. ___	19. ___	20. ___	21. ___	22. ___	23. ___	24. ___
25. ___	26. ___	27. ___	28. ___	29. ___	30. ___	31. ___	32. ___
33. ___	34. ___	35. ___	36. ___	37. ___	38. ___	39. ___	40. ___
41. ___	42. ___	43. ___	44. ___	45. ___	46. ___	47. ___	48. ___
49. ___	50. ___	51. ___	52. ___	53. ___	54. ___	55. ___	56. ___
TOTALS	___	___	___	___	___	___	___

MENTAL TOUGHNESS PSYCHOLOGICAL SKILLS PROFILE

	Confidence	Physical Arousal	Attention Control	Arousal Control	Imagery Use	Commitment	Self-Talk Use	Physical Condition
35 –								
31 –				YOU'RE IN COMMAND				
30 –								
25 –				YOU PASSED MUSTER				
20 –								
15 –				NO MEDALS YET				
10 –								
5 –				BASIC TRAINING TIME				
0 –								
	Confidence	Physical Arousal	Attention Control	Arousal Control	Imagery Use	Commitment	Self-Talk Use	Physical Condition

What does your MTPSP mean?

Your score will be easier to understand after you have read this book and become more familiar with the psychological aspects of performance. For now, here is a brief description as an introduction:

Confidence describes the degree of faith you have in your ability to respond effectively in any situation.

Physical Arousal represents how positive your physical and psychological arousal is during a mission.

Attention Control describes how well you believe you can stay focused during your mission and response.

Arousal Control reflects the degree to which you can control the effects of the adrenaline rush so that they do not interfere with your performance during a mission.

Imagery Use describes the degree to which you can use mental imagery or mental rehearsal to prepare yourself for responding in various aspects of an assignment as a means of preparation for that mission.

Commitment refers to your degree of satisfaction and positive involvement with being a leader.

Self-Talk relates to a specific psychological performance factor that affects how your thinking influences your performance during a mission.

Physical Condition is a brief measure of how well you act to optimize your physical condition.

The higher your score, the stronger is your psychological skill in that area. Specifically, scores in the range of:

31-35 are highly positive and suggest that you're "in command" of those skills.

25 to 30 suggest that you "passed muster;" your skills are maturing.

15 to 24 are ok, but you haven't earned any medals yet; improvement in these areas is still needed.

14 or less, indicates your skill needs a lot of basic training to reach a level of proficiency.

No matter what your level on a given psychological skill, this book seeks to help enhance your performance. A low score suggests an opportunity to add a new dimension to your response and leadership skills. Even if you're "in command," this book can help you understand your skills better, refine them, and use them more effectively.

We challenge you to be the best warrior and leader possible and open to learn anything that improves the quality of your skills. Although some of the techniques discussed in the book might seem odd or uncomfortable at first, the challenge is to not automatically dismiss them, but consider possible use or adaptation.

If you do not accept the challenge for yourself, we challenge you to maximize your skills for the other warriors you lead or with whom you serve in critical and difficult situations. Finally, we challenge you to be your best for the community you serve, the country you defend, the people who are close to you, proud of you, and anxiously await your safe arrival home.

2
chapter

Fit for Duty:
Physical Conditioning and Mental Toughness

Iron rusts from disuse,
stagnant water loses its purity...
ever so does **inaction sap**
the vigor of the mind. – Leonardo DaVinci

It's an overdone analogy to say that the human body is a complex biological machine. Nonetheless, the truth is that the body is your machine, your most basic piece of equipment. It needs attention, care and conditioning.

It may seem odd to find a discussion on physical conditioning in a book about psychological skills. However, it does not require much reflection to recognize why this is important. Tennis great Jimmy Connors has stressed the importance of physical condition:

> **People say I am still around because I have a lot of heart,**
> **but I know all the heart in the world couldn't have helped**
> **me if I wasn't physically fit.**

Because the brain (and the mind) exists in the environment of the body, the quality of that environment is an essential factor in the quality of psychological function. It's a major focus of this book to describe how the mind and body are intertwined, interact and how they need to function in synchrony for optimal mental toughness. True fitness for duty is a combination of physical and mental excellence.

There are many issues to maintaining the machine, everything from performance nutrition, to sleep deprivation, to how mood affects the body's function. For our purposes, however, we will comment briefly on only two areas: exercise and substance/drug use.

EXERCISE AND PHYSICAL CONDITIONING

The importance of body conditioning is clear when we acknowledge that combat and hi-risk calls by the military and police are intense physical and psychological operations. While there are other professions or activities that can be equally intense, military and police response is unique in that physical intensity can initiate immediately, without warning or preparation. (In contrast, athletes arrive two hours before a competition to warm-up and maybe even get a rub-down before they commence their activity). Few other endeavors can require such lengthy and protracted efforts under such immediate and high-stress conditions.

The First Ultra-Athlete/Soldier?

Ultra-performance and ultra-endurance have always been areas of aspiration and awe for elite performers. The Athenian Phidippedes may have been the first model of ultra-endurance. He ran 280 miles from Athens to Sparta to request aid for the Athenians during the Battle of Marathon. After that, he marched and fought in battle in full armor. He then ran 26 miles to Athens to deliver the news of victory after which he collapsed and died of exhaustion. The marathon races of today pay homage to Phidippedes and the Battle of Marathon. Sports science has endeavored to increase performance while safeguarding survival.

Benefits for the Body

The evidence is now clear and abundant that exercise and good physical conditioning produce important benefits. The effects of exercise, especially cardio-vascular conditioning, can reduce resting heart rate, blood pressure and can improve the capacity and efficiency of the heart under stressful conditions. In well-conditioned individuals, the heart rate returns to resting levels more quickly when physical demands are completed.

Exercise improves the power of respiratory muscles, which results in deeper respirations per breath. Untrained individuals must meet their oxygen need by increasing the rate of respirations, which can more quickly lead to respiratory fatigue. The efficiency gained from exercise is therefore important to the warrior. Additionally, exercise benefits cholesterol levels, blood sugar levels, bone health, and the like.

Benefits for the Mind

Research has now shown that exercise is also associated with positive psychological benefits. It can reduce feelings of depression and anxiety and increase one's self-esteem. Regular exercise promotes the release of endorphins (the body's own naturally occurring opium-like substances), which are associated with improved mood and pain tolerance. The release of other substances, such as phenylacetic acid, has been linked to energy, mood and attention. Research now shows that exercise increases blood flow in the part of the brain known as the dentate gyrus, which helps create new blood cells. This area of the hippocampus is involved in memory (Carmichael, 2007).

Individuals who are not fit have greater sympathetic arousal (stress response), while well-conditioned individuals have shown decreased responses to stressors, such as cold and noise. Overall stress tolerance is greater in well-conditioned individuals; they demonstrate a more stable mood and they show clearer mental functioning under stress.

The increases in endurance, strength and flexibility are particularly important. Consider the following. You're questioning a subject during a vehicle stop on the side of the road when, without warning, he bolts and runs down an alley. You pursue him all-out for about 200 yards before you're able to tackle him. Now is when you need the endurance, strength and flexibility to subdue him (and maybe even to survive the encounter). If you're out of shape and depleted by the run, you're in trouble. Even the ensuing tussle can drain your energy quickly if you're not in good physical condition. Clearly, maximal physical condition is a foundation for your success and survival.

In summary, it might be said that physical toughness and mental toughness are closely related. Enhanced physical condition is associated with improved physical and psychological functioning. Here are the effects most relevant to military and police activity:

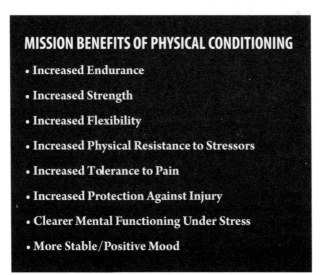

MISSION BENEFITS OF PHYSICAL CONDITIONING

- Increased Endurance

- Increased Strength

- Increased Flexibility

- Increased Physical Resistance to Stressors

- Increased Tolerance to Pain

- Increased Protection Against Injury

- Clearer Mental Functioning Under Stress

- More Stable/Positive Mood

Specificity of Exercise

The Law of Exercise Specificity (Nasi, 2006) is an important aspect of physical conditioning that is gaining notice. It's also been called Functional Conditioning (Coombs, 2008). The concept says that that there should be a relationship and similarity between physical training and the type of field task or skill it's supposed to improve. Besides training just for strength, functional conditioning also considers and integrates speed, agility, power, and movement mechanics into the training.

For example, running ten miles is excellent for aerobic conditioning, but is less effective for training for the intense briefer burst of energy needed to charge a target or engage in a foot chase. There can be significant benefit in assuring that your workout routine reflects your real world of action.

The "ice treadmill" for hockey players is one good example of functional exercise. The Cornell University Men's Hockey Team trainer says that "hockey guys aren't runners." So the ice treadmill simulates skating movements, which develops strength and endurance conditioning for the precise activity in which the players engage. (De Los Rios, 2007).

The Importance of a Warm-Up

One last aspect of maintaining or perhaps preparing the body for a mission deserves mention. It was joked earlier that military and police personnel don't have the luxury of getting to a stadium two hours early to warm-up like athletes. However, this doesn't meanthat it's impossible to warm-up to stimulate physical and psychological performance.

One good reason why athletes and exercisers warm-up prior to their physical activity is because sudden strenuous exertion can create cardiac ischemia, that is, restricted blood flow to the heart, an event that can occur even in healthy individuals. Barnard and his colleagues (1973) demonstrated that without a physical warm-up period, 60 percent of the healthy males in his sample (including some firefighters) showed ischemia or restricted blood flow when engaged in sudden strenuous exertion. This occurred under conditions (sudden intense treadmill) that simulated the kind of bursts of energy that might be needed in an emergency. However, when subjects did warm-ups first, none showed decreased heart blood flow with the strenuous exercise.

Smith (2007) has rightly emphasized the importance of this research for prevention of heart attacks in police officers and the benefit of warming-up when possible. While this momentary reduction of blood flow may not be a problem for healthy conditioned individuals, it can be dangerous for those with underlying heart disease, especially so for people with undiagnosed heart disease.

There are a variety of subtle but effective exercises that can be done in many, if not all situations. The table below contains some possible examples. As noted, these exercises can be done for Cardiovascular (CV), Stretching (S) or just general Warming-Up (WU) purposes. Their mission relevance can vary from preparing to lift and carry heavy equipment, to running up steps, to climbing a steep grade.

Warriors fail to warm-up not because situations don't allow it or because it's without benefit, but rather because doing so has rarely been considered.

MISSION PHYSICAL WARM-UPS

Exercise	Purpose	Response-Relevance
Shoulder Circles	CV, S, WU	Carrying, Lifting
Heel/Toe Taps	CV, S, WU	Steps, Run
Scapular Retractions	S, WU	Carrying, Lifting
Forward Neck Rolls	S, WU	Carrying, Lifting
Back/Side Bends	S, WU	Carrying, Lifting
Toe Raise/Semi Squat	CV, S, WU	Steps, Run

Do it Because it's Good for You

Regular exercise is essential for overall health and longevity. Concerned by increasing accounts of younger officers in their 30's and 40's experiencing heart attacks after strenuous activity on the job, Officer Kathy Vonk in her excellent article (2007) on police and cardiovascular disease presents some controversial but sobering statistics on heart disease and law enforcement:

- Police officers live an average of 15 years less than the average American.
- Death is 25 times more likely from heart disease than from a suspect's actions.

Hoiberg (1985) reported data many years ago suggesting that Navy pilots, on average, were three years younger at the onset of their cardiovascular disease than other Navy officers. He proposed intervention programs to modify lifestyle factors of pilots. Vonk suggests you have the power to control your own destiny by the preventive actions of healthy nutrition and consistent physical conditioning.

SUBSTANCE USE AND ABUSE

We hope it's not necessary to emphasize the problems with substance (drug) use on military and police performance, although it may be more necessary to do so when it is recognized and admitted that alcohol is also included on the list of substances. It's also important to discuss the issue because it often seems that if one uses a substance "to improve performance," warriors and others see it as less problematical and somehow different from "street use."

As an indication of this, one only needs to review the reporting of the Congressional testimony on the use of performance enhancing drugs and steroids in baseball. In all the discussion as to the severity of penalties that should be levied by Major League Baseball against a using player, there was hardly any mention that the substances are illegal and subject to criminal charges. It's a misconception that using drugs to enhance performance is somehow morally and legally different than other forms of substance abuse.

For our purposes here, we don't need a detailed discussion of all the issues surrounding performance-enhancing or mood-altering substances; however, a brief review of the issues with *non-prescribed and medically unmonitored* substance use seems warranted before moving on to psychological techniques for performance enhancement.

Performance Enhancing Drugs	We also recognize that extreme combat and operational circumstances may necessitate the use of certain substances to maintain or maximize performance. Military physicians may prescribe medications such as stimulants or sleeping medications for the health and performance of warriors. The use of antidepressant medication during deployment to help manage the stress and trauma of war is reaching heretofore unseen levels of acceptance and use (Thompson, 2008). However, co-author Lt. Col. Dave Grossman warns that the use of performance enhancing drugs is always subject to exigent circumstances, a risk-benefit analysis, and the recipients' awareness and acceptance of the risks involved. Most importantly, use should always be under the direction and monitoring of a physician.

Alcohol

The social, recreational, and problematic aspects of alcohol aside, some believe that it's a performance enhancer and a source of energy. More often, there is the perception that alcohol is a good general relaxant for performance. Some believe that it can be used to "steady nerves."

The realities are that performance enhancement is unlikely to be a result of alcohol use, especially for military missions and police operations. Alcohol lacks nutritional benefit, it's a source of weight gain, it's a deconditioner, it's addictive and an irritant to the nervous system. As for performance, it slows reactions time, reduces inhibitions, and negatively affects cognition. (While some amounts of alcohol may positively impact some skills to a degree, the amount and effects are variable and difficult to manage).

It's also important to recognize that alcohol-related impairment is associated with tunnel vision. Your visual field starts to narrow at one-half the typical legal limit of .08 blood alcohol level. Ultra-fine muscles that coordinate eye movements become less able to simultaneously process elements from the periphery of your visual field and from your focal point. These effects have been noted as significant in driving skills (Mills, 2005).

Amphetamines and Stimulants

Amphetamines and related stimulants can be controversial when related to performance. Expectations are that they reduce fatigue, increase alertness, and increase confidence. While amphetamines can have these effects, there are major concerns with their use. There can be problematic physical side effects, such as dizziness, rapid heartbeat, dry mouth and nausea. Heat exhaustion is more likely in hot environments and paranoia develops with prolonged use.

Performance effects are problematic because the nature and degree are unpredictable, as are the side effects. Many factors can affect response, from the purity of the drug, to a person's physical condition, to one's unique physiology. It's easy to become overstimulated, "wired," or have a "hair trigger." Leach (1994) notes that methamphetamines can induce perceptual narrowing (tunnel vision/hearing) just like stress.

Caffeine

Caffeine is the "less lethal" form of amphetamines. Although not always thought of as having "performance enhancing" effects, the expectations of caffeine are much the same as those from amphetamines: a reduction of fatigue, increased alertness and resulting increased performance. Caffeine has been shown to decrease rifle-sighting time in conditions of high stress and extreme sleep deprivation, but had no effect on measures of accuracy (Tharion, et al., 2003).

Mullins (2003) discusses his study of the effects of caffeine use in a shoot-don't-shoot Hogan's Alley scenario. Results indicated that the use of caffeine affected fine-motor skills and decision making. Even low doses of 100 mg in 24 hours were enough to impair shoot-don't-shoot decision making. Moderate doses of 300 mg in 24 hours led to decreased performance on motor skill tasks and the highest doses of 600 mg in 24 hours (4 to 7 cups of coffee, depending on the degree of caffeine) were associated with the poorest decision making. Overall caffeine users did worse on all measures and at all levels. Mullins also found decreased performance when regular caffeine users were deprived of using caffeine.

Much like amphetamines, the side effects that are problematic with caffeine include increased heart rate and arrhythmias, blood pressure, urination, panic attacks and insomnia. Because caffeine is an addicting substance, withdrawal effects include increased agitation and headaches. Unpredictable levels of stimulation are a problem for caffeine use, as well.

Anabolic steroids

Given the frequent use of anabolic steroids as performance enhancers (different from corticosteroids prescribed by physicians for various conditions), caution needs to be expressed so that you do not get enticed into using steroids in an attempt to enhance your performance in your duties. The basic expectations from anabolic steroid use are increased strength, weight, bulk, and performance.

The reality is that even with anabolic steroids, you still need to train to produce useful strength and weight gain, and you still need to practice to translate gains into skill and performance enhancements. Use of steroids can lead to negative health effects, such as increased blood pressure, increased cholesterol, hepatitis and liver cancer. In males, there can be worsening acne, decreased sperm, testicular atrophy (shrinking of the testicles), and gynecomastia (development of larger, more feminine-like breasts). In females, the voice may lower, body hair can increase, and there can be menstrual changes. More rapid aging occurs, too.

The psychological effects of steroid use are profound. There can be an increase in general aggression, acute episodes often called "roid rage," as well as, paranoia and psychotic symptoms. Additionally, an opposite but similar problem to anorexia nervosa can also occur. Anorexia involves a distortion in body image such that no matter how much weight a person loses or how thin a person is, the self-view is that of being fat. With steroid use, one can experience a condition called megarexia, in which no matter how strong, cut or ripped an individual becomes, they see themselves as thin, puny, and weak.

While steroids are well-known for being psychologically addicting, it's becoming apparent that they can be physically addicting, as well. Increasing doses are needed to achieve the same result, and athletes have said that they cannot stop using the substance; those who do have reported depression (University of Michigan Health System, 2004).

Physiology or Psychology?

It seems that an individual's expectation, in addition to the biological effects of the substance, may be an important part of performance enhancement. In a study of track athletes, results showed that believing one had taken a performance enhancing substance resulted in times almost as fast as the effects from the drug itself. In contrast, taking the drug without knowing they were doing so yielded no significant performance improvement (McClung & Collins, 2007). As with most things in life, the quick fix for performance is not quick, safe or effective.

However, it's possible to enhance performance in ways other than by just practicing harder. That is the subject of *Warrior Mindset*. For most types of performance enhancement sought by substance use, there are psychological techniques that can also move you to that goal. The next table shows typical performance enhancement goals and the psychological techniques that can help achieve them.

Warrior Mindset is about integrating physical and psychological skills and training for the development of the complete warrior. An interesting model for the recognition of the importance of this is found in Michelangelo's statue of David. According to Dr. Nancy Sherman, who was the inaugural holder of the Distinguished Chair in Ethics at the United States Naval Academy, this statue is probably the best-known representation of the warrior or athletic body. She goes on to state, however, in her book, *Stoic Warriors* (2005), that "Yet in this great statue physical control is at the same time mental control."

David is poised for action and military strategy. His piercing gaze emits determination and focus against a assumed Goliath.

PSYCHOLOGICAL TECHNIQUES FOR PERFORMANCE ENHANCEMENT

	Mood	Increasing Strength & Endurance	Concentration	Confidence	Relaxation/ Arousal Management	Increasing Pain Tolerance
Attention Control Training			X	X	X	X
Biofeedback					X	X
Centering	X		X	X	X	X
Concentration Training			X	X		
Imagery	X	X	X	X	X	X
Music	X	X		X	X	X
Muscle Relaxation					X	X
Selective Association	X				X	
Visuomotor Behavior Rehearsal	X	X	X	X		
Self-Talk	X	X		X	X	X
Physical Conditioning	X	X		X		X

Adapted from Asken, M. (1990). Dying to Win: Preventing Drug Abuse in Sport. Minneapolis, MN: Community Interventions, Inc.

On Alert:
Arousal and Mental Toughness

Victory always *starts in the head. It's a state of mind.*
It then spreads with such *radiance* and such *affirmations*
that destiny can do nothing but obey.

– Douchan Gersi

Military missions and police operations are ultimately about control: control of the target/area, control of damage or injury, and control of the outcome. It's also about leaders and personnel controlling themselves.

AROUSAL

A fundamental requirement for a successful mission is to understand and control arousal, that state that allows you to fight or flee danger at maximum capacity. Arousal is related to the now well-known "fight or flight" response (although there is a third reaction, which is to "freeze"). Much of this is the result of adrenaline and other stress chemicals released in the body during high-stress situations. The effects of the release of these substances — a phenomenon often termed "adrenaline dump" — is well-recognized in military and police missions. It's so well-recognized that it has been said that the "holy grail" for firearms instructors is teaching the management of the effects of adrenaline on performance (Williams, 2004).

Arousal can be physical or psychological, and it's called by different terms, such as "being up", "being pumped," "activated," or experiencing a "preparatory readiness." Let's look at two types of arousal: primary and secondary.

Primary and Secondary Arousal

Primary arousal results from the performance demands of the mission; it should provide the necessary preparatory readiness to respond. Increased energy and enhanced alertness are part of this preparatory readiness and primary arousal.

Secondary arousal results from aspects of the mission unrelated to directly meeting the challenge. It may occur as a result of:

- not feeling ready or prepared.
- concern about danger.
- fear of failing.
- fear of looking bad in front of others, such as squad members or superiors.

The problem with secondary arousal is that it's not skill-focused. Its occurrence and intensity are unpredictable, it's harder to control, and it tends to inhibit effective action in military missions and police operations. For example, a rookie being closely monitored by his field coach on his first high-risk traffic stop may be so concerned about looking good and impressing the trainer that he exaggerates his command presence and his situational awareness techniques.

THE RELATIONSHIP OF AROUSAL AND PERFORMANCE

The concept of arousal is important because it directly relates to how well you may function during a mission. There are two theories about the relationship of arousal and quality of performance.

Drive Theory

The first is called Drive Theory; its relationship to performance is shown here. Drive Theory says that when arousal is low, performance will also be low or poor. It says when arousal is high, performance will be high or good. In short, the higher your arousal is, the better your performance. It suggests that it can never be too high and

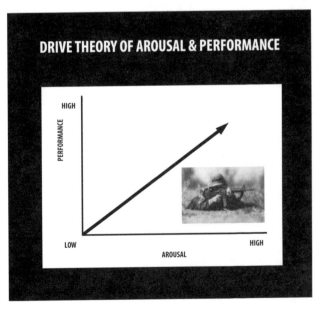

DRIVE THEORY OF AROUSAL & PERFORMANCE

that more is better. This may be akin to football linemen who pound each others' pads and bang helmets to get fired up.

Upside-Down-U or Inverted-U Theory

There is another theory of arousal and performance called the Upside-Down-U or Inverted-U Theory. The formal name is the Yerkes-Dodson Law (Yerkes was involved with psychological military research in the early twentieth century).

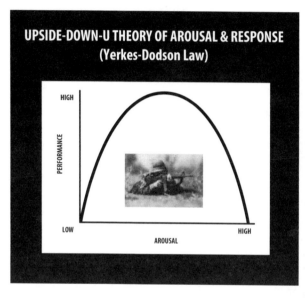

UPSIDE-DOWN-U THEORY OF AROUSAL & RESPONSE
(Yerkes-Dodson Law)

The Inverted-U Theory says that for any skill, task or situation, there is an optimal level of arousal that leads to peak performance. If there is too little arousal, performance will be poor. Likewise, if there is too much, performance will also be poor. Too little arousal fails to make you sharp enough to perform well while too much becomes distracting, gets in your way, and impairs performance.

Which theory do you think is correct?

It appears most support is for the Inverted-U theory of arousal and performance. (Know that "too little arousal" is not the same as being cool under pressure. Too little means there is a lack of sufficient, even minimally necessary physical and psychological readiness to respond to a situation effectively.) Pargman (2006) notes that there is also a model called "Catastrophe Theory" which posits that quality of performance follows the inverted-U curve. However, catastrophe theory suggests that the drop-off in quality of performance after the ideal level of arousal is exceeded is dramatic and precipitous, rather than gradual.

Hancock (Hancock & Szalma, 2008; Hancock, 2009) proposes another variation on the inverted-U curve and its relationship to quality of performance. In a critical tone, he argues that there is not a smooth increase and decline in performance, but rather a flat plateau-like "platform of performance" across which response stays relatively stable. He proposes that when adaptive abilities reach the "edge of exhaustion," performance decreases rapidly and precipitously; this state is characterized by a variability in performance. In recent work Tennenbaum et al. (2008) have tried to mathematically predict the probability of quality of performance related to placement on the arousal curve (U).

In what was truly pioneering work, but today is more of a historical and contextual interest than accurate, *Sharpening the Warrior's Edge* author Bruce Siddle (1995 attempted to link this theory and performance to heart rate based on work by Leavitt (1972, 1973). As can be seen below, he proposed that when heart rates approach 115 beats per minute, fine motor skills deteriorate, and when heart rates approach 145 beats per minute, complex motor skills deteriorate. He notes that when heart rates reach 175 beats per minute or more, there can be, among other problems, a "catastrophic failure of cognitive processing."

115 BPM
Fine motor skills deteriorate

145+ BPM
Complex motor skills deteriorate

175+ BPM
"A warrior can expect to experience auditory exclusion or loss of peripheral vision and depth perception. This initiates a catastrophic failure of cognitive processing capabilities, leading to fatal increases in reaction time or hypervigilance (freezing in place or irrational acts)."
p.7-8

Perhaps more important and predictive of performance under stress than heart rate is heart rate variability. In its simplest form, heart rate variability (HRV) refers to variations in time (measured in milliseconds) between an individual's heartbeats. A growing amount of research suggests that high HRV is a good thing and related to improved health and performance. HRV is seen as an indicator of the degree of reactivity of a person's autonomic nervous system.

Mastering control of HRV has been used to train athletes to readily enter the competitive mindset and peak performance state. While more research is still needed, HRV training may be the next evolution in training maximal response (Asken, et al, 2009).

In *On Combat* (2004), co-authors Grossman and Christensen adapted Siddle's work suggesting that different levels of arousal (as represented by increasing levels of heart rate) can also help or hinder performance. Following Remsberg (1986) and using a system popularized by Colonel Jeff Cooper, they assigned different conditions or status levels as noted below. They suggested that conditions yellow, red and possibly gray (in highly skilled individuals) are optimal for most responses. For example, some Air Force pilots stick yellow dots on their watches or in their cockpits to remind them to stay in Condition Yellow.

The work by Siddle, while pioneering, needs to be considered with caution because the original research on which he based his conclusions was limited. Further, newer research has shown that some elite performers can tolerate higher heart rates without deleterious effects on their performance. For example, in *On Combat*, Grossman and Christensen (2004) wrote that NASCAR drivers can sustain heart rates of around 175 beats per minute in competition.

They also discussed research on elite Special Forces operators tested in stress-inducing close-quarter combat scenarios where performance excelled despite heart rates around 175 beats per minute. However, some skills like threading flex-cuffs (plastic handcuffs) were less efficient at these high rates. Bruce Siddle has recently (2008 re-emphasized this by noting that it is *precision* skills that are highly susceptible to disruption by stress. This is especially true for medics and EMS personnel who have "multiple precision needs" including precision in

STRESS, HEART RATE & PERFORMANCE

200	
180	CONDITION BLACK
160	CONDITION GRAY
140	CONDITION RED
120	
100	CONDITION YELLOW
80	
	CONDITION WHITE

perception, processing, treatment and demeanor. The interested reader might want to look at innovative military and police trainer Chris Sarkis Ghannam's work (2007, 2008) who is involved with developing new training methods that allow individuals to function more optimally at higher heart rate levels.

It also essential to differentiate between heart rates that are elevated because of physical exertion, such as sprinting, (not what we are talking about here) and those elevated due to psychological/emotional stress.

Research with firefighters also shows the differences between exercise versus emotion-induced arousal and how mental challenge can magnify stress responses in the body beyond those with just physical demands. Researchers (Webb, et al., 2006) studied firefighters in two conditions: One was exercising to 60 percent of breathing capacity (physical challenge); the other was also exercising to 60 percent of breathing capacity while simultaneously doing a computerized fire strategy and tactical drills decision challenge (physical plus mental challenge).

There were two findings of interest. First, firefighters in the physical plus mental challenge condition perceived the workload to be harder than in the physical challenge only condition. Further, with the addition of mental stress, there was an elevation of the firefighters' stress hormones: epinephrine (adrenaline), norepinephrine, and cortisol. Thus, the mental or emotional component of stress responses should be differentiated from physical stress. (See Vonk, 1994 for a further discussion on the difference between exercise-induced elevated heart rate and stress-induced elevations on performance).

Nonetheless, Siddle's ideas, especially as refined by Grossman, do reflect the accepted and useful concept that arousal can affect performance and that there is probably an ideal level of arousal for maximum performance for each individual.

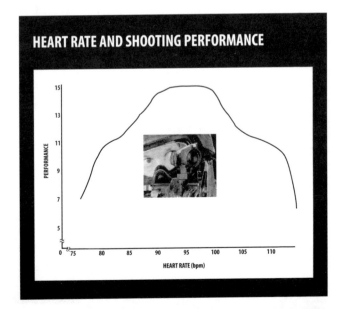

HEART RATE AND SHOOTING PERFORMANCE

As another example of the application of the Upside-Down U theory, research by Landers and Daniels (1985) has found a similar relationship between heart rate and performance for elite-level shooters. As shown below, shooting performance is best with moderate elevation of heart rate.

Janelle & Hatfield (2008) describe the inverted-U effect related to cortical activation (brain activity) and aiming a weapon. They report that while inability to control arousal (too much activation) impedes performance, somewhat surprisingly too much relaxation in shooting can be detrimental, as well. They suggest that excessive relaxation can be seen in shooters prior to deciding to abort a shot.

The inverted-U effects are not limited to physical skills. Essential in any mission is what is called "situational awareness." This has been characterized (Johnson & Proctor, 2004) as the perception of the elements in an environment within a volume of time and space, the comprehension of their meaning, and the projection of their status into the future. This is a fancy way of saying you need to be aware of what's out there, what it means and what it's likely to do, in order to provide an effective response (situational assessment and action selection). The point is that situational awareness is also is affected by level of arousal. Where there is too much, necessary information cannot be effectively processed; where there is too little arousal, the individual loses vigilance. The inverted- U principle has also been found to describe the quality of memory (Staal, et al., 2008) under stressful situations (hurricanes).

However, moving beyond Siddles's pioneering efforts, we find that the relationship between arousal and performance of any type is a bit more complex than just heart rate. There are several factors that affect the relationship of arousal to the quality of performance.

- Nature of skill or task
- Complexity of skill or task
- Experience with skill or task
- Individual characteristics

Nature of the Warrior Skill

Different skills or tasks can allow or actually require different levels of arousal to be performed in an optimal manner. Oxendine (1970) first noted this as it relates to sport. Consider the following.

This chart displays several sport skills and a scale ranging from 5 to 1. Assume that the number 5 represents very high levels of arousal, i.e., you're as pumped as you can get. Also assume that the number 1 represents very low levels of arousal, i.e., you're almost asleep. Write in where you would place each sport skill in terms of how much arousal is needed to perform it well.

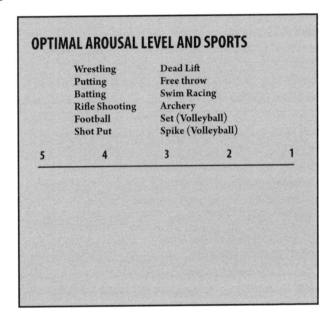

OPTIMAL AROUSAL LEVEL AND SPORTS

Wrestling	Dead Lift
Putting	Free throw
Batting	Swim Racing
Rifle Shooting	Archery
Football	Set (Volleyball)
Shot Put	Spike (Volleyball)

| 5 | 4 | 3 | 2 | 1 |

Here are suggestions as to where the sports skills might be placed for optimal performance.

Wrestling   Dead Lift
Putting   Free throw
Batting   Swim Racing
Rifle Shooting   Archery
Football   Set (Volleyball)
Shot Put   Spike (Volleyball)

5	4	3	2	1

Wrestling   Batting   Putting

    Football   Shooting

Shot Put   Free throw

Dead Lift   Swim Racing   Set   Archery

    Spike

Many references are made in this book to athletes and athletic performance. Of course, there are huge differences between military missions, police operations and sport competition, not the least being the difference in salaries and lifestyle of athletes despite never having responsibility for the welfare of society, safety of others, or having to risk their lives.

Nonetheless, human performance in any arena shares common characteristics. Much of the work done with athletes holds promise for effective translation to other situations. Officer Lou Ann Hamblin, an avid mountain bike officer and competitor, has been reported as commenting on the unfortunate lack of transfer and application of sport psychology performance skills to police work (Murray, 2004). Keyes (1996) has made an application to shotgun shooting. Sherman (2005) notes the ancient Romans, and indeed the ancient Olympics, intertwined military and athletic cultures. Wells (1988) reports that combat pilots, especially during the World Wars, often described sportsmanship and love of sport as part of their combat experience. Nadelson in his book, *Trained to Kill: Soldiers at War* (2005), also notes the similarities between sport and combat and complimentary roles in training required skills. The U.S. Army (2005) has highlighted similarities between soldiers and athletes in their recruiting efforts. Holmstedt (2007) in her accounts of American female warriors in Iraq, reports Captain Amy "Krusty" McGrath, marine aviator, cited as her inspirational role models original Project Mercury Astronauts John Glenn and Alan Shepard. She also named professional athletes, Johnny Bench, Terry Bradshaw and David Robinson. Several years after sport and human performance psychological concepts were introduced into police training, the Journal of Military Psychology published a special issue (Fiore & Salas, 2008) devoted to "understanding expertise in sports and its relevance to training and performance in the military." So with appropriate cautions it is hoped that the principles learned from sport competition and other areas of high-level human performance can enhance military and police response.

Let's consider the same issue of arousal with warrior skills. In the following chart, place each of the skills under the number that represents the ideal level of arousal for their optimal performance. The number 5 represents high arousal and 1 represents low arousal.

OPTIMAL AROUSAL LEVEL AND WARRIOR SKILLS

Breaching Ram	Sighting for Shot
Communicating to Others	Head Lock
Driving Response	Processing Information
Setting a Charge	
Covert Clearing	

5	4	3	2	1

Here are examples of where these skills might be placed.

OPTIMAL AROUSAL LEVEL AND WARRIOR SKILLS

Breaching Ram	Sighting for Shot
Communicating to Others	Head Lock
Driving Response	Processing Information
Setting a Charge	
Covert Clearing	

5	4	3	2	1
Breaching Ram	Head Lock		Driving Communication Covert Clearing Processing Info	Sighting Set Charge

There is no right or wrong response. The point here is to consider that different skills may be performed better at different levels of arousal.

COMPLEXITY OF THE WARRIOR SKILL

Complexity of the task is another important factor as to how levels of arousal affect the quality of performance. Simple tasks use and tolerate more arousal than complex ones. This is why football lineman can and need to get pumped up. Without wanting to insult them in any way, blocking someone as a lineman is less complex than the job of a quarterback, which requires reading the defense, scanning the field, looking for the receiver, defining the target, making a split second decision and throwing the ball to the receiver, all while the field is in a dynamic state of rapid change.

Therefore, in conditions of high arousal, such as a police situation that requires an officer to use his baton, there might be a tendency to use simple skills. The next chart shows data Siddle (1995) reported from research by Garcia (1989) in which officers, in fact, did use more simple techniques than complex ones.

REPORTED FREQUENCY OF USE OF SIMPLE VS. COMPLEX TECHNIQUES FOR THE SIDE HANDLE BATON

Spins	794	34.5%
Jabs	562	24.4%
Chops	296	12.9%
Basic Blocks	182	7.9%
Power Blocks	113	4.9%
Armlocks	238	10.4%
Hooking Techniques	114	5.0%

Strength skills require more arousal than communication skills. But you may also see that simple skills like breaching a door can allow more arousal than more complex skills like setting a charge or processing information.

PRACTICE, EXPERIENCE AND WARRIOR SKILL

Here is another consideration in the relationship of arousal and performance. Skills that have been well-practiced allow higher levels of arousal without becoming impaired than do newly learned skills. That is why experts may still function in a "condition gray" that would likely be disruptive to someone less skilled and practiced.

Proper experience and training engrains a skill so that it's much harder to disrupt under any condition, including one of stress and arousal.

WARRIOR INDIVIDUALITY AND WARRIOR SKILL

The level of arousal varies by individual, by the uniqueness of every warrior. Some warriors perform better with more arousal, while others need to be as relaxed as possible to perform their best. Steve Cauthen, the great racing jockey, says:

> I don't psych myself up. I psych myself down. I think clearer when I'm not psyched up.

Co-author Loren W. Christensen notes that over the years he has watched individual police officers and individual martial artists vary in their arousal levels, sometimes dramatically so, though all performed optimally. He says that at any martial arts tournament you see competitors — newbies and high-ranking veterans — prepare for their competition in a variety of ways. Over in one corner of the arena, you find a fighter sitting cross-legged, hands clasped in his lap, eyes partially closed, as he follows his slow, rhythmical breathing in meditation. Another fighter in the opposite corner psychs up and burns off nervous energy by slamming hard kicks and punches into his training partner's hand-held pads.

Loren says that he often combined both extremes during his competition years. He would spend the first hour at a tournament sitting quietly in the bleachers or outside on the lawn, maintaining a sense of calm and stillness as he repeated affirmation statements (See Chapter 9 on affirmations) to himself: "I am calm," "I am relaxed," "I am performing well," (keeping such statements in the present tense) "I am fast," "I am powerful" and so on. But then about 20 minutes before his event, he would pace near his competition ring, clenching and unclenching his fists, deliberately accelerating his breathing, and conjuring a sense of controlled rage throughout his body and mind (See Chapter 4 on increasing arousal).

Loren found that maintaining a sense of calm up to the last few minutes before his competition helped him conserve his energy and allowed him to better control his nervousness. Additionally, it helped him during the psych-up moments before his event to better ignite his energy, adrenaline and his sense of ferocity. This approach served him well for years in the tournament arena.

During his police career, Loren says that he saw all extremes of arousal among officers preparing to ram a door on a drug house, when facing an angry mob, serving a dangerous warrant and driving into a volatile, gang-infested area. Some would sit calmly and chat quietly with one another in the office prior to going out. Others would call home and talk to their families.

One image that comes to Loren's mind is that of a SWAT officer, a giant, barbell-trained man with tattoos, a buzz cut and a thick, snake-like vein that curled down the center of his forehead and disappeared into a bushy eyebrow. While other officers in the room talked and laughed loudly in edgy anticipation of the mission, the big man, dressed in full regalia, talked quietly on the phone to his three-year-old daughter. Hunched over the desk, his bear-like paw dwarfing the receiver, the SWAT behemoth spoke in tender baby talk to his child about the cuddliness of her little stuffed zebra.

Some patrol officers listened to hard rock all day in their patrol cars while others listened to classical. Some officers began their shift parked on a sleepy residential street reading the newspaper while others charged themselves with three or four cups of coffee at the local diner. Two partners who worked the next beat over from Loren Christensen's would head to a Starbucks right after roll call where they would each gulp several shots of espresso. (Remember the cautions expressed about excessive caffeine use in Chapter two; the above is a description – not necessarily a recommendation!)

Define Your Optimal Arousal Level

One of the biggest mistakes that coaches, leaders, or officers make is to believe that everyone needs the same level of arousal, to be either really pumped or really mellow to perform well. This is not so. The key is to find the optimal level of arousal to maximize your performance. Where do you perform your best? This is what athletes refer to as "getting psyched-up," and playing "in the zone." Feeling some arousal should be seen/felt as a good thing, as a sign of readiness to respond and perform at your best.

THE ZONE

The zone is associated with what is sometimes called the "flow experience," a state where everything seems to click and the effort seems flawless (Csikszentmihalyi, 1990). Here are the characteristics (Gauron, 1984) usually associated with flow:

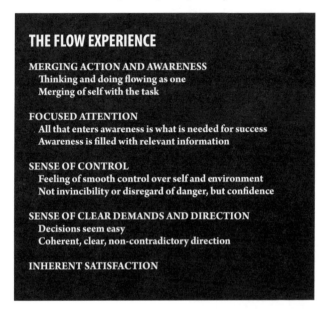

THE FLOW EXPERIENCE

MERGING ACTION AND AWARENESS
Thinking and doing flowing as one
Merging of self with the task

FOCUSED ATTENTION
All that enters awareness is what is needed for success
Awareness is filled with relevant information

SENSE OF CONTROL
Feeling of smooth control over self and environment
Not invincibility or disregard of danger, but confidence

SENSE OF CLEAR DEMANDS AND DIRECTION
Decisions seem easy
Coherent, clear, non-contradictory direction

INHERENT SATISFACTION

Siddle (1995) describes the flow experience related to warriors and tactical skills:

> **The warrior class has recognized the existence of a higher plane of combat performance for thousands of years. It is a level of performance where physical skills are executed with little effort, cognitive processing becomes so efficient that perception of time distorts and the warrior experiences virtually no fear or anxiety.**

Goleman (1997) notes that Csikszentmihalyi (who first described the flow) describes a relationship with Flow Experiences that reflects the Inverted–U curve. He says flow is most likely to occur when someone finds a task with which they are skilled and that slightly challenges their ability. Too little challenge leads to boredom and too much challenge can yield anxiety. Flow is said to occur in that "delicate zone between boredom and anxiety."

Perry (2005) suggests that the flow cannot be forced or directly created. It occurs when skills and abilities match the task.

Science Supports the Existence of the Zone

Recent research (Ferrell, 2006) lends evidence to the existence of an actual performance mental zone state, one that is different from other performance states. Using brain scans called Functional Magnetic Resonance Imaging (FMRI), researchers were able to show differences in neural activation between recall of zone (high level) performance and non-zone (regular) performance. The researchers feel that this initial data supports the reality of the "...palpable, yet enigmatic sensation that many athletes refer to as the 'zone' when performing at high levels."

Scott Sonnon (2001), an expert in the martial arts, especially the fighting art of Samba, emphasizes the importance of flow in combat sports. He describes an upward or enhancing performance spiral that leads to flow and being in the zone. He also cautions about the potential downward performance spiral called the "vortex," which drags a warrior down and results in sub-optimal or even dysfunctional response. He proposes that the goal is to promote the zone in oneself while sending the opponent in the psychological/physiological/behavioral vortex.

With experience, you will become more aware of your Optimal Arousal Level or Ideal Performance State. We like to call this zone of optimal readiness for maximal performance the **O-ZONE**, or your *Optimal Zone of Natural Excellence*. Just like the earth's ozone layer, it is protective and facilitative at the right levels: too close and it is dangerous and too far it is not protective of our planet. Recognizing your personal performance O-ZONE and mastering the techniques to put you in it is a personal "force-multiplier" for excellence and victory. You can help determine it in one or both of two ways.

First, think about your most successful missions. On a scale of one to nine, where one represents being very relaxed and nine represents being really revved up, how high was your arousal? Then think about a mission where you did not perform the way you would have liked or things did not go well. Where was your level of arousal on that one?

Analyzing the relationship between the quality of personal performance and the level of arousal on past missions may show a pattern of consistency indicating what level is associated with your best performance. Famed Russian sport psychologist Yuri Hanin calls this defining your Individual Zone of Optimal Performance (IZOF) and found that athletes can recall with great accuracy past performances, their level of arousal and the quality of that performance (Pargman, 2006).

It's also useful to do multiple or repeat training scenarios in which you respond at different levels of arousal: high, low, or in-between. Then consider these questions: Where did you feel most comfortable? Where did you do your best? Where was your thinking the clearest?

Another term for O-ZONE is Individual Affect-Related Performance Zone (IAPZ). There is some suggestion from work in this area (Tennenbaum, et al., 2008) that on a scale from one to nine, optimal performance is most likely to occur in a perceived range of 5.2-6.5. Performance is likely to be decreased with excessive arousal above a rating 6.8 and insufficient arousal below a rating 4.0. However, remember that the nature of the task and your nature as an individual are important moderating factors in the arousal–performance relationship.

As will be discussed later, while the adrenaline dump under stress can have life-saving and performance-enhancing effects, it can also degrade performance to dangerous levels. Coming to recognize your best levels of arousal and then using the techniques discussed throughout this book to achieve them can help maximize your performance.

Condition Black:
chapter **Stress, Fear and Mental Toughness**

*No passion so effectively robs the mind
of all its powers of acting and reasoning as **fear***.

– Edmund Burke

The biggest challenge in a military mission or police operation is typically to control or manage too much arousal that is often innate to such actions. However, there are times when under-arousal, or too little arousal is the problem.

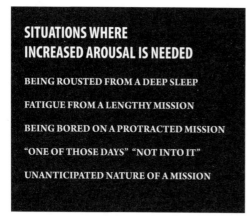

SITUATIONS WHERE INCREASED AROUSAL IS NEEDED

BEING ROUSTED FROM A DEEP SLEEP

FATIGUE FROM A LENGTHY MISSION

BEING BORED ON A PROTRACTED MISSION

"ONE OF THOSE DAYS" "NOT INTO IT"

UNANTICIPATED NATURE OF A MISSION

UNDER-AROUSAL AND OVER-AROUSAL

Insufficient Sleep

High-stress situations rarely occur at convenient or comfortable times. Often there is the late night, all night or early morning mission or crisis. Being awakened from a deep sleep and/or not having had enough sleep can lead to under-arousal. "Sleep inertia" refers to the ten to thirty minutes needed to become fully awake and clear when roused from a deep sleep. Clearing sleep inertia and getting into an optimal level of arousal as soon as possible can be important for performance.

Long Missions

Fatigue from a lengthy mission can cause arousal to drop below levels where performance is enhanced. Being bored, or being bored and fatigued, can cause arousal to become insufficient to promote optimal response.

Off Day

Unusual or high-stress situations can occur on one of those days when you're already feeling that your performance is less than ideal. We all have a natural variation in alertness, mood and enthusiasm for work. If a mission is required on one of those days when we "just aren't into it," adequate arousal may not be present and, therefore, techniques to boost arousal may be useful. While in some jobs an off day may result in inconvenience or frustration; an off day in military or police operations can be lethal and tragic.

Unanticipated Nature of the Mission

Optimal arousal may also be difficult to obtain due to the unanticipated nature of a mission. A "routine" patrol that encounters resistance, the "routine" sentry duty that encounters an intrusion, or the "routine" domestic call that becomes a hostage situation, can quickly impact your arousal. While such situations often lead to an uncontrolled skyrocketing of arousal when the threat becomes clear, summoning an adequate amount can be an issue, as well.

Those Vulnerable Moments After the Mission

One final situation where maintaining arousal (if not increasing it) can be crucial is in the moments when the action of a mission or a call seem to be over. This can be a time of great danger if your focus and readiness are relaxed too soon. This was cautioned about in *On Combat* by citing the comments of Napoleon, who said:

The moment of greatest vulnerability is the instant after victory.

Combine this with the observation of Wes Doss (1994) noting the effects are both physical and psychological:

Exhaustion and confusion are typical after-effects from being involved in a high-stress situation, even for trained individuals.

Survival expert Laurence Gonzales (2003) has called this the "Whew Factor," that sense of relief that occurs when a crisis is resolved. He cautions that this letting down of one's guard may occur prematurely.

These comments warn that the physical letdown and/or relaxing too soon after a mission is concluded may be problematic, if not lethal. What is often called "consolidation and reorganization on the objective" should include maintaining adequate levels of arousal. Arousal and focus need to be maintained until an area of responsibility is truly secure. SWAT teams and the military use the acronym L.A.C.E. (liquids, ammunition, casualties, equipment) to promote appropriate actions and, hopefully, arousal levels. Psychological skills can be used to maintain such readiness in spite of the reported tendency to let down your guard. Use these techniques to stay ready. As Yogi Berra said:

It ain't over 'til it's over.

All of these situations call for ways to increase performance arousal. There are several techniques elite performers use to self-regulate and induce higher levels of arousal when needed to successfully meet the challenges they face:

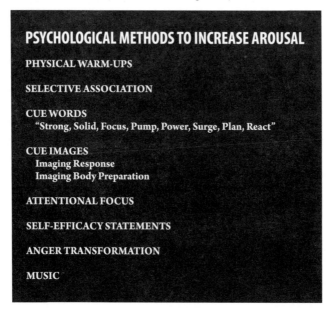

PSYCHOLOGICAL METHODS TO INCREASE AROUSAL

PHYSICAL WARM-UPS

SELECTIVE ASSOCIATION

CUE WORDS
"Strong, Solid, Focus, Pump, Power, Surge, Plan, React"

CUE IMAGES
Imaging Response
Imaging Body Preparation

ATTENTIONAL FOCUS

SELF-EFFICACY STATEMENTS

ANGER TRANSFORMATION

MUSIC

Physical warm-ups
While not purely a psychological technique, physical warm-ups, like those discussed earlier, can be useful for increasing arousal. The mind and body are connected, so physical activation can spur psychological activation, as well.

Selective Association
Selective association refers to being with others who have the level of arousal you need. If you need to increase your arousal, it's best to be around those who are the loudest, joke the most, back slap, and so on. But if you need to reduce your arousal, isolate yourself more and associate with those who are quieter during pre-operation. We react to the behavior of others. Gladwell (2000) reports research by Condon and others on "cultural microrhythms" where individuals will come to synchronize

aspects of their behavior with each other, like physical gestures or rates of speech. Use others to help you gain your optimal performance state, not get distracted from it.

Cue Words

These are words or phrases you say to yourself to increase arousal. They may include: "pump," "power," "surge," "react," "focus," "think," "clear," and "plan."

Bill Kipp is a leading expert in scenario-based adrenal stress response training, and among many other accomplishments, served in the elite 3rd Marine Recon teams specializing in counterterrorism and security testing at top-secret military installations. In an interview (Christensen, 2004), co-author Loren Christensen ask him about ways to summon intensity and master fear when needed.

Kipp responded that one of the best mechanisms to "fire up the fear-into-power response at will" is to use a word or sound to trigger adrenaline. He reports that he has a specific word in his head that "instantly prepares me to be ready for anything." This occurrs because of training that engages the mind, emotions and body to anchor effective survival responses. He further suggested that training with such trigger words is more effective when also done during a fatigued state, when under duress and when physically and mentally tapped out.

Cue Images

Cue images are mind pictures/movies of you responding well. They may also be mind pictures/movies of your body being ready to respond. For images of speed, some performers may superimpose images on their legs of the flowing muscles of a cheetah speeding across a plain. Some of you may remember "Popeye the Sailor" transforming from mild and meek to muscled champion of his lady — Olive Oil —by "eating his spinach." Or some of you may remember the "Incredible Hulk" bursting through his clothes as he transformed into a champion of justice. Some performers superimpose such images on their own bodies to prepare mentally for their challenges. Seeing your muscles bulging or your brain "lit up" and "electrically charged" may seem silly at first, but it has been used successfully to induce arousal and readiness.

Attentional Focus

Attentional focus means to consciously focus on the mission skills at hand. It's a conscious attempt to block out irrelevant thoughts and bring all your energy to bear on your response.

Self-Confidence Statements

Thoughts like: "I'm feeling ready," "I'm feeling sharp" are used by many warriors to instill a powerful sense of confidence.

Anger Transformation

Anger transformation is used by some to help energize themselves by getting angry or ticked-off about something and then drawing on this energy to respond. The great Pittsburgh Pirate player Roberto Clemente confided:

> **If I would be happy, I would be a very bad ballplayer. With me,**
> **when I get mad, it puts energy in my body.**

While there is some controversy about using anger as a self-regulation technique for psyching up, Dr. Nancy Sherman, in her book, *Stoic Warriors* (2005), states that the importance of anger in performance, particularly in war, dates back to the ancient Roman Stoic philosophers. She reports that Plato in *The Republic* sees anger as the "special province of the warrior class and that it was felt to be the fire in a warrior's belly (or actually the thumos, the spirited part of the soul)."

She feels that the *Iliad* is "arguably about warrior anger — about the fury of a warrior such as Achilles." She also writes that the Roman Stoic Seneca wrote that anger "whets the mind for the deeds of war."

If anger works well for you, OK. Just know that this is a controversial self-management approach that is generally not recommended. Research (Murphy, 2005) suggests anger may increase performance on strength-related tasks for some individuals (those who have strong physiological responses to anger imagery). However, this data is not conclusive. The problem is that the amount of anger/energy produced can be unpredictable and uncontrollable. Additionally, being angry during a response can be distracting or disruptive.

Goleman (1997) provides further support that anger may not be the best psychological preparation technique. He says that catharsis (getting anger out) may be a problem because contrary to what many believe, it does not dispel anger; it pumps up the brain; it prolongs thinking about the anger situation. Finally, your anger may trigger or set off an aggressive response in the target or subject that might not have otherwise occurred.

In *Stoic Warriors*, Sherman notes that Seneca also *cautioned* about anger in war. She writes that "unlike weapons and armor, anger, warns Seneca, is not easily thrown off after the battle." She describes anger as a "runaway emotion, easy to turn on but hard to turn off." She suggests that its unpredictable effects may lead to adjustment problems post-action or post deployment, especially domestically. She suggests that combat veterans can "bring home a rage that has lost its targets and finds new ones that are far less appropriate." She quotes Cicero from the Tuscalan Disputations:

> **And what about when your warrior's anger goes home? What is**
> **it like with his wife and children? Is it useful then, too?**

If anger transformation is used, you must be sure about your ability to control it and convert it to useful energy. If you don't need it then don't induce it. If it's already present then transform it into useful energy.

There is one exception to the cautions about using anger to induce arousal; this is when your survival is imminently threatened and death is certain if you give up or cease your struggle. For example, if you are engaged in close-quarters combat and about to be overwhelmed, muster all the unbridled anger, even rage, power, and determination possible. Anything that works is valuable when survival is at stake.

Music
Music is the most popular method of psyching among athletes: hard pounding rhythms to get up and mellow tunes to relax. When you can, use it to stay awake as you return to base and then use it to help you get to sleep.

Mansfield (2005) has collected reports of American soldiers in Iraq using music to prepare for missions, for battle and for motivation. CD players may be hooked into a tank's communication system and fed through helmets. He quotes one American soldier saying:

> **It's the ultimate rush, cuz you know you're going into the fight to begin with, and then you got a good song playing in the background and that gets you real fired up. Ready to do the job.**

He quotes another soldier:

> **We picked 'The Roof is on Fire' because basically it symbolized Baghdad bein' on fire and at the time we wanted it to burn to get Saddam and his regime out. The roof is on fire …we don't need no water…let [it] burn.**

Depending on the situation, police officers and SWAT team members report using music to prepare psychologically. Co-author Christensen recalls a small clique of police officers at one of the precincts playing Wagner's "Ride of the Valkyries" (popularized by the helicopter assault scene in the motion picture *Apocalypse Now*) on a large boom box in the locker room prior to a dangerous mission. Some might argue that that particular piece of music, and the resultant psyche, is not in the best interest of public servants since it so easily brings to mind that violent scene depicted in the movie. Nonetheless, the officers in question, all of whom had 10 to 15 years of experience, always carried out their missions in a highly professional manner.

Loren says that during the years he worked skid row, he would drive to work listening to hard rock on his car radio – and he hates hard rock. But he used it as a psyching device to prepare for his driving and walking beat. However, after eight hours patrolling in what he has called, "an insane wild west show" where every imaginable stimulus assaulted his eyes, ears, nose and brain, he drove home after work in complete and joyous silence.

McDonald (2006) reports comments from a police sergeant that illustrate an example of the police equivalent of psyching up or mentally preparing for performance (or duty):

> **Before every shift I do the same thing. As soon as I get in my own**
> **personal vehicle, I turn off the radio and run through three things:**
> **A high speed pursuit, first aid/CPR and a barricaded person scenario.**
> **For example, I go through when high-speed pursuits are permitted,**
> **what you can and cannot do, what questions I would ask, etc.**
> **I do that every shift.**

Another similar example of pre-performance routines is given by Holmstedt (2007) in her riveting accounts of U.S. female soldiers in Iraq entitled Band of Sisters. She reports that before taking off in their helicopters, the pilots and co-pilots set up their cockpits in what is referred to as "cockpit management." She specifically describes the routine of Captain Vernice "Junk" Armour, USMC, the first African-American female pilot in Marine Corps History, and first black female combat pilot in the history of the Department of Defense:

> **Armour had the same routine every time she went out…**
> **She put her gas mask and NVGs behind her left shoulder and**
> **stored her emergency procedures book behind her left elbow.**
> **She removed a cushion from where her left arm would rest**
> **and replaced it with maps. Armour placed her NVG mount on top**
> **of the dash. She stuck extra batteries in the cracks beside her on the**
> **right. On the inside of her body armor behind her right elbow**
> **was an inverted M-4…**

The point is that just as elite athletes go through psyching-up rituals to prepare for performance by calling forth the proper competitive mindset, it's essential for you to do the same but in preparation for survival. At some point, you need to make the transformation from the lower-ready state of being off duty to the focused high-ready state of the mission. You need a means of "throwing a switch" that lights up and energizes your mind. It's your choice whether it happens when you walk out of your home or your barracks, through the door of the station, or when gearing up.

Is Psyching-Up for Real?

While it's tempting to just look to testimonials from (thousands of) athletes (and other performers) who practice psyching-up on a regular basis as to how effective it can be, there is also research data available.

One typical study (Shelton & Mahoney, 1978) was on the effects of psyching-up on grip or hand strength. At a national weight lifting championship, weight lifters were divided into two groups: a psyching group and a non-psyching group. First, their grip strength was measured by a hand dynamometer followed by each group participating in three trials.

In the first trial, individuals in both groups were told to immediately grip the dynamometer as hard as possible on the "go" signal. On the second trial, individuals were told to count backwards from 100, subtracting seven each time (e.g. 100, 93, 86, 79...) until they heard the "go" signal (always thirty seconds later) when they again gripped the dynamometer as hard as possible. This was done to distract the weightlifters and prevent them from psyching-up on their own before gripping.

The difference was in the third trial. This time, the psyching group was told to psych-up until they heard the "go" signal (thirty seconds later) and then grip the dynamometer as strongly as possible. The non-psyching group was again made to count backwards from 100 (so they could not psych up) until they heard "go" (also thirty seconds later) and then grip as strongly as possible.

The purpose was to compare the strength results in the third trial of the group that psyched-up first and the one that didn't.

PSYCHING AND STRENGTH

TRIALS	1	2	3
PSYCHING GROUP (EXPERIMENTAL)	52.13	51.46	54.93kg
NON-PSYCHING GROUP (CONTROL GROUP)	50.85	50.65	49.12kg

As can be seen from the results, the psyching group demonstrated greater hand grip strength (54.9 kilograms) than the non-psyching group (49.12 kilograms). It's also noteworthy that the psyching group showed the greatest strength on their third trial, which was the only trial during which they psyched-up. The results also show that it's unlikely that "practice" was a factor, because the non-psyching group demonstrated decreasing strength across the trials.

Finally, it may be of interest that a colleague and I (Asken & Goodling, 1986) were able to replicate the effects of psyching-up using this model even in a seventy-nine year-old patient on a hospital rehabilitation unit! Even though admitted for a stroke, having other medical problems, and never having been an athlete or even a regular exerciser, her performance improved in both the hand weakened by the stroke and the unaffected hand when psyching. In the unaffected hand, she was able to show, when psyching, an average increase in grip strength of 1.37 kilograms and a total increase overall of 8.25 kilograms. Even in the stroke-affected (weakened) hand, she was able to show, when psyching, an average increase in grip strength of 1.21 kilograms and a total overall increase of 7.25 kilograms. Psyching can work!

STRESS AND RESPONSE PEFORMANCE

The polite translation of FUBAR is *Fouled* Up Beyond All Recognition. Stress has the distinct capability to create emotional FUBAR during military missions and police operations. Performance expert David Pargman (2006) writes that stress exerts a "substantial" effect on performance — usually negative. Further, the effects of stress are undifferentiated, meaning that they cut across a broad band of types of performance. As Pargman writes, "Stressors make no distinctions among their targets."

Learning the psychological techniques to manage stress not only reduces discomfort but can enhance performance, as well. Mission stress can be seen in this manner:

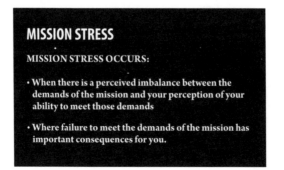

MISSION STRESS

MISSION STRESS OCCURS:

- When there is a perceived imbalance between the demands of the mission and your perception of your ability to meet those demands

- Where failure to meet the demands of the mission has important consequences for you.

While this definition is a bit long and complex, it contains several important principles that are necessary to understand response stress, particularly, how it works, and how to control it.

The Influence of Perception

First, stress is very much the result of perception; how we view a situation. In fact, there are four parts to any response stress situation:

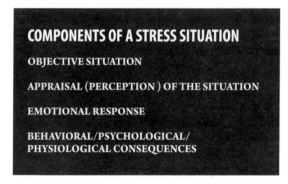

COMPONENTS OF A STRESS SITUATION

OBJECTIVE SITUATION

APPRAISAL (PERCEPTION) OF THE SITUATION

EMOTIONAL RESPONSE

BEHAVIORAL/PSYCHOLOGICAL/ PHYSIOLOGICAL CONSEQUENCES

The objective situation refers to the nature of the mission, the facts of it, something that can be largely agreed upon by everyone. Faced with an objective situation or challenge, you then make an appraisal of the situation and evaluate your ability to deal with it. This leads to an emotional response that has behavioral, psychological, and physical reactions that affect the quality of your performance.

Balance Between the Demands and Your Readiness

Where your appraisal/evaluation is such that you feel prepared to act, your stress will be minimal, you will feel confident and you will have optimal arousal. However, whenever you feel ill-prepared (by lack of training, experience, information, equipment, back-up, or whatever) your stress will increase. The specific impact of this is described shortly.

Why People React Differently

The fact that perception determines your stress levels explains why people have such differing reactions to the same situation. Hopefully, there is congruence between the objective situation and the ability to handle it. However, because perception plays such a large role, some individuals will feel unready to respond when, indeed, they might be very capable. Others may feel very confident, when perhaps more caution is warranted.

Importance of the Outcome to You

This definition of mission stress also points out that stress occurs only when you care about the consequences of not succeeding in the challenge situations. Where the outcome matters, you're invested in doing well, and may be more likely to feel some stress. When you don't care about the result, no stress will occur.

When you can learn to manage your perceptions, you can better manage your stress.

What Makes a Situation High Stress?

There are situations that are stressful and then there are situations characterized by *high* stress. The specific characteristics of high-stress situations have been described by Driskell, Salas, & Johnston (2006). These include:

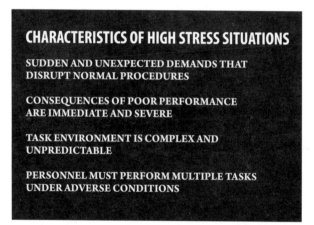

CHARACTERISTICS OF HIGH STRESS SITUATIONS

SUDDEN AND UNEXPECTED DEMANDS THAT DISRUPT NORMAL PROCEDURES

CONSEQUENCES OF POOR PERFORMANCE ARE IMMEDIATE AND SEVERE

TASK ENVIRONMENT IS COMPLEX AND UNPREDICTABLE

PERSONNEL MUST PERFORM MULTIPLE TASKS UNDER ADVERSE CONDITIONS

Unexpected Demands

High-stress situations often occur suddenly and unexpectedly, placing demands on us that were unanticipated (such as expecting a quiet night when instead all kinds of the stuff hits the fan). Events can unfold quickly, usually requiring an immediate response. Consequently, normal and routine procedures are interrupted.

Severe Consequences from Poor Performance

High-stress situations have critical consequences and effects. They demand a full and efficient response. Poor performance or failure will have a dire impact during and/or after the response, all of which impacts the individual, squad and/or others.

Complex Situations

High-stress situations are typically complex, dynamic, variable, and often unpredictable; their cause or immediate nature may be unclear. An effective response may be outside of standard operating procedures and require adaptations or creative reactions.

Multiple Tasks

High-stress situations typically require people to perform multiple tasks quickly and even simultaneously. These demands can include assessing, formulating a response and responding to this dynamic situation. Such situations can be further complicated and strained by adverse conditions, such as time pressure, noise, darkness, inclement weather and fatigue. Unchecked, extreme stress is "an emotional and physical carnivore..."

A similar description of what constitutes extreme stress conditions comes from the field of High-Velocity Human Factors engineering and psychology, which, as noted before, seeks to maximize human-machine and human-systems interactions in high-stress conditions. They term a non-stress situation an "equilibrium event" and a high-stress situation a "non-equilibrium event."

Non-equilibrium events are said (Rahman citing Orasanu et al., 1993) to be made up of:

- events that unfold rapidly (high-velocity events).
- events that fluctuate in chaotic and unruly ways, described as "non-linear dynamics."
- events that are irreversible once a certain threshold has been achieved.
- events that are high stakes.
- events that occur in naturalistic settings.

The physical signs of stress are familiar to most warriors and include what has been characterized as the "pucker factor." These include reactions such as those listed here.

ACUTE SIGNS OF STRESS

STOMACH UPSET
    Butterflies
    Nausea

INCREASED HEART RATE

INCREASED BLOOD PRESSURE

INCREASED PERSPIRATION

INCREASED RESPIRATION

SWEATY PALMS

BOWEL/BLADDER URGENCY

MUSCLE TIGHTNESS

DIZZINESS

VISUAL CHANGES

DRY MOUTH/THROAT

FATIGUE

RESTLESSNESS

CONCENTRATION PROBLEMS

WORD-FINDING PROBLEMS

CHEST PAIN

TREMORS/SHAKES

DECREASED EMOTIONAL CONTROL

High-stress missions and events have also been said to be characterized by "Fog and Friction." Fog refers to the lack of clear or complete information (Grunow, 2006) and friction refers to physical impediments faced by the operator in the field (Kramer, 1965).

Stress can affect our reflexes and make them hyperactive. Grillon, et al., (1993) found the magnitude of our startle blink reflex was greater when subjects expected a negative event (receiving electric shock) compared to a neutral event (no shock). Whether heightened reflexes are good or bad for performance will depend on many factors, but managing performance stress and its impact is the critical skill.

Gonzales (2005) notes that the effects of out-of-control stress have been likened to a "knife fight in a phone booth." He also extended Plato's analogy of stress as a model of a jockey and race horse in the starting gate.

> **The human organism, then, is like a thoroughbred at the gate. He's a small man and it's a big horse, and if it decides to get excited in that small metal cage, the jockey is going to get mangled, possibly killed. So, he takes great care to be gentle. The jockey is reason and the horse is emotion…**

The jockey is your rational self and the horse is your emotional self. When under control and in a optimal arousal state, your performance is maximal. However, if "spooked" and rampaging in the stall, the horse (your emotions) is out of control and performance is negatively affected.

Positive and Survival-Based Effects

Amidst all the discussion of the potential negative effects of stress as expressed in the adrenaline dump, it seems important to re-emphasize that the body's stress response (adrenaline release) has positive and survival-based effects. These are well illustrated in the story (Koster, 2007) of the "incredible bulk," Royal Marine Colour Sergeant Carl Tatton.

At the time of the incident, Colour Sergeant Carl "Tatts" Tatton was serving in southern Afghanistan as a physical training instructor with J Company, 42 Commando. Fellow Royal Marine Mark Farr's legs were trapped when a mortar round flipped a two-ton truck on top of him in a water-filled ditch in which he was working. After an initial yell for help, Marine Farr was dragged under the surface in three feet of water.

As incoming shells continued to fall, Colour Sergeant Tatton jumped into the ditch with Marine Farr just seconds from drowning. Despite the danger and overwhelming odds, he was able to lift the truck to save his fellow Marine. Speaking of the adrenaline rush that allowed him to lift a vehicle thirteen times his own body weight, Color Sergeant Tatton said "When you see one of your mates in danger, you just react." Marine Farr nicknamed Tatton the "Incredible Bulk." Indeed, marshalling and using the effects of adrenaline can have profound effects on performance

Recognizing that some arousal in itself is not a bad thing as discussed in the arousal-performance curve, Dixon (1976) quotes Israeli General Moshe Dayan as saying:

> **It is better to struggle with a stallion when the problem**
> **is to hold it back, than to urge on a bull which refuses to budge.**

It's essential, therefore, to recognize that the effects of adrenaline and other "stress chemicals" released in demanding situations can have positive effects on strength and energy. Almost everyone is familiar of tales of "superhuman" acts that someone showed during an emergency, as did Colour Sergeant Tatts above. However, as the horse and jockey analogy describes, understanding and controlling these effects is necessary to insure that the impact is performance enhancing rather than performance destroying. Control of excessive arousal is the key as suggested by Williams (2006) who has described the struggle with stress in this manner:

> **The fight or flight mechanism is for animals or the untrained,**
> **not the warrior prepared for danger or death.**

Training and Restraining Excessive Arousal

The failure to understand, control and channel the effects of physiological arousal can not only impede performance, it also lead to extreme actions that can be problematic. Excessive arousal may be an important factor in both military and police overreactions that lead to tragic and highly publicized results. For example, many believe that the tragic friendly-fire death of ex-NFL football star and Army Ranger Pat Tillman (discussed later) might have been related to excessive adrenaline/arousal effects leading to tunnel vision and impulsive thought and action.

Here Marine Physician Richard Jadick provides an example of how the effects of stress and adrenaline on thinking can result in a rush to action:

> **Word came back: wounded marines. Johns handed off his weapon, grabbed his med bag and started sprinting the 150 yards to the lead truck. "I wasn't even thinking about it for the first hundred meters," Johns recalls now, "but then it hit me. This is how they initiate ambushes. We're going to get hit right now, and I'm running down the middle of the road by myself."**

Examples of how excessive adrenaline effects can lead to ingrained but potentially dangerous, deadly and tragic actions like "rescue fever" are validated by research like that from Dr. Matthew Sztajnkrycer, an emergency medicine physician and police and emergency response unit medical director (2008). His research is concerned with helping responding officers make good decisions when confronted with an injured colleague in a kill zone that is still hot (Force Science News, 2008).

Dr. Sztajnkrycer emphasizes that "injuries under conditions of active threat" are "… simply another tactical consideration and do not necessarily take precedence over other tactical priorities." Further, he notes that "good medicine can be bad tactics." However, the sight of a wounded teammate or fellow officer "raises primal emotions" and this can lead to problematic actions, namely rushing in and exposure to danger where it is not necessary or even of value.

In one scenario, where the victim officer was clearly dead, he reports "every group of tactical operators approached the downed officer, despite the fact that the officer showed no signs of life, and had a simulated head injury with exposed brain." No team attempted remote assessment in an organized fashion. He provides several examples of tragic consequences of an emotion and adrenaline-driven rush to aid without a "calculated analysis" of the situation.

Another example is given by coauthor Loren Christensen (2002) in his book *Crouching Tiger*. Here he describes how a high baseline of stress can add to arousal problems and how excess arousal can lead to more intense reactions in stressful situations.

OUT OF CONTROL

Dispatch said to see the sergeant at the Saigon jail about picking up a guy to transport to the prison in Long Binh. Since Long Binh was about 35 miles from Saigon, Brett and I were pleased to get the call because it would eat up the entire day. We always enjoyed the drive to the prison and back because the country air was fresh and we found the rice paddies and rich green of the countryside to be a nice break from the sweltering concrete and stench of Saigon.

We needed the break, too. Ten months of military police duty in the busiest, most polluted, crowded and violent city in the world had pushed us to the breaking point. We didn't know a thing about stress in those days, but looking back on it now I can see that I was near the end of a rapidly burning fuse. Even the occasional good night's sleep didn't help my aching physical fatigue; my brain, as well as my spirit, were toasted from working twelve- to sixteen-hour shifts. In ten months, we had enjoyed a grand total of two days off.

It was a thankless job where the Vietnamese as well as most American servicemen hated our guts. The bold, white "MP" letters on our black helmets and black armbands, and the authority that that gave us, made us the constant target of verbal insults, physical assaults and even an occasional sniper round. The job was violent, dangerous and frightening. Making all this even worse was that sleep, even on a good night, was fitful because of the oppressive heat, noise and constant buzz of activity.

Although happy to get the radio call to transport the prisoner, I was in a cranky and miserable mood. I had jungle rot on my toes, ringworm on my butt, an old sprained finger that wouldn't heal, and I was nauseous and wilted from the day's one hundred-degree-plus temperature. During the past two days I had been in four fights, been puked on by a drunken sailor, spit on by a doped-up marine, chewed out by my sergeant for knocking the spitter on his rear, and a Vietnamese policeman had pulled his gun on me because I had tried to get an American soldier's money back from a prostitute who had rolled him. I was in a black mood and Brett wasn't feeling any better.

The desk sergeant was waiting for us in the compound area, one of his beefy hands gripping the arm of a skinny, pimply-faced kid. We climbed out of the jeep and walked up to the sergeant, who greeted us with a nod; the kid sneered his lip and looked at Brett and me as though we were mess hall garbage cans. His shirt was without shoulder patches and his brown hair was as long as a hippy's, indicating he had been hiding in the back alleys of Saigon for a few months. The sergeant said that he had refused to give his name and from what unit he was AWOL. I instantly disliked the kid, especially the way he was looking me up and down with contempt.

We replaced the sergeant's handcuffs with ours and helped the prisoner into the backseat of our jeep, all the while he continued with the smirking. I told him to knock it off, but he didn't, adding a few snorts to underscore his disdain. Brett slid in behind the wheel and I sat in the front passenger seat, turned partially so I could keep an eye on the prisoner. We threw the sergeant a mock salute and headed out of the compound.

Thirty minutes later, we had progressed no farther than a mile from the jail compound. Saigon's exhaust-choked traffic was especially bad and for the umpteenth time that day, we were caught in an immovable jam of bicycles, motorcycles, military vehicles, taxis and a cacophony of horns, engines and curses. Everyone had a ride but no one was going anywhere.

A monster-sized, Vietnamese army truck inched along side of us. Every few seconds the impatient driver leaned his forearm on the horn, sending out a twenty-second, eardrum-shattering blast, which didn't help the jam but did make Brett and I angry. We yelled at the driver to knock it off or we would rip his horn out and stick it where it would make him walk funny. The driver yelled something back in Vietnamese and, though we didn't understand, it was clear that it wasn't nice. Just as I started to say something back, our jeep rock slightly.

My gut instinct told me instantly what had caused the movement even before I twisted around and looked dumbly at the empty backseat. "He's escaped!" I yelled. "There," Brett said, pointing at the jam of traffic behind us. "He's running around that bus."

That was all it took to bring my rage, stress and fatigue together like a thunderclap. I leapt from the jeep with a loud curse. Losing a prisoner was at the top of the list of embarrassing things that could happen to a military policeman.

I zigzagged through traffic, trying not to lose sight of the kid. I executed a perfect two-handed vault over the hood of a taxi but rammed into a motorcycle, knocking it, the old man straddling it, and all his baskets to the pavement. I muttered "Sorry" and sprinted off.

When the kid ran into a less congested alley, the distance between us began to increase. His hands had been cuffed behind his back, but somehow he had maneuvered them to his front. He was at least a half block away now and, just as I thought he might elude us, one of his laceless boots flew off, making him stumble. He regained his balance quickly and sped up in spite of his hobble.

I drew my .45 semiautomatic, thinking that the whine of a bullet over his head would scare him into giving up. I aimed as best I could while running and squeezed the trigger. The Colt jammed.

Bam! A shot came from behind me.

I instinctively ducked and twisted around, worrying for a moment that the prisoner had an ally. It was Brett, running right on my heels, holding his .45 in the air; he squeezed off a couple more rounds. *Bam! Bam!*

When I turned back, the kid had stumbled and fallen, a swirl of dust lifting into the air around him. Dozens of Vietnamese, who had been walking, riding their bicycles or just socializing in the alley, fled in every direction, no doubt convinced they were in the middle of a firefight, not with the Viet Cong, but one between crazy American servicemen. MPs to boot.

I reached him just as he was trying to climb to his feet. A hard kick sent him head over heels into the dirt, and follow-up kicks kept him from getting up. When Brett caught up a few seconds later, we both rained wild punches and kicks on him. The kid fought back desperately with his cuffed hands and bare feet, not in an attempt to escape, but to survive our terrible onslaught. The more he fought to defend himself, the more we attacked as if possessed. We yelled and cursed and punched and kicked.

As the kid's fight began to weaken, ours' grew stronger, but only for
a moment before Brett and I grew so weak we could beat him no more.
Spent, we collapsed across his bleeding, semiconscious body.

The three of us lay together for several seconds, our chests heaving,
all of us coughing, sweat saturating our fatigues. Beneath us, the kid
whimpered and moaned as blood streamed from his nose and mouth.

After two minutes passed, or maybe twenty, Brett sat up and removed
a plastic handcuff strip from his pants pocket. I feebly restrained
the man's legs while he wrapped the cuff around the kid's ankles,
an unnecessary precaution since he was too injured to run anyway.

After he was bound, Brett and I sat in the dirt for a moment, letting our
breathing return to normal and looking at our prisoner. "How we going
to get him back to the jeep?" I wheezed.

"I've already thought of that," Brett said, struggling to his feet.
He staggered over to an old mamasan who had been watching us
from a short distance away as she balanced a long pole across her
shoulders, a bucket of water hanging from each end. Brett talked to her
for a moment, pointing once toward the prisoner and once toward me.
She nodded, lowered the pole from her shoulders to set the buckets on
the ground, and then slid the pole away from their handles. She handed
it to Brett and he handed her a coin.

"I've rented us a prisoner transport system," he said proudly on his
return. I didn't immediately understand until he ran one end under
the prisoner's plastic ankle cuff and the other through his wrist cuff,
slinging him like a slain deer. We lifted the pole, placing an end on
each of our shoulders, and began walking down the alley, the prisoner's
sagging rear bumping the ground with our every step. The old woman
trailed behind us, calling for everyone to look, so that by the time we got
back to the street, we had an entourage of twenty chattering Vietnamese.

We carried our prized catch through the traffic jam, which had just
unclogged and was moving at a snail's pace. Our jeep, left in the middle
of the street, was now causing most of the problems as a myriad
of vehicles struggled to maneuver around it, including a large,
blue American military bus with a sign over its front window that
read "Bien Hoa Airport."

The bus was crowded with freshly arrived American Servicemen from the United States. Their virgin faces pressed against every window, eyes wide as they watched Brett and me carrying the beaten, bleeding prisoner slung from the wooden pole. At first glance, they probably thought we had captured a Viet Cong, but when it was clear that he was an American, their eyes widened even more.

Brett smiled at the gawking faces and nodded toward the prisoner with a bob of his eyebrows. "Welcome to the 'Nam boys," he said. "Don't break the law during your visit."

This time I didn't take my eyes from the kid, who we placed, minus the pole but still bound, in the backseat. Brett once again fought us through traffic and eventually to the highway. The prisoner screamed and cursed most of the way to Long Binh, and whenever it got too annoying, one of us would reach over our seat, slap his shoulder and tell him to hold it down.

At the jail, we were met by a booking sergeant outside, who looked with mild curiosity at our whimpering injured prisoner, met us outside. I told the sergeant that the kid had gotten hurt when he fell out of the jeep on an especially sharp curve. He nodded that he understood, and said, "Yes, that happens quite often. Actually, it happens a lot." Then he winked.

When the prisoner realized he wasn't getting any sympathy, he spat a hunk on the big man's chest followed with a curse at the sergeant's mother. This was not a wise decision by the kid, since Long Binh jailers, who were oppressed by their own stress, didn't treat disrespectful prisoners as nicely as Brett and I. In a flash, the big sergeant grabbed one of the prisoner's feet and yanked him out of the jeep, his butt and head hitting the ground with a sickening *whump!* A second jailer suddenly appeared and began kicking the prisoner as the booking sergeant drug him by his feet through a door and into a holding cell.

A couple of hours later, we were on the highway again heading back to Saigon. It was a peaceful ride and we even stopped for a while to watch an old farmer plow a rice paddy with his water buffalo. As I gazed at the serene scene, I thought about stories I'd heard of American helicopters flying over Vietnamese farmland as the door gunner, an extraordinarily stressful and dangerous job, just for giggles, or release, gunned down farmers' water buffaloes.

I recalled a boot camp drill sergeant saying once that the most vicious person in the world was a nineteen-year-old American soldier in Vietnam with an M-16. Judging by what I did and saw others do, there was much truth to his words.

The question that has to be asked is this: Did Vietnam cause it or was it there all along? My experiences in Vietnam taught me that viciousness is part of an uncontrolled warrior spirit, and the horror of such a place can act as a catalyst with some people to bring its ugliness to the surface. While war brings out the best and the worst in us, it also brings out the best and worst of one's warrior spirit.

I'd like to think that today, decades after Vietnam, I could experience such a place with control and humaneness. Well, the chance of my ever finding out is slim to none at my age. So I can just kick back and tell myself that those days were another time and another place.

Two more contemporary examples of the impact of excessive emotion on behavioral reactions are provided by Army LTC Carl Grunow, senior U.S. advisor to the Iraqi Army. He describes the Iraqi "death blossom," which he says has been seen by every U.S. soldier who has spent time in Iraq. He offers that any enemy attack on the Iraqi Army, whether mortar, sniper or IED, leads to the "average Iraqi soldier" emptying his thirty-round magazine or "whatever belt of ammunition happens to be in his machine-gun." He says that "ninety percent of the time, there is no target." He, further, notes that while soldiers always agree on the danger of this action and the waste of ammunition, they continue to do it.

Another example is what is termed the "death burst." This occurs in the context of the death of a comrade during an attack. In apparent reaction to such events, there can be a bullet-filled "rampage," often through a civilian community by surviving Iraqi soldiers. He reports this "return fire" has lasted up to ninety minutes in response to one deadly sniper shot.

Examples of such reactions are not limited to Iraqi forces. Marine physician Richard Jadick described a similar situation where hyperarousal almost led to tragedy, but was averted:

The 1/8 Marines set up what was called a CMOC, a civilian military operations center, in Mosul, to start coordinating construction. It was a good idea and the right thing to do. There hadn't been any heavy fighting here, and there was no reason for us not to get along with the population. But things couldn't have gone worse. The Marines were nervous: and this

> was their first time in a war zone. They had been trained for war and
> Special Ops, but not for handing out job applications and dealing with
> upset civilians who wanted someone to shout at.
>
> The situation turned south very quickly. A crowd had gathered outside
> of the CMOC and they started chanting, wanting jobs, wanting money,
> wanting the Marines and the United States to provide them these things.
> The situation intensified as more and more demonstrators grew angry
> before the Marines even managed to get set up. Then, from the rear of
> the crowd, there was a flurry of gunfire. The Marines reacted the way
> they had been trained — they opened fire.
>
> I wasn't there when it happened but I saw the results. These young Marines
> were trained as warriors: they were pumped up and Oorah-ed to the hilt,
> ready to get into shit and kick some ass. Then they were asked to work
> a job fair and handle an angry mob. If you egg on a dog until it is in
> a frenzy, that's not a good time to ask him to go play with children.
> Somebody's going to get bit.

While surely difficult to know for certain, excessive arousal effects may be an important factor in the tragic events in the killings at My Lai and Haditha, or the beating of Rodney King. Human Factors psychologist Moin Rahman (2007) noted:

> The savage nature of war and the adrenaline fueled psychology
> of the warrior in combat combine to form a lethal symbiosis,
> a tsunami of violence, which can maim both men and their minds."

He believes that this, rather than "a few bad apples" among soldiers or police officers, may account for this behavior. He goes on to state, however, that "This phenomenon is poorly understood, particularly by civilian leaders who have never been in combat."

THE IMPACT OF STRESS ON PERFORMANCE

From a performance perspective, the common physical disruptions of stress include:

COMMON PHYSICAL DISRUPTIONS WITH STRESS

CHOKING

FREEZING

DEATH GRIP

MUSCLE TENSION AND FATIGUE

DISRUPTED COORDINATION

BLURRED VISION

Choking

Elite performers are well aware of certain physical effects that occur with stress that directly affect the quality of their action. Choking refers to performance failure at a critical moment. While it refers to any type of "failure" response, it comes from the sensation of being unable to breathe or swallow under stress.

Carlstedt (2004) developed what he calls the Theory of Critical Moments, which is described as "instances or situations that are pivotal to the successful outcome." He identified specific traits that he believes can predict who will perform well at such times and who will choke.

He reports that those who fare well in high-stress situations (don't choke) are low on hypnotic ability/absorption — a measure of hypnotic ability; low on neuroticism — the tendency to fixate on catastrophizing thoughts and negative emotions; and high on repressive coping — a left-brain hemispheric localized behavioral tendency that has been shown to inhibit the inter-hemispheric transfer of negative affect (emotions) between hemispheres of the brain. As a complicated as these traits are to understand, they are even more complicated to measure (assessment is typically done by Dr. Carlstedt). More importantly, he believes that specific training can mediate these traits to maximize performance at such critical moments.

Freezing

Most people are aware that stress leads to the fight or flight response: the body prepares to fight or flee at maximum capacity to effect survival. Often forgotten, however, is the third "F," which is to freeze under stress, called temporary paralysis by Duran & Nasci, (2000) below.

Dr. Ken Mills (2005) has reported work with driving skills that suggests that when eyes fixate (under stress) too long on an object (like a car skidding out of control in snow in front of the driver), the driver's hands will also freeze. Another example is when a driver freezes by hitting the brakes in response to a stimulus, such as when he sees a speed trap. Mills says that distracted drivers miss or are slower to react to more red lights, they break harder to compensate, and they take more risks.

Feeling frozen, whether seen in the death grip or feeling as though one cannot move or perform skills, can be overcome. Perhaps you have seen *Apocalypse Now* that classic motion picture about Vietnam and remember the iconic helicopter assault scene choreographed magnificently to Wagner's "Ride of the Valkyries." As the choppers began to descend into an extremely hot landing zone, Lance, the surfer, froze in his seat, refusing to get out, screaming. "I'm not going, I'm not going, I'm not going." He did exit, but only after another soldier who was on the ground yanked him out. Lance then went on to do what was needed in the battle.

Wingert & Evans (2006) reported the story of Dr. Richard Jadick (who was referred to earlier) from the Iraqi War. As Marines were headed out to war, Jadick was a "bored physician pushing paper." Earlier in his life, he had hoped to attend West Point but was denied due to poor depth perception. He subsequently went to college on an ROTC scholarship, served as a communications officer in the Marines but left after seven years, frustrated he had missed the Gulf War. He then went to medical school on a Navy scholarship and later, when a shortage of doctors led to a question of who could be sent to be the physician for the First Battalion, Eighth Marine Regiment, he volunteered.

He recounted his first reaction to that first contact.

> **I can't tell you how scared I was. My legs wanted to stay in that vehicle, but I had to get off...I felt like it took me hours to make the decision to go.**

He said it felt like he was "walking through water." But he got up and went, and among the times he did, he saved thirty lives in one battle and was awarded the bronze star.

Wells (1988) wrote about the feelings of an Air Force pilot as he was diving on enemy positions during the Vietnam War. They are noteworthy for their candor and in representing, in one instant, many of the stress responses described before — fear, freeze, time distortion and mastery:

> I felt a sort of cold numbness throughout my body as I rolled
> in on the muzzle flashes below. The tracers came up the way
> heavy hail comes down from a thunderstorm. I was scared and
> breathing hard. The pass seemed like an hour, but only seconds
> passed until I was pulling up and jinking away.

Co-author Loren Christensen saw an officer freeze when they were taking down a subject who had just emptied a shotgun into a psychiatrist's face, reloaded and fired again into his chest. In another incident, Loren's partner froze when a massive suspect being arrested by them began to violently resist. When an observant citizen saw the officer's inability to move, he reached into to their cruiser and called for help over the police radio. Another officer Loren knew froze at the dinner able at his home and was unable to go to work that afternoon. Loren, personally and courageously, admits to freezing in his cruiser once such that he could not reach for his mic to take a call about a bar brawl. Loren says that as far as he knows, none of these officers, including himself, had further problems with freezing.

Death Grip
The death grip — holding on to something too tightly and longer than needed or desirable — is also a form of choking or freezing. We are reminded of people who, during swim training in treading water while holding a weighted block, would panic when fatigued, and grip the block until it dragged them to the bottom of the pool. Rather than just letting go and floating to the surface, they would have to be rescued by someone prying loose their grip on the block.

Loren Christensen notes that many times an officer will continue to hold onto his notebook and pen when the subject being interviewed is clearly growing agitated. Even when the person becomes so agitated that he begins to advance threateningly, the officer continues to hold onto the items; sometimes he even grips them more tightly. Then when force is necessary to take the person into custody, the officer struggles to control him while still gripping the notebook. Loren says he has seen officers grapple with one hand while extending the one gripping the notebook out of the way of the scuffle.

Muscle Tension and Fatigue
Fluid movement, flexibility, speed and explosive power in skills such as defensive tactics and close-quarter combat occur most readily when muscles are loose and relaxed. Muscle tension interferes with and degrades these aspects of maximal technique. Unfortunately, a very common effect of stress is tightening of our muscles (muscle-tension headaches are an extreme but not uncommon example of the impact of stress on our muscles). Further, when muscles are tight they expend more energy and fatigue occurs more readily.

Disrupted Coordination

Stress can affect coordination. As noted, stress often leads to muscle tightness. This can also affect coordination by disrupting the quality of response as just described. This tightness can also lead to injury as described below.

Blurred Vision

Stress can affect vision which inhibits performance. We discuss tunnel vision later but also know that stress can cause a loss of near vision that can make it hard to effectively sight your weapon. When this occurs, it may be difficult to effectively use your pistol sights, though it's less of a problem with a rifle since its front sight is farther away.

The effects of stress on human performance in all areas are well-recognized. These are summarized here.

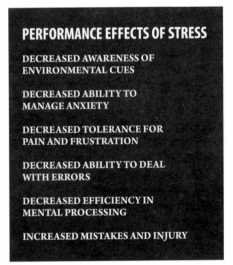

PERFORMANCE EFFECTS OF STRESS

DECREASED AWARENESS OF ENVIRONMENTAL CUES

DECREASED ABILITY TO MANAGE ANXIETY

DECREASED TOLERANCE FOR PAIN AND FRUSTRATION

DECREASED ABILITY TO DEAL WITH ERRORS

DECREASED EFFICIENCY IN MENTAL PROCESSING

INCREASED MISTAKES AND INJURY

Decreased Awareness of Environmental Cues

This means that you become less aware of what is going on around you. It's often a manifestation of tunnel vision where you visually focus on a limited area or just one object.

Mills (2005) describes this as it relates to driving skills, saying that the "eyes stick" and "target fixation" occurs. Target fixation, also called a "zoom" response, is similar to tunnel vision, and can occur when our eyes lock onto a new, unfamiliar event, especially one that is potentially a threat. It's noted that professional drivers learn to avoid such target fixation.

Mills refers to observations by Paul Whitesell that during an actual police car pursuit there can be perceptual narrowing of up to seventy percent. There can also be impaired depth perception, impaired ability to track multiple stimuli, and impaired night vision, among the other effects of stress.

The potential problem with typical reactions like tunnel vision has been well described by Leach in his book *Survival Psychology* (1994):

> Perceptual narrowing appears to be a manifestation of restricted attention. There is a narrowing of awareness coupled with an intensification on only one task. While this intensification enables a person to concentrate on a selected task, there is no guarantee that the task so selected is the most appropriate one in the circumstances. Furthermore, the task can overwhelm the victim, blocking out other, perhaps vital, information needed for effective functioning and limiting the number and limiting the number of alternative responses available…

There is also a physiological component to what is called tunnel vision or perceptual narrowing (Janelle & Hatfield, 2008). A constriction of visual field occurs when anxiety or arousal increases. Along with this, gaze becomes more eccentric and fixated on peripheral views to detect relevant from irrelevant cues.

There can be tunnel hearing, also called auditory exclusion, where we seem to hear only selected words or sounds. People firing a weapon often say that the sound was muffled, it just made a "pop" or firecracker sound. Grossman and Christensen (2005) say that recent work suggests that this may occur because of an "auditory blink" (like an eye blink) that affects the sound of one's own gunfire. Recent brain imaging work from the Johns Hopkins University reported by the Force Science Research Center shows that when an area of the brain focuses, as in sighting, other areas like those involved with hearing become less active. (An excellent resource for cutting edge research reports is Dr. Bill Lewinski's Force Science Research Center at Minnesota State University at Mankato, Mankato, Minnesota; Info@forcescience.com).

Sensitivity to Your Anxiety
When your awareness becomes tunneled, you might become more focused and sensitive to signs of anxiety in your body. So instead of being focused on the challenge, you're distracted by butterflies in your stomach, the shakes in your hands, or the need to defecate. You have a decreased ability to manage or tolerate anxiety and stress.

Decreased Tolerance For Pain and Frustration
Stress decreases your tolerance for pain and frustration. Military missions and police operations, especially those of a protracted nature, involve discomfort from fatigue, uncomfortable tactical positions and uncomfortable weather conditions. Stress reduces your ability to tolerate them, and increases the chance you will act more quickly and impulsively to reduce your discomfort.

Decreased Mental Processing, More Errors

Stress can affect your mental efficiency so that your decisions become less clear and harder to make. You might have trouble remembering details or names of equipment you need. Along with the potential for more errors is the potential that you might focus on them.

Increased Injury Potential

Because stress can reduce your ability to focus and causes you to make more errors, there is an increased chance for injury. Adding to the problem is that under stress your muscles tighten, decreasing your flexibility and increasing the chance for muscle-related injury.

Research (Rogers & Landers, 2005) has shown that peripheral narrowing of vision (tunnel vision) under stress is indeed a likely factor in injury. Comparing athletes during non-stress (practice) and stressful (games) situations, peripheral visual narrowing was a major contributor to injury. However, psychological coping skills moderated the effects of life stress on injury.

Sudden-Stress Syndrome

Duran and Nasci (2000) define Sudden-Stress Syndrome as:

> **Physiologic changes that occur as a result of sudden and extreme stress, as well as, the effects the changes can have on your perception and your motor skill performance."**

These reactions have been well documented. For example, typical perceptual changes in high-stress situations include (Duran & Nasci, 2000):

PERCEPTUAL DISTORTIONS WITH SUDDEN STRESS

AUDITORY EXCLUSION; DIMINISHED SOUNDS:
Muffled Gun Shots
Failure to Hear Shouts, Directions

INTENSIFIED SOUNDS:
Cylinder of a Weapon Turn and Lock

TUNNEL VISION
Tunnel on the Gun Not Center Mass

HEIGHTENED VISUAL CLARITY
Objects in Tunnel are Highlighted

AUTOMATIC PILOT

TIME DISTORTION
Slow Motion Time
Fast Motion Time

MEMORY RELATED DISTORTION
Forgetting Events
Inserting Events that Did Not Occur

DISASSOCIATION

INTRUSIVE DISTRACTING THOUGHTS
Friends and Family

TEMPORARY PARALYSIS

It's important to emphasize that while these effects can profoundly affect the quality of your response in an emergency situation, they are not abnormal or infrequent. Data that co-author Dave Grossman provided from the work of Artwohl & Christensen and Klinger is summarized below where it can be seen that these reactions can be quite frequent. Both Grossman and Christensen (2004) and Ken Murray (2004) have described their nature and impact. Because of this and because the focus of this book is on preventing or managing such reactions, they will not be discussed in more detail here.

FREQUENCY OF PERCEPTUAL DISTORTIONS UNDER STRESS

Artwohl & Christensen		Klinger
85%	DIMINISHED SOUND/AUDITORY EXCLUSION	82%
80%	TUNNEL VISION	51%
74%	AUTO PILOT	
72%	INCREASED VISUAL CLARITY	56%
65%	SLOW MOTION TIME	56%
51%	MEMORY LOSS FOR EVENT	
47%	MEMORY LOSS FOR ACTION	
40%	DISSOCIATION	
26%	INTRUSIVE THOUGHTS	
22%	MEMORY DISTORTION	
16%	FAST MOTION TIME	
16%	INTENSIFIED SOUND	20%
7%	TEMPORARY PARALYSIS	

Bilateral Symmetry

This is another effect of stress (Grossman & Christensen, 2004). Bilateral symmetry means that what you do on one side of your body, you also do on the other. The term *sympathetic contractions* and *mirror movements* have also been used to refer to involuntary contractions that may occur in the muscles of one limb when the muscles in another limb are performing an intended forceful action.

This is typically seen in infants who, when startled, jerk both hands and legs out to the sides simultaneously (the Maro reflex). Under stress, adults can do this, as well. Therefore, you must be cautious in situations in which you grab for something or someone with one hand while holding your weapon in your other with your finger on the trigger.

In a series of experiments, Heim and his colleagues (2003, 2006) have empirically demonstrated this tendency and found that unintentional trigger pulls can be set off by a variety of physical movements, such as jumping or kicking. Involuntary movements may occur due to sympathetic contractions, loss of balance, or as a startle response. However, there may be other factors, as well, such as perceptual and psychological states.

This research also found that not only are unintentional trigger pulls related to other physical actions, but officers often inadvertently place their finger on the trigger (rather than outside the guard) despite regulations and intentions counter to this.

Twenty percent of officers had their finger on the trigger at some point during a test scenario. Further, none of the officers were aware of doing so and maintained they had not done it (Heim, Niebergall, & Schmidtbleicher, 2008).

Doin' What Comes Naturally: A Return to Basic Responses
A final important effect of stress is the return to not only more simple responses but to those that are most basic, preferred, or dominant. When calm, your brain requires eight to ten seconds to process each piece of complex and novel information. If there are no immediate responses for the situation, your mind searches for the "first fix in its library of habits" (Time, 2005).

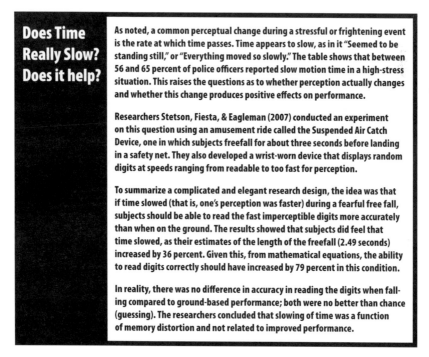

Does Time Really Slow? Does it help?

As noted, a common perceptual change during a stressful or frightening event is the rate at which time passes. Time appears to slow, as in it "Seemed to be standing still," or "Everything moved so slowly." The table shows that between 56 and 65 percent of police officers reported slow motion time in a high-stress situation. This raises the questions as to whether perception actually changes and whether this change produces positive effects on performance.

Researchers Stetson, Fiesta, & Eagleman (2007) conducted an experiment on this question using an amusement ride called the Suspended Air Catch Device, one in which subjects freefall for about three seconds before landing in a safety net. They also developed a wrist-worn device that displays random digits at speeds ranging from readable to too fast for perception.

To summarize a complicated and elegant research design, the idea was that if time slowed (that is, one's perception was faster) during a fearful free fall, subjects should be able to read the fast imperceptible digits more accurately than when on the ground. The results showed that subjects did feel that time slowed, as their estimates of the length of the freefall (2.49 seconds) increased by 36 percent. Given this, from mathematical equations, the ability to read digits correctly should have increased by 79 percent in this condition.

In reality, there was no difference in accuracy in reading the digits when falling compared to ground-based performance; both were no better than chance (guessing). The researchers concluded that slowing of time was a function of memory distortion and not related to improved performance.

It is highly recommended that every warrior read the following pioneering and essential works to fully understand these most critical aspects of their careers: *On Combat: The Psychology and Physiology of Deadly Conflict in War and Peace* by Lt. Colonel Dave Grossman and Loren Christensen (2004); *On Killing: The Psychological Cost of Learning to Kill in War and Society,* also by Grossman (1995); and *Training At The Speed of Life: The Definitive Textbook for Military and Law Enforcement Reality Based Training* by Murray (2004).

A university professor was asked to investigate "unexplained" scuba diving deaths — instances where divers drowned despite having adequate air in their tanks. These deaths can likely be explained by the above principle of a return to basic or dominant responses under stress. The dominant response for human beings when choking or having trouble breathing with something in or something covering their mouths is to (often frantically) remove it to clear the air intake. The maneuver is effective on land but has the opposite effect when a panicked scuba diver frantically removes the mouthpiece/regulator under water.

Murray (2004) reports that 74 percent of police officers go to their dominant responses under stressful (shooting) circumstances. Siddle (1995) reports research also showing that stress promotes a return to more basic or dominant responses as shown in the following:

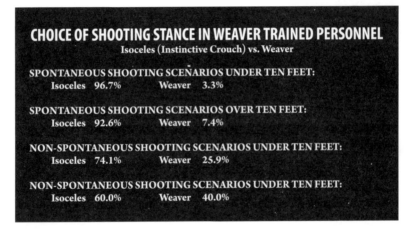

CHOICE OF SHOOTING STANCE IN WEAVER TRAINED PERSONNEL
Isoceles (Instinctive Crouch) vs. Weaver

SPONTANEOUS SHOOTING SCENARIOS UNDER TEN FEET:
   Isoceles 96.7%   Weaver   3.3%

SPONTANEOUS SHOOTING SCENARIOS OVER TEN FEET:
   Isoceles 92.6%   Weaver   7.4%

NON-SPONTANEOUS SHOOTING SCENARIOS UNDER TEN FEET:
   Isoceles 74.1%   Weaver   25.9%

NON-SPONTANEOUS SHOOTING SCENARIOS UNDER TEN FEET:
   Isoceles 60.0%   Weaver   40.0%

In this study, the Isosceles Stance (triangular position with both hands on the weapon in front of you) is the instinctive position and the Weaver Stance (a bladed position with the body angled to the side) is the trained response. As the data shows, under the more stressful spontaneous shooting scenarios, there was a much greater return to the basic Isosceles Stance, while under the less stressful non-spontaneous shooting scenarios, the trained Weaver Stance was maintained much more often.

Another example of regression to more basic and "comfortable" behavior and away from needed responses is seen in a study on the types of commands issued by police officers in high-stress versus low-stress situations by Dr. Mark Houlihan (2006) at Minnesota State University at Mankato. The study looked at the frequency of "Alpha commands" (Get down, Get on the ground, Drop your weapon, Stay in your vehicle) versus "Beta commands" (Move, Don't make me shoot you, Don't be stupid). It was found that, in non-violent situations, 84 percent of the commands were Alpha commands, but in violent situations, only 16 percent were Alpha commands.

The point is that Alpha commands are more direct and clear than Beta commands (just what exactly should or shouldn't a suspect do to not "be stupid"?). But it appears that in violent, high-stress situations, there is a strong tendency for officers to revert to more emotional and vague directives, opposite from what would be more effective. It's noted that the emotional tone is also seen in the increase of profanity and use of the F-word in their commands.

The presence of such effects of stress and their uniqueness to a given individual (everyone should not expect exactly the same reactions) is described by Marine Officer Nathaniel Frick (2005):

> **I was afraid for the first time in Iraq. Against the white noise of the blood rushing through my head, I heard my feet tapping involuntarily on the Humvee floor. My knees stitched up and down like a sewing machine. My mouth felt dry and gummy. Everything seemed to pass in a blur. I thought of war stories that talked about hyperclarity in combat, seeing every blade of grass and feeling colors more intensely than ever before. But for me, whole city blocks faded into a gray fuzz. I feared I was processing information too slowly, seeing only one of every ten things I should. I felt short-changed. I wanted hyperclarity, too. (p.204)**

This description also demonstrates why it's so important to understand the performance effects of stress. Without this knowledge to serve as a foundation for training, warriors may become perplexed and distracted, and misinterpret what is happening to them under stress. They may see normal responses as abnormal and feel they are "losing it." They may have "heard things" about how they should or should not respond in a high-stress situation and then be upset if they don't respond similarly. However, by understanding stress effects on performance, the warrior is allowed greater flexibility in dealing with intense situations.

The astute reader will also realize that the very point of assault tactics used in situations like drug raids and other surprise missions are designed to produce exactly these kinds of stress responses *in the targets*. Surprise, speed, and noise through flash bangs and/or aggressive shouts and commands, are meant to induce stress and dysfunction. The key is to produce such reactions in others, while the officers and soldiers have learned the psychological skills needed to perform under stress.

This book is not about general stress, life stress, or cumulative stress per se. However, it is important to realize that ongoing levels of stress in your life can affect acute stress responses. High levels can accelerate stress reactions in demanding missions.

The Pat Tillman Tragedy

The importance of these perceptual and performance effects of stress (and the need for their control) is sadly illustrated, in the story (Lindlaw & Mendoza, 2006) of tragic American hero, Pat Tillman. As many are aware, Pat Tillman had a successful and multi-million dollar career playing professional football for the Phoenix Cardinals. So greatly affected by the events of September 11, 2001, Pat gave up his career and joined the military to become an Army Ranger. His brother Kevin joined with him, giving up his own chance to play pro baseball. Pat was deployed to Iraq in 2003 and then sent to Afghanistan.

Although he shouted "Cease fire! Friendlies! I am Pat (expletive) Tillman, damn it!" he and an Afghan ally were killed by friendly fire by Rangers from his own Black Sheep Platoon. While the exact reasons for the tragedy are still being explored at this writing, comments from the Rangers who shot Tillman seem unfortunately representative of the perceptual and psychological effects of high-stress situations.

One Ranger said that he was "excited" by the sight of rifles, muzzle flashes and "shapes." The squad leader reported he had tunnel vision. He described the scene as one of being "amid the chaos and pumping adrenaline," and "hammering" what he thought was the enemy but was actually the allied Afghan fighter next to Tillman. He said: "I zoned in on him because I could see the AK-47. I focused only on him."

Whatever the details of the tragedy eventually prove to be, the unfortunate result has been described as "Chaos broke out and communication broke down. A humvee packed with pumped-up Rangers opened fire, killing the friendly Afghan and Tillman."

For these reasons, realistic training and training to levels of what has been called "unconscious competence" (Murray, 2004) is critical. Smith (2006), however, has recently suggested that while the engrained habits of unconscious competence are for sure critical, remaining at a level of "conscious competence" is more likely to maintain critical awareness and avoid complacency. Grossman and Christensen stressed the importance of these types of competency in *On Combat* (2004) by saying:

You don't rise to the occasion,
You sink to your level of training.

Therefore, training in both physical skills and psychological skills is essential to minimize stress effects during responses.

This critical importance of learning to control the effects of the adrenaline dump was recently summarized and reinforced by Drs. Audrey Honig and William Lewinski in their excellent article on human factors in lethal force encounters:

> **Critical to performance under stress is the ability to quickly control the stress reaction and, hence, reduce the release and effect of adrenaline on the system.**

FEAR

Let's briefly address a topic that is not discussed as much as it should be: The presence of fear during military missions and police operations. Dr. Roger Solomon, one of the leading experts on police post-shooting trauma, notes that every police officer has "experienced fear to some degree." He defines it as an automatic emotional reaction to a perceived danger or threat characterized by a high state of arousal. While there are some individuals who in most situations experience little, or possibly no fear, this is the exception.

Courage without Fear?
Rachman (1990) raises the interesting point that it may not be possible to demonstrate courage without feeling fear. He suggests that while there may be individuals who are fearless, this is not the same as courage, which requires feeling, confronting and overcoming fear. Reflecting Rachman's point, retired police lieutenant and Vietnam combat veteran, Dave Grossi (2004) quotes General Douglas MacArthur as saying:

> **"If bravery is a quality which knows no fear, then I have never seen a brave man."**

> ## Trained & Restrained
>
> **While the adrenaline dump can aid survival and performance, it will do so consistently and effectively when it's trained and restrained. A dump that is untrained and unrestrained is more likely to be unpredictable, unwieldy and unproductive to survival and success.**
>
> **As Brasidas, a Spartan Commander in the 429 B.C. Peloponnesian Wars, said, "Fear makes a man forget and skill which can not fight is useless."**

General George Patton said:

> **And every man is scared in his first action. If he says he's not,
> he's a goddamn liar.**
>
> **The real hero is the man who fights even though he's scared.
> Some get over their fright in a minute, under fire; others
> take an hour; for some it takes days…**

Gonzales (2003) describes the pre-flight briefing given to pilots aboard the Carrier Carl Vinson by LSO (Landing Signal Officer) Mike Yankovich:

> **It *will* scare the living shit out of you. If you taxi to the cat and
> you don't have a knot in your stomach, there's something wrong.**

Marine physician Lt. Commander Richard Jadick describes his experience with fear:

> **I stepped off the truck and noticed that everything was heavy.
> *Holy fuck, am I even going to make it?* Fear is like deep water.
> Slowing every step….(p. 41).**

Fear is our emotional equivalent of warning lights. It's a complex emotion and topic that can fill hundreds of pages of discussion (408 pages in Gavin DeBecker's excellent book, *The Gift of Fear*). The interested reader will also find an important discussion of fear in military personnel in *On Combat*.

For our purposes, fear can be seen as the ultimate stress; it involves excessive arousal that can inhibit effective functioning. However, fear also has positive aspects. For the military and police it can function to produce a readiness to respond and it can, importantly, signal the need for caution in certain situations. In *On Combat*, co-authors Grossman and Christensen note that some degree of fear can be present with various levels of arousal: condition "red" relates to some fear and condition "black" to intense fear.

Williams (2006) also suggests that fear can be a positive or negative force, but it's likely always present in dangerous situations:

> **Fear is an ever-present factor in a dangerous situation…**
>
> **It is not the absence of fear, but an understanding of it that
> allows the body to continue to function or, indeed, increase
> its ability to function when fear is present.**

Fear can show itself in different ways. Many of the symptoms of stress are the same as those of fear, though for the latter it's often more intense, i.e., the hand tremor from stress that begins to shake uncontrollably from fear. There are also performance indications of fear. Some as described by Feigley (1989) are listed here:

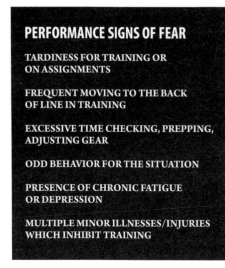

PERFORMANCE SIGNS OF FEAR

TARDINESS FOR TRAINING OR ON ASSIGNMENTS

FREQUENT MOVING TO THE BACK OF LINE IN TRAINING

EXCESSIVE TIME CHECKING, PREPPING, ADJUSTING GEAR

ODD BEHAVIOR FOR THE SITUATION

PRESENCE OF CHRONIC FATIGUE OR DEPRESSION

MULTIPLE MINOR ILLNESSES/INJURIES WHICH INHIBIT TRAINING

Performance Signs of Fear

Most warriors tend to be highly motivated and enthusiastic about what they do. Therefore, continual absences or lateness to training should raise a suspicion that something is not as it should be. Likewise, excessive time prepping that delays joining into training or action may signify uneasiness with responding. Unusual behavior may signify a fear problem. This may show itself in behavior that is not appropriate to the circumstance of the mission, by being distracted or by excessive joking and sarcasm. Or it may show itself by behavior that is odd for the individual, i.e., the typically quiet warrior who becomes boisterous to distraction, or the typically animated individual who becomes quiet and withdrawn.

Much like stress, fear can create multiple minor discomforts. When these cause the warrior to miss training excessively, be slow to respond, leave training early, or perform below expectations, the problems should be evaluated (medically and behaviorally). Finally, a typical manifestation of fear, one that is most often seen in training settings, is the individual who avoids full and repeated participation in training activities.

The complex nature of fear and performance is seen in an excellent discussion of the different types described by performance expert Dr. David Feigley (1989). Awareness of them is crucial not only for identifying fear's presence, but also for providing the most appropriate intervention to help with it. The type of fears and psychological techniques for helping to manage them are presented here:

PSYCHOLOGICAL TECHNIQUES FOR MANAGING FEAR

REALISTIC FEAR	FEAR OF THE UNKNOWN	ANXIETY	ILLOGICAL FEAR	FEAR OF FAILURE	FUN FEAR
Increased/ Adjusted Training	Imaging Alternate Responses	PMR	Self-Talk	Shaping	None Needed
Goal Setting	Exploration Time	Tactical Breathing	Negative Thought Stopping	Self-Talk	
Imagery	Simulation	Biofeedback		VMBR	
Simulation				Counseling	

Realistic Fears

These have a basis in reality as there is a potential for pain, injury or death if performance is inadequate. Realistic fears may be related to specific skills or situations (falling while rappelling or a weapon jam, for example). Each specific realistic fear should suggest its own solution.

Realistic fears are often a sign that more training is needed (remember, stress occurs when one doesn't feel prepared to meet the challenges of a given situation). These fears tend to subside with experience and the resulting confidence. Other factors that can fuel realistic fears include past failure, negative or traumatic experiences, or bad and inadequate training experiences.

Increased training can help, but more of the same isn't always better. A different approach and/or different techniques may be needed. Simulation training is always an excellent tool. Simulated or live exposure to a greater variety of situations, such as fire, malfunctioning equipment, being lost, or getting dressed down can broaden experience and confidence. Appropriate goal setting in training that allows success can help with realistic fears. Tactical imagery (see Chapter Seven) can also be helpful in creating confidence for dealing with unlikely, unforeseen, or unusual but worrisome situations.

Fear of the Unknown

This is a specific form of realistic fear. Not knowing what to expect is frightening, though the anticipation of a situation is often worse than the actual situation itself. Experience is the best antidote for fear of the unknown. In fact, it's recognized that what makes an "expert" isn't so much being brighter or quicker than everyone else, but rather having more experience in a given area. An expert knows what he is looking at and, because he has seen similar situations so many times before, he can quickly and effectively respond. The unknown for him has become well-known.

Fear of the unknown is also related to the uneasy or often terrifying "what-if" questions. "What if I screw up?" "What if someone dies?" "What if I don't react quickly enough?" "What if I don't pick-up on the danger signal that is so obvious to everyone else?"

What-if questions should always be answered and have a response, even if it's not favored or pleasant. Answering this type of question provides a plan and reduces the fear that lingers or increases if it remains unanswered. Always answer any what-if questions with a good tactical answer and plan.

Simulation is an extremely useful approach for fear of the unknown, as well. Sometimes just having time to explore or be in fearful situations at one's own pace can reduce uneasiness. Simply working with or having time to "explore" new equipment can begin to create greater comfort. Imagery can also be useful in preparing for unknown or unusual situations by confronting them and mentally rehearsing responses for that situation.

Language can be important in managing what-if fears, which is discussed later in greater depth (Chapter 8). However, as an example, it's useful to change the what-if proposition to an If-Then: *If* X occurs *then* I will react… Even better is a When-Then statement: *When* X occurs, *Then* I will react…)

Anxiety

If anxiety isn't strictly a type of fear, it's related to it. It's sometimes said that fear occurs when there is uneasiness about a specific object or situation, whereas anxiety is a diffuse uneasiness (fear) without specific focus. It can also be seen as arousal that has become too intense or occurs from the wrong sources (unrelated to the immediate challenge).

There can also be a "secondary anxiety." This is anxiety about having anxiety. While this may sound a bit silly, it makes sense. Knowing that becoming anxious can affect performance and maybe jeopardize a situation can actually create its own anxiety. This is often made worse when a warrior believes that he should never feel any anxiety or anxiety-related arousal during a mission. Of course, this is unlikely, unreasonable and unwise, as we have discussed previously that some arousal is needed to perform well. However, if one believes that there should be no uneasiness at all, the first signs of any degree of arousal can precipitate a rush of anxiety (often about "losing it," losing control of himself or the situation).

The key is to understand and manage arousal, not attempt to prevent or eradicate it.

Anxiety can also result from being advanced too quickly. A warrior may appear to have objectively good tactical skills, but may need more training, modeling, exposure or graded entry before feeling comfortable in a live response or leadership position.

The nature of the anxiety should help suggest a solution. Stress management techniques like Progressive Muscle Relaxation, Tactical Breathing or Biofeedback can be useful for managing the symptoms of anxiety or a high level of arousal. Adequate training, simulation and recognition of the nature of anxiety and secondary anxiety can also prevent negative performance impact.

Illogical Fear
This is a fear that is out of proportion to objective realities and is often seen in self-doubts that are greater than what they should be. Illogical fears result from a distortion (usually an exaggeration) in perceptions of a situation. Warriors experiencing illogical fear use words like "never" or "always" when referring to a situation or themselves. Comments such as "I always screw up when X is in command" or "I never do well with search operations" represent illogical fear. It's illogical because human beings rarely "never" or "always" do anything, including screwing up. Words like "never" and "always" are usually exaggerations but are so powerful that they create fear and concern. The use of self-talk and negative thought stopping (discussed in Chapter Eight) can be helpful in managing illogical fears.

Fear of Failure
This is a complicated fear, but not uncommon among highly motivated and achieving individuals. This is because high motivation can come from one of two sources:

- The Motive to Achieve Success (MAS).
- The Motive to Avoid Failure (MAF).

While both of these can produce high levels of motivation and performance, there are big differences as to how they relate to performance and how they affect the individual.

If you are driven by the MAS:

- you enjoy challenges.
- you don't mind problems; you like to solve them.
- you don't mind setbacks; it just drives you harder.
- you enjoy the process of meeting challenges so as to see what you're capable of doing, as much as you like seeing the outcome of your effort.
- you volunteer for new activities and you're the first to try new things.

If you're driven by the MAF:

- you also work hard to succeed but not because you enjoy the challenges and seek success.
- you're driven because you fear and because you want to avoid the embarrassment of failing.
- you perform, but do so under great pressure, discomfort and worry.
- setbacks and changes are seen as horrific catastrophes because they impede you from reaching your goal and raise the specter of failure.
- you don't enjoy the process of the challenge.
- you strive for the relief of obtaining a successful outcome.
- you tend not to volunteer for new activities, as this only puts more pressure on you.
- you don't enjoy your accomplishments as much as you feel relief that you made it through without screwing up too badly.

Most warriors are a blend of both MAS and MAF. The Motive to Avoid Failure leads to fear and discomfort. Much of this is related to experiences while growing up and experiences during training. Positive training, the kind that emphasizes development, tends to foster MAS, while negative, critical or failure-based training fosters MAF.

Dealing with fear of failure can be quite complicated because its roots penetrate deeply into one's development. At a minimum, it requires understanding that mistakes are part of learning and an opportunity to get better. It also requires separating one's self-concept and self-worth from a single performance situation.

Specific techniques to try include shaping skills, that is teaching skills in small achievable steps to experience success. A positive training philosophy can mediate fear of failure and self-talk can help at times, as well. Other times psychotherapy is needed.

Fun Fear

Rollercoaster riding and skydiving are examples of fun fear activities. Actually, so-called fun fear more accurately represents activity that induces arousal, rather than fear. Certainly arousal can be pleasurable; indeed, many warriors do what they do because they enjoy the feelings of arousal. Persons who enjoy such arousal have been called "adrenaline junkies."

Remsberg (1986) offers the comments of one police officer that demonstrate this point:

> **I like the edge, the challenge. I get a high off it. You're out**
> **there in the concrete jungle or the cornfield jungle.**
> **You know the guy you're up against has no regard**
> **for authority or society. I like the element of danger.**
> **It makes me feel alive.**

However, there is a difference between fun fear/arousal and fear. Fun fear has the common element of control and mastery: It assumes the rollercoaster, despite its speed, will not jump its tracks. It assumes that driving fast, despite its inherent danger, is under the control of the driver. Fear occurs when these things are out of control.

Competitors use potentially deadly techniques in martial arts tournaments and full-contact cage fighting where winning is defined by dominance. Injury or death is always a distinct possibility. However, even here, the presence of a referee provides a sense of control that reduces the levels of arousal that would be present in a street fight to the death.

The importance of control in fun fear can be further seen in Remsberg's officer's further comments:

> **But I don't expose myself to danger blatantly… I'm**
> **prepared tactically. That's what the rush comes from.**

Consider these points:

- Fun fear or arousal induced from an amusement park ride are usually interpreted as pleasurable and need no intervention.
- Fear induced by military missions and police operations can be controlled by tactical and psychological preparation.

Barriers to Fear Management

Despite the commonality of fear and the techniques to learn to manage it, it's well-recognized that it isn't always easy to address fear. The primary barrier is denial of fear's existence, something that warriors often do for many reasons, not the least of which is that military and police environments typically see fear as a weakness. Those with fear might be of the (erroneous) belief that no one else has experienced such feelings. There may be concern about looking weak, not having the "right stuff," or being seen as wacko by others. Despite being two different things, fear is often confused with cowardice, perhaps the greatest of any military or police sins.

This is an unfortunate perception, for as Solomon (1990) states:

> **The ability to understand the dynamics of fear**
> **in such critical instances is the first step to controlling fear**
> **and using it to one's own advantage.**

The second barrier is the denial of fear by others, especially trainers and command personnel who avoid it. Avoidance may stem from the same reasons that make an individual reluctant to discuss fear. It may result from faulty understanding about human psychological function or the lack of understanding of how to deal with the fear issue. Whether from macho philosophy, embarrassment or ignorance as to what to offer to help warriors manage fear (other than comments like "get over it"), the issue is too often ignored.

Bill Kipp, the scenario-based adrenal response training expert, 3rd Marine Recon veteran, martial artist, stuntman, bouncer and bodyguard quoted earlier, eloquently summarized the issue of fear (Christensen, 2004) for performance and the impact of avoiding fear discussions and training:

> **Fear is one of our greatest God-given tools. Without it**
> **our species would not have survived to this day. Fear is**
> **an inevitable and important survival response for anyone**
> **experiencing any sort of intense situation. But without**
> **proper training, fear can be a warrior's biggest enemy,**
> **causing an internal freeze or flight response in the heat of battle.**
> **Unfortunately, most modern day warrior training dances around**
> **the topic of fear. Adding fuel to the fire, many warriors are taught**
> **by society that fear is unacceptable and "umanly."**

The World War II pamphlet *Army Life* cautioned that because of uncertainty and thoughts of being killed, "You'll be scared" (Sherman, 2005). There was no mention in the pamphlet about how to manage this fear.

More likely to be discussed is the topic of courage as the opposite of fear. The interested reader might find Shalit's (1988) presentation a useful and interesting discussion of courage in military operations, which complements and provides further perspective on the issue of fear. Castro (2006) also discusses military courage and what he calls the "Battlemind" model of courage.

The term "Battlemind" has been adopted by the Army (Castro, 2007) as the name for its programs and efforts to help soldiers with stress pre-deployment, during deployment, and post-deployment.

Evidence of changes in the attitude about discussing fear is found in the "Battlemind" program (Castro, 2007), and in particular, in a list titled "8 Facts and Battlemind Concepts." It suggests that "fear in combat is common" and reports that two thirds of Army Silver Star recipients for gallantry in action reported increased fear as the battle progressed.

While a little brief on how to actually deal with fear, it's recommended in "Battlemind" literature that soldiers focus on what they have learned in training for combat, that they admit and joke about fear, and that they remember that fear is not a mental disorder. It's emphasized that "Even heroes feel fear."

A quote from General SLA Marshall cited by Grossman seems appropriate:

> **Fear in combat is ever present, but it is uncontrolled fear that is the enemy.**

Fear's Ultimate Embarrassment? Physiological Dyscontrol

There is also a particular aspect to fear that is almost as reviled as cowardice, though it's a normal response in a fearful situation and, like fear itself, requires discussion. Stress and fear can affect our bladder and bowel function. Co-authors Grossman and Christensen addressed it in *On Combat* but it's worth revisiting.

In *On Combat* it was reported that research shows that if you have a "load" in your bowels during a highly stressful or fearful situation, it's likely going to go. What do you do if that happens? You keep on fighting.

The American Soldier, the official study of the performance of U.S. troops in World War II, tells of one survey in which a quarter of all U.S. soldiers in World War II admitted that they had lost control of their bladders and an eighth of them admitted to defecating in their pants. Yet this is rarely talked about. Most warriors are too macho, or uninformed, to believe that such things happen, let alone happen to them. But they are wrong and, when it does happen, they feel shame and think something is wrong with them. But they are wrong about that, too.

If we look only at the individuals at the tip of the spear and factor out those who didn't experience intense combat, we can estimate that approximately 50 percent of those who did experience it admitted they had wet their pants and nearly 25 percent admitted they had messed themselves.

Those are the ones who *admitted* it, so the actual number is probably higher, though we cannot know by how much. One veteran told co-author Grossman, "Hell Colonel, all that proves is that three out of four were damned liars!" That is probably unfair and inaccurate, but the reality is that the humiliation and social stigma associated with crapping yourself probably results in many individuals being unwilling to admit the truth.

Dave notes that although this is happening, denial, lack of discussion and education about it continues. He reflected and asked: Have you ever heard about it in all the war stories told at the VFW? Can you imagine an old vet saying, "Yeah, Billy Bob, I remember the night I messed my drawers!" Or, 30 years after the war when you are bouncing your grandbaby on your knee and the child looks adoringly into your eyes, and asks, "Grandpa, what did *you* do in the war?" The very last thing you are going to say is, "Well, grandpa crapped himself!"

No, says Dave, you will never tell your grandbaby about the degrading, demeaning, debasing, humiliating things that happened to you in combat. Instead, you will fill him with popcorn and sunshine. The problem with this is that 20 years later when he is in combat and has just messed his drawers, he will ask himself, "What's wrong with me? This didn't happen to grandpa and it didn't happen to John Wayne. There must be something terribly wrong with me!"

Co-author Loren Christensen wrote an article for a major police magazine about the effects of stress on police officers forced to defend themselves in deadly shootings. The editor accepted and loved the piece but deleted the section about the possibility that officers might soil themselves.

Co-author Dave Grossman says the myth is perpetuated across the generations. Remember, the data indicates that most veterans of intense combat didn't experience this, but for that large minority who *did*, it can be their deep, dark secret. And there is power in knowing that it might happen. "I will go see a war movie," said one Vietnam veteran, "when the main character is shown shitting his pants in the battle scene." Have you ever seen a movie that depicted a soldier defecating in his drawers in combat?

It may be well to repeat the experience of a federal agent during the terrorist attack on the Twin Towers that was originally described in *On Combat*. A few months after the September 11, 2001, attacks, Dave had the privilege of training a group of federal agents. He described it this way:

> One of them had been at the World Trade Center during the attack. He came up to me after I had taught about loss of bowel and bladder control, and said, "Thank you. Now I understand what happened to me." Then he told me his story.

> He and the other agents in his office were able to evacuate the building after the hijacked airplane had hit it. They were wearing their tactical gear and assisting local police when the first building began to come down. At first they didn't know what to do, and then they realized that they had better, as he put it, "Run like hell." He said that a black cloud of smoke and dust enveloped them and darkened the sky. He couldn't breathe and was losing consciousness. Then the cloud passed and he turned around and went back in to help.

> Then the second building began to collapse. I found myself admiring his ability to find humor in the situation as he said, "By now we'd gotten to be experts at falling buildings, and we knew exactly what to do. We turned and ran like hell." Again a black cloud enveloped him and darkened the sky, and again he thought he was dying as he began to lose consciousness. But when the cloud passed, he once again turned around and headed back in.

> A few hours later, as he was climbing through the rubble, someone tapped him on the shoulder and said, "I'm your relief," and he was directed back to a cleanup point in a gym.

> "The thing that I always wondered about," he said, "was why everyone there had crapped themselves, except me. Now I understand. You said, 'If there's a load in the lower intestines, its gonna go.' Just before those bastards hit our building, I had taken a really good morning visit to the bathroom."

Probably no event in human history has been reported and studied more than the 9/11 attacks, and yet almost no one knows that, apparently, most of the survivors lost bowel and bladder control. Does this diminish their courage? Not in the least. But if it ever happens to us, it would be good to know that it is perfectly normal.

Professionals who work with addictions often talk about the problem in the family being like an "elephant in the living room." There is this gigantic disruption in their lives that they try to ignore, walk around, and deny, but addiction clearly impacts functioning. Fear and its management in military and police settings is much like that elephant. It's time to cut through the baloney and learn what really happens in combat so that a generation of warriors is raised to be mentally and emotionally prepared to go into the toxic realm.Siddle (1995) notes that even the coolest of gunfighters in the old west were not without emotions; it was their control that was the key to success.

> …with such men it was not a case of lack of nerves as some try to make it appear; it was a matter of having everything in the way of impulse and emotions absolutely under control at the psychological moment…"

> …no disturbing influence was great enough to throw them out of normal balance, no danger no matter how great or close, interfered with their positive movements, properly controlled, correctly timed and accurately directed."

Machowicz (2002) describes fear in SEAL training during Hell Week and the will to manage it.

> Some guys try to act cool… Those are the guys who think they're going waltz in and breeze through this – it often turns out they're the first ones to quit. On the other side are the guys who are really nervous – I was one of them. But I tried to keep my body relaxed and tell myself, whatever it is, you've just got to do it.

The key is to acknowledge, understand, manage and use the natural emotion of fear. Famous test pilot Chuck Yeager is quoted as saying:

> I was always afraid of dying. Always. It was my fear that made me learn everything I could about my airplane and my emergency equipment and kept me flying respectful of my machine and always alert in the cockpit.

In *Dune*, author Frank Herbert describes confronting fear this way:

> **I must not fear. Fear is the mind-killer. Fear is the little-death that brings total obliteration. I will face my fear. I will permit it to pass over me and through me. And when it has gone past, I will turn the inner eye to see its path. Where the fear has gone, there will be nothing. Only I will remain.**

Chaplain Lt. Colonel Douglas Etter spent 18 months in Iraq in a forward position embedded with his unit, helping carry their ammunition and supplies. He poignantly noted both the normalcy of fear and then the diminishing of fear with time:

> **Fear is an expected part of what we shoulder, but like the weight of our body armor, we have grown so accustomed to it, we almost don't notice it anymore.**

Chief Kevin Nelson, one of the people I respect most for his performance excellence, captured a philosophy of accepting and transforming fear in saying:

> **You replace fear of a situation with respect for its challenges.**

Room of a thousand terrors
We are reminded of one last lesson about mastering fear called the "room of a thousand terrors." I don't remember where I heard it or even if the legend has any truth, but it seems most relevant.

It was well-known that to become the holiest of yogis in Eastern mysticism takes years of study, self-sacrifice, and ascetic living. However, it's said that the years of austerity can be circumvented by crossing through "the room of a thousand terrors." It was said that after one would enter the room he had only to get to the door on the other side to exit. But as soon as he entered, his deepest and darkest fears would become live and large to challenge him, torment him and drive him back from his crossing.

It was also said that there was a means to thwart the fears and attain the other side. This was "to keep your mind clear (focused) and your feet moving." In doing so, you would eventually come to the other side.

In moving from fear of a situation to respecting it, psychological skills training integrated with physical training can help create that transformation to keep your mind focused and your feet moving.

MANAGING AROUSAL, STRESS AND FEAR

Given that high-stress missions can create normal but problematic reactions for warriors, it's essential to control and minimize them. As noted, experience is the usual way adaptation to the stress of missions occurs.

The Importance of Experience
Individuals who are experienced with a given set of skills show a different pattern of arousal from those who are less experienced with the same set. This figure from Fenz and Epstein (1967) shows the pattern (chart from Asken, 1993) of arousal between experienced skydivers and inexperienced skydivers.

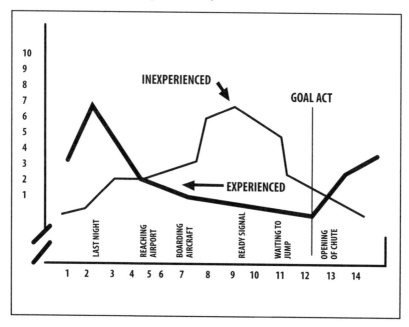

Note that inexperienced skydivers have rather low levels of arousal when there is still considerable time until the jump. But as they begin to prepare, approach the airport, begin their ascent in the plane, and receive the ready signal, their level of arousal increases significantly. After the jump is (safely) over, arousal declines once more... almost in a sense of relief.

For experienced skydivers, however, the pattern is different. Their arousal is actually higher the night before as they enthusiastically anticipate doing the jump. As they approach the airport, board the plane and receive the ready signal, they gain control over their arousal as they focus on their mental checklist, just as a pilot goes over the preflight checklist. Their arousal lowers with this focus until after the chute opens and they feel the exhilaration of the jump. This a typical pattern found in many areas of human performance when comparing experienced performers with rookies.

Research with police officers shows the effects of experience on arousal, as well. Vonk (1994) reported that while experienced and less experienced police officers both showed the same inverted-U pattern to arousal and performance, experienced officers showed lower levels of arousal overall.

Of course, becoming experienced requires time and assumes an adequate number of missions in general and an adequate number of missions of the same type for familiarization with their nature. Additionally, the mission needs to have gone well or at least not have been traumatic. Unfortunately, despite many similarities in mission situations, there are so many possible differences, that it can take awhile to become an expert in just one kind.

Reality Training

Simulation or reality-based scenario training and tactical performance imagery (discussed in Chapter Seven) are excellent approaches to gaining experience and exposure to various types of missions. Repeated training can help dampen arousal and strengthen emotional control. Unfortunately, time and access may limit training of this nature. Therefore, using the psychological skills described next adds a further dimension to your training for performance excellence by developing greater control for self-regulation of emotion and arousal.

Does Scenario Training Really Simulate Stressful Conditions?

When it comes to inoculating warriors against stress, training such as reality-based scenarios (and experience) are unsurpassed. Tactical Arousal Control, Tactical Performance Imagery, Stress Inoculation Training and the other psychological skills discussed in this book facilitate the process and results.

A question that is often raised, however, is whether simulations can really induce stress since trainees "know " the situation "is not real." Research has tried to address this question.

Objective evidence of stress during scenario training is found in physiological monitoring during such training. Increases in heart rate and blood pressure significantly greater than normal daily levels occur across training scenarios from vehicle pursuits to intervening in domestic disturbances (McCraty et al., 1999). Additionally, subjective reports corroborate these findings with perceptions and feelings of stress.

Participants at an advanced topics training for police crisis negotiators (Asken et al., 2008) were asked to complete questionnaires on various aspects of training and performance before engaging in reality-based scenarios and/or after the scenario portion of the training was completed. Trainees were asked to answer all questions using a 1 to 10 rating scale where 1 indicated little agreement or minimal effect and 10 indicated the most agreement or maximal effect.

Results showed that crisis negotiators reported they do experience stress during actual call-outs and their negotiations and the intensity of the stress was rated at an average of 6.2 out of 10. They reported the stress they felt during scenario training to be 6.1 out of 10, almost exactly the same intensity of stress as they reported they experience during actual call-outs and crisis negotiations. Further, they rated the degree of realism of the scenario experience to be an average of 7.9 out of 10.

Other research (Asken & Yunk, 2006) found similar results. The same model as above was applied to undercover/ narcotics agents undergoing training. The participants rated the stress of the reality-based scenarios to be 5.8 out of 10.

Thus, scenario training is rated by participants as very realistic and stressful. For crisis negotiators, the amount of stress generated by scenario training was almost identical to that experienced during actual police negotiation incidents.

chapter

Mental Attack Plan:
Tactical Arousal Control Techniques and Mental Toughness

Watch your thoughts; they become words.
Watch your words; they become actions.
Watch your actions; they become habits.
Watch your habits; they become character.
Watch your character; it becomes your destiny.

– Anonymous

Succeeding with the goal of preventing or managing reactions, such as those perceptual distortions that occur in high-stress situations, involves controlling your arousal so that your O-ZONE can be achieved and maintained. This is tactical self-control using Tactical Arousal Control Techniques (TACT).

Anti-terrorism expert and trainer John Giduck writes (2008) about the critical importance of being able to remain relaxed in confrontations, including hand-to-hand combat. He says that "the single most important thing" that Russians (specifically the Spetsnaz special forces) stress in close-quarter combat is " the need to relax in combat; to relax in the face of threat or conflict." (We would emphasize that it is the self-regulation of your O-ZONE that is crucial, but relaxation is typically part of arousal control and does have its own benefits as Giduck notes in the following).

Here are effective methods for Tactical Arousal Control:

TACTICAL AROUSAL CONTROL TECHNIQUES

TACTICAL MUSCLE RELAXATION

RELAXATION RESPONSE

MEDITATION

YOGA

TACTICAL PERFORMANCE IMAGERY

SELF-HYPNOSIS

AUTOGENIC TRAINING

BIOFEEDBACK

Tactical Muscle Relaxation (TMR) and Tactical Performance Imagery (TPI) are discussed in detail later in this book. We mention other approaches only briefly in the event you wish to learn more about one or more of them. All have potential benefits and are useful.

Remember the insights of John Giduck (2008) who writes that "the single most important thing" that Russians (specifically the Spetsnaz special forces) train in close-quarter combat is "the need to relax in combat; to relax in the face of threat or conflict." He goes on to say that experience from training done by his Archangel Group shows that removing tension from the mind and body increases the force that can be generated by the muscles. It is more difficult to hurt the relaxed combatant and relaxation prior to and at initial engagement can save oxygen and energy to be used later to dominate a depleted enemy.

The Relaxation Response

This is a form of "Americanized" meditation developed by Dr. Herbert Benson of the Mind-Body Institute and Harvard Medical School. The Relaxation Response involves sitting comfortably in a quiet setting and repeating a word or phrase that suggests relaxation to you. In traditional meditation, this word or phrase, called your mantra, is usually spoken in Hindu, though any word or phrase suggesting calmness, relaxation and focus is effective.

This is a passive method of inducing relaxation, meaning that it's important to focus on the word or phrase and let the relaxation happen. You cannot force it, which many people try to do. Relaxation involves "letting go" to allow a calmer state to evolve. Forcing is the opposite of this.

Initially, The Relaxation Response was created to help treat people with high blood pressure who were not responding to medication. Because of its success in this area, it has been applied to other stress-related disorders, such as tension headaches and those situations where a state of relaxation is desired to help treat or cope with the problem situation. Dr. Benson has done some fascinating and important research on the power of meditative techniques, which is discussed later.

Meditation and Yoga

These ancient Eastern techniques are highly effective ways to control and quiet the body. While at first they may seem strange to Americans and Westerners, which is why Benson adapted them to form the Relaxation Response, they can nonetheless be highly effective. In fact, it was the yogis and practitioners of these arts who taught Western Medicine that it's possible for an individual to control functions in the body that were believed to be only controllable by medication, such as heart rate, blood pressure, and muscle tightness. These were named "autonomic responses," as it was believed they were automatic and could not be controlled.

The Fab Four's Contribution	Begley (2007) feels that the musical group the Beatles helped legitimize the scientific study of meditation and yoga in Western Medicine. In 1968, the four Beatles went to study with the Maharishi Yogi, a journey well covered by the press. Begley writes, "Their visit popularized the notion that the spiritual East has something to teach the rational West."

The military application of yoga is ancient. One form called kundalini yoga was passed through Sikh warriors for generations. It is reported that the warriors of a great Indian yoga of the seventeenth and eighteenth centuries, Guru Gobinde Singh, were known to generate terror in their enemies by the focus and fearless attitude they displayed going into battle as a result of such training (Alexander, et al., 1990).

Meditation is based on concentrating or chanting a mantra (or special phrase) and yoga is based on rhythmic breathing techniques (Tactical Breathing is discussed later) in conjunction with dynamic body postures. While still controversial, some research suggests that several forms of meditation can improve concentration, reaction time, learning and memory (Walsh & Shapiro, 2006). Other research (Anthes, 2008) has found that regular practice of meditation increases performance on target recognition tasks, increases awareness of nearly simultaneous targets and appears to result in using less mental energy while engaging in such tasks.

Ruge (2005) writes of the value of mantra use in police skills, in survival, and in preparing "the mind for battle."

Despite the skepticism that many police officers and soldiers have about meditation and yoga, there is nonetheless a growing acceptance of its value and effectiveness. For example, Nelson (2006) profiles an Annapolis graduate and SEAL who participates regularly in yoga training, enjoying both the physical and psychological benefits. He describes the breathing-based techniques as helpful with diving, being comfortable when working in contorted and difficult positions, remaining focused on-task longer, and functioning for long periods in confined spaces.

Of Monks, Mind, Meditation, Mastery and Drying Sheets

Dr. Benson, of Harvard Medical School and developer of the Relaxation Response, and his team studied the ability of Tibetan Monks to use a form of Meditation called Tum-mo to master the metabolism and other physiological processes in the body (Cromie, 2002). The demonstration took place in northern India in a chilly room of forty degrees Fahrenheit.

After the monks entered a state of deep meditation, they were draped in wet sheets that had been soaked in cold water (49 degrees F). Rather than developing the hypothermia and uncontrolled shivering that would affect most of us, the monks continued to meditate with little reaction. More remarkably, steam began to rise from them as the cold sheets reacted to the meditating monks' body heat. The sheets dried in about an hour. Each monk dried three sheets over the course of the demonstration.

In other studies, the monks warmed the temperature of their toes and fingers by as much as seventeen degrees. They were also able to slow their metabolism through meditation by sixty-four percent. (When we sleep, our metabolism slows about 10-15 percent. Other forms of simple meditation find metabolism decreases of about 17 percent.)

As a final example of self-regulation through meditation, wearing only woolen or cotton shawls, the monks slept through a February night on a 15,000-foot Himalayan mountain ledge, with temperatures at zero degrees Fahrenheit. They did not huddle together, they showed no shivering, and at dawn they walked back to their monastery.

Co-author Loren Christensen, Vietnam veteran, retired police officer, and a martial artist since 1965, meditates daily, sometimes for 15 minutes and other times for two 25-minute sessions. He says that it's a wonderful way to enhance your mental facilities and improve your physical skills. Think of it as self-mastery, a highly sought after quality that all warriors want. It's a powerful device that Loren says declutters your mind and relaxes your body so that you're able to think faster, learn quicker, make decisions better, and stay focused and on task even when extremely fatigued.

Many warriors imagine that they have to sit in the lotus position and burn incense to meditate. Not so, Loren says. You can do it in your easy chair at home, in a quiet place at work, in a squad car, leaning against a sandbag, in bed just before you go to sleep, or just after you awaken. You can even do it while walking. Loren says that there is nothing weird, new age or even mystical about it. It's simply a powerful, natural and effective way to sharpen your warrior skills.

Hypnosis or Self-Hypnosis

These words often bring up strange images of a stage hypnotist or swami putting people under their spell. Actually, self-hypnosis is a form concentration control. In hypnosis, one area of focus is so strong that everything else seems blocked out. Nowicki (1994) defines it as a state of relaxation characterized by heightened awareness, restricted mental focus and increased suggestibility.

We often engage in a form of self-hypnosis in our daily lives through distraction. For example, if we ask how your shoes feel, you could tell me if they are comfortable, tight, or pinching. However, chances are that prior to my asking, you were not thinking about them at all; you didn't even feel them or your feet. The distraction of your attention away from your feet (by reading and concentrating on this book or by daydreaming) is a form of self-hypnosis, that is, the act of concentrating so intently that other distractions are blocked out. The interested reader should examine Cohen's (1998) *The Stuff of Heroes* in which he suggests that hypnosis is valuable for performance enhancement.

Autogenic Training

This relaxation technique, developed in Germany in the early part of the last century, uses self-suggestions of warmth and heaviness in your body to induce relaxation. You begin in a quiet setting and relaxed position, and make self-suggestions of body regulation. For example, you would say: "My arms and legs are heavy and warm." "My heart rate is slow, calm and regular." Repeat these several times, consciously feeling the heaviness and calming. Try using calming statements, such as "I am at peace." (Lichtenstein, 1988). Use of suggestions of heaviness and warmth in the abdominal area has shown to be associated with decreased stomach motility (reduced sensations in the stomach).

Biofeedback

Biofeedback incorporates any relaxation technique to inform you via a biofeedback instrument (machine) if your body is relaxed. A device attaches to your body that measures a physiological response related to stressed or relaxed states. Usual examples are heart rate monitors, blood pressure monitors, brain wave monitors (as some types of brain waves relate to relaxation) or skin temperature. Biofeedback systems can monitor a single body reaction or several body responses at the same time.

For example, warmer skin temperature is associated with relaxation and reduced stress. Stress decreases skin temperature in your hands, hence the cold sweat you feel in your palms. While you practice your relaxation technique, the biofeedback device gives you information (feedback) as to whether your body is responding and, if so, how much. You learn to raise your skin temperature using feedback lights, sounds or numbers from the instrument. Since it's impossible to be stressed and relaxed at the same time, learning to control and raise your skin temperature can help prevent or abort a stress response.

Biofeedback has been successful in treating a variety of stress-related health conditions. It has also been widely used in training athletes.

Targeting Specific Bodily Reactions with Biofeedback	Biofeedback is also used to make athletes more aware of and to be in control of specific physiological reactions in their bodies during performance (Helin & Sihvonen, 1987; Janelle, Hillman, et al., 2000; Tremayne & Barry, 2001). A variety of studies in shooting sports, including rifle, pistol, and archery competitions, have found changes in brain waves, visual gaze and even cardiac rhythm related to level of expertise and best versus worse performances.
	For example, there is often found an increase in alpha rhythm in the left hemisphere of competitors' brains, suggesting a quieting (relaxation) of the thinking-verbal areas and increase in the spatial relationship areas as targets are sighted. Janelle & Hatfield (2008) report research on precision pistol shooting with midshipman at the U.S. Naval Academy which showed decreased left-hemisphere (thinking) activity after the sixteen weeks of training. Related to heart rhythm, there has been found a deceleration in heart rate before firing. Biofeedback training, including Neurofeedback (brain waves), is used to teach athletes to control such responses to maximize performance.

Biofeedback is also used to help astronauts learn self-regulation for managing the stress of extended missions and maintaining attention (Pope & Prinzel, n.d.).

An Example of Adaptation and Application

Beckett (2008) presents a very interesting description of using psychological techniques (including anger) to control pain. He makes an important distinction between types of pain; acute and immediate severe pain, milder but extended pain, and chronic pain.

Acute and immediate pain, such as the trauma of a physical attack or accident. As Beckett says, really "LARGE" pain. In this situation, he describes anger used as a coping mechanism; the greater the pain the more intense the anger that is mustered. It's described as "anger looking out through your eyes at the threat," like a loudspeaker facing towards the inside of your skull, and a sound tone that is savage like a roaring lion. In fact, the associated imagery is that of a wounded lion turning on the hunter. It's a physiology of fighting and survival, crawling, kicking, whatever is needed. The greater the pain inflicted, the greater the anger amassed, the less pain perceived and the harder one is to defeat.

The second type of pain, that which is milder but more extended, is exemplified by dental or medical procedures performed without anesthetic and throbbing joint or muscle injury while healing after injury. The approach suggested here is "disassociation" or psychologically stepping "outside yourself" and watching what's going on. The more the discomfort the farther you step away. Distraction can also be used here, like focusing on a song (Beckett suggests Carly Simon's "I Haven't Got Time for the Pain").

For chronic pain like arthritis, Beckett suggests hypnotic-like manipulations. He describes intentionally focusing on the pain and feeling the different components, but then changing them. For example, he makes the pain a color and puts it "in a box." If the color is envisioned as becoming brighter, the pain increases and as the color dims, the pain wanes. Change the color to a more soothing green, tropical island azure or upbeat yellow, and the pain moderates.

The above description is not provided as a specific prescription for dealing with pain, though it may be useful for many people. It does demonstrate a situation where anger might be used to cope and survive (although, once gain, caution in control and the target of such anger is critical). It's mainly provided to illustrate the personal adaptation of techniques, the use of different and multiple techniques and how psychological training and approaches can be used to influence physical, emotional and performance states.

TACTICAL MUSCLE RELAXATION (TMR)

Applicable to Police and Military Needs

Experience shows that Tactical Muscle Relaxation (TMR) is effective and easily used by police, the military and emergency personnel. In fact, while it often takes patients and civilians many practice sessions to gain proficiency at more traditional progressive muscle relaxation, my (MA) experience is that people who work in high-stress situations often experience good control and relaxation the first time they try it.

Unlike some forms of relaxation training that involve just "thinking" and being passive, TMR is a physically and mentally active approach. This fits better with the more action-oriented nature of military and police duties, and the expectations of officers and soldiers. It provides a good point of focus and is shown to be superior to other relaxation techniques.

Muscle Tensing and Relaxing

Traditional Progressive Muscle Relaxation has its roots in Dr. Edmund Jacobson's work in the 1920's. A simple technique, it begins with tensing and then relaxing different muscle groups in the body. For example, the procedure begins with relaxing muscles in the hands and arms, proceeds to the shoulders and neck, further progresses down to the chest, stomach, legs and into the toes. See Appendix I for the specifics.

The initial training session takes about 15 to 20 minutes. Once mastered, you move to the next level, called "letting-go." This involves relaxing without tensing the muscles first; you just let go of the tension. See Appendix I for a good description of this process.

TMR works because tensing and relaxing the muscles trains them to relax and release tension. When muscles relax, other parts of the body respond, as well. Heart rate slows, blood pressure decreases, and breathing becomes slower and easier.

Training in TMR also helps warriors recognize signs of tension in their muscles, whether from stress, posture or both. Initiating relaxation at the earliest signs of muscle tension makes it easier to reverse it, rather than waiting until tension is high and muscles are tense.

Creating a Command Word

The process of "conditioning" your mind and body allows TMR to work fast, sometimes in a matter of seconds. The first step involves focusing on a command word or phrase that you say aloud or think to yourself. (This may also be referred to as a "trigger" or "trigger word.") This can be any word or phrase, as long as it suggests relaxation and concentration. Words like "focus," "smooth," "easy," or "relax" are fine.

In traditional Progressive Muscle Relaxation, using words like "Hawaii" or "Blue Sky" helps create relaxation. However, it's probably best that warriors are not thinking about these things in the middle of a mission. So choose a control word that fits better with the environment and the action of a mission.

Focusing on the command word or cue, while creating relaxation in your body and mind, conditions or creates an association between that command word and controlled relaxation in your body. So, with practice, just thinking the command word or whispering it will cue the start of your relaxation. You will not have to spend twenty minutes tensing muscles to achieve relaxation. Thinking or uttering your cue word will be a bit like flipping on a light switch or a relaxation switch.

Co-author Christensen has used the command word for years as a device to create a sense of relaxation and calm. Sometimes he uses it simply as a way to bring on a sense of ease when he is feeling agitated, while other times he employs it as a device to start the relaxation process quickly when he is about to meditate. Christensen calls it his "Keyword." Here is what he said about it in his book *The Mental Edge, Revised*:

Keyword is a nifty device that quickly and easily gets you started into a state of relaxation...Choose any word you like, such as "relax," "calm," or "tension go." I use my middle name, Wayne. I seldom hear it, and I use only my initial when I write my name. Best of all, I can remember it.

First, you need to develop a comfortable level of expertise with one or more of the relaxation methods just discussed. When you are deeply relaxed and susceptible to autosuggestion, tell yourself that whenever you say the word "relax," or whatever word you choose, you will immediately experience a sense of deep relaxation wash over you. You may have to tell yourself this for several sessions until it takes hold. Even after it's working for you, you should continue to practice the relaxation and keyword to keep the conditioning strong.

An alternate term for the cue or key word is that of "anchor." Anchors are cues that recall patterns of behavior (Alexander, et al., 1990). It is useful to realize that anchors can be verbal, visual or physical. For example, relaxation cueing can be enhanced by also associating a physical anchor with the relaxing training or the key word. Making a fist, or extending the fingers, or touching a particular spot on the body would be examples of physical anchors that could be conditioned and used to recall and stimulate relaxed states.

Pavlov and Conditioned Control

Training in TMR is actually the reverse process of how stress and tension are conditioned during missions. Much of human emotion is the result of an association developing between feelings in our body and some outside stimulus. Our understanding of this comes from the work of the Russian physiologist, Ian Pavlov. You may have heard about "Pavlov's dogs."

Pavlov was able to get dogs to salivate to a stimulus/cue that in no way should cause a dog to salivate. Here is the process:

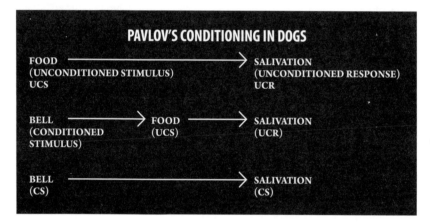

If you show food, especially meat to a dog, it begins to salivate, as this is a "wired" or innate response. Because there is no learning involved with this reaction, food is an **un***conditioned stimulus* and salivation is an **un***conditioned response*. (Conditioning means "learning" and conditioned means "learned" in behavioral psychology terms).

Pavlov wanted to see if he could get the dog to salivate to a stimulus that normally would not produce salivation, like the sound of a bell. To produce the association or conditioning, he would ring the bell before presenting the food. The dog would of course, salivate only upon presentation of the food. However, Pavlov found that after several sessions, the dog would salivate at the sound of the bell, even before the presentation of the food. The bell, a formerly neutral stimulus, brought on salivation. (Actually, the dogs would often salivate just at the sight of Pavlov or his laboratory assistants!) At this point, the bell is a *conditioned stimulus* and the salivation is a *conditioned response*.

While this may be interesting, though not so exciting in itself, its importance is in its applications. As noted, this seems to be the model for how much of human emotion is learned, including stress in military missions and police operations.

How Psychological Conditioning Impacts our Behavior

Pavlov's model applies to most human emotional situations. For example, many people begin to react emotionally when entering a dentist's office (some react just thinking about going to the dentist); some react when they hear the sound of the drill or see the needle. This is not because they are emotionally weak. More likely it's because in the past they experienced pain at the dentist, which has become associated with one of these aspects of the office.

Did you ever eat bad seafood and then puke your guts all night long? What are the chances that you went out to eat more seafood as soon as you felt better? Probably unlikely – even if someone else was buying! Looking at seafood probably made you feel queasy and it was probably a while before you were able to enjoy it again. This is not a result of being hysterical or wimpy. It's a conditioned response between the seafood and the night of nausea.

In Stop Teaching Our Kids to Kill Dave Grossman and Gloria Degaetano (and Dave in *On Combat*) importantly describe the dangerous conditioning that occurs when kids play violent video games. Such play also sharpens shooting skills (as noted in several school shootings) and desensitizes kids to the suffering of others. However, just like Pavlov's dogs, the games (and other media) condition a toxic association between having fun (being with friends, food, partying) and killing, maiming, and spilling another's blood, including police officers.

Psychological conditioning also occurs for positive emotions. If you feel a surging river of pride whenever you hear the national anthem, this represents a conditioned response to the flag's symbolism for you. If you and your significant other share a special song, it's likely that you experience warm positive feelings whenever you hear it. This is result of the pleasant times the two of you spend together (or a particular behavior you engaged in) in the presence of the song.

A police officer told me of a situation where he was involved in a lethal ground fight with a suspect. He was beginning to tire and thoughts of giving up were entering his mind. Then, he began to hear the faint but intensifying sounds of the backup officers' sirens. He felt his energy and motivation intensify to the point where he was able to sustain the fight until they arrived.

Pinizotto and his colleagues (2006) report the case of a police officer shot in the head, hand and back. He related to them that he felt that he was going to die. He also reported that:

> **I remember in the ambulance looking out the back window,**
> **and it was a sea of red and blue lights following me to the hospital.**
> **And, that was actually quite comforting.**

He survived.

Here is the model for conditioned arousal/anxiety in response to a threat:

HUMAN CONDITIONING OF AROUSAL/ANXIETY

THREAT **(UCS)**	⟶	**AROUSAL/ANXIETY** **(UCR)**
READY ORDERS **"GO COMMAND"** **(CS)**	⟶ **THREAT** **(UCS)** ⟶	**AROUSAL/ANXIETY** **(UCR)**
READY ORDERS **"GO COMMAND"** **(CS)**	⟶	**AROUSAL/ANXIETY** **(CR)**

As described earlier, there are varieties of reactions that represent stress, arousal or anxiety that occur in our body when confronted with a threat. The threat (a pointed gun, aggressive posturing, or being under attack) is the unconditioned stimulus; the arousal is the unconditioned response. For military and police warriors, the threat is preceded by orders to get ready, a "go" command, gearing up, or by entering transport vehicles.

These aspects of the response are like the ringing bell and can become the conditioned stimulus. When preceding or being paired with threats on a mission often enough, feelings of arousal are set off by these aspects even before the actual threat is encountered. At this point, the mission or police call (and almost any part of it) become the conditioned stimulus; the arousal or anxiety the conditioned response. This process intensifies when there are negative, problematic or traumatic aspects to the mission. (Success and effective performance can condition positive feelings and cognitions).

Multiple exposures to successful missions can actually create confidence and desensitize you to some of the mission-related anxieties – though be cautious about complacency. TMR can aid the process of comfort and confidence. The same process explains why TMR works to create relaxation or a "counter-condition" to the arousal/anxiety that is conditioned by the mission. This is the process:

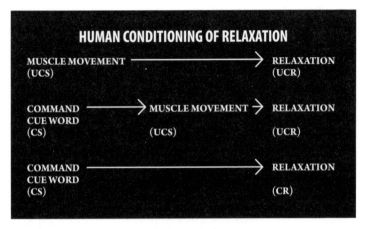

HUMAN CONDITIONING OF RELAXATION

MUSCLE MOVEMENT (UCS)	⟶	RELAXATION (UCR)
COMMAND CUE WORD (CS)	⟶ MUSCLE MOVEMENT (UCS) ⟶	RELAXATION (UCR)
COMMAND CUE WORD (CS)	⟶	RELAXATION (CR)

Your Command Word is a Conditioned Stimulus

In relaxation training, tensing and relaxing the muscles create relaxation throughout your body. The muscle movement is the unconditioned stimulus and relaxation is the unconditioned response. Thinking or saying your command word before or while doing the muscle movements is like ringing the bell. The command word is the conditioned stimulus. With adequate practice and training, you condition the association between the command word and the feelings of relaxation, such that thinking your command word leads to the relaxation (without having to tense and relax your muscles). The command word is the conditioned stimulus and the relaxation is now the conditioned response.

Cautions

There are some cautions in training relaxation. First, mastering relaxation and creating effective conditioning takes practice to both develop and maintain relaxation effects. Secondly, relaxation is a fundamental skill; it's not a cure-all or substitute for other skill training. You have to be smart about the application of this training, especially if you become very good at producing relaxation. Use caution that you don't produce excessive relaxation before or during a mission. While it's unlikely that this would happen, remember, your goal is to be at your optimal arousal level. Use relaxation as part of the process to achieve it.

Relaxation techniques are usually without side effects and are even used to treat many medical and psychological conditions. However, if you have a health concern (especially if you have a history of trauma-related psychological problems or post-traumatic stress disorder), it's best to check with your physician before intensely pursuing relaxation training.

Benefits of Tactical Muscle Relaxation Training
Here is a summary of the benefits to learning tactical self-control via TMR:

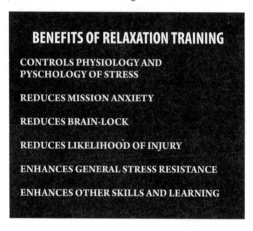

BENEFITS OF RELAXATION TRAINING

CONTROLS PHYSIOLOGY AND PYSCHOLOGY OF STRESS

REDUCES MISSION ANXIETY

REDUCES BRAIN-LOCK

REDUCES LIKELIHOOD OF INJURY

ENHANCES GENERAL STRESS RESISTANCE

ENHANCES OTHER SKILLS AND LEARNING

Your objective here is to get control over the physiology of stress. Where you feel the stress as anxiety, TMR helps to manage and reduce it. Being relaxed facilitates thinking, concentration, prevents brain-lock and reduces the likelihood of injury from overly tight muscles. Although we are focusing on the application of PMR related to military missions and police operations, the regular practice of relaxation enhances general stress resistance in other areas of your life. Finally, a relaxed state can help in all types of learning, as a relaxed focus enhances attention to and retention of material and skills.

Ways You Can Use TMR During a Mission
We have looked at the general stress/arousal controlling effects of TMR and creating a more relaxed state. However, there are mission-specific uses of relaxation:

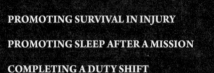

MISSION-SPECIFIC USES OF TMR

CONSERVING ENERGY

MANAGING ANGER AND FRUSTRATION

AIDING PERSONAL REHAB AND RECUPERATION

PROMOTING SURVIVAL IN INJURY

PROMOTING SLEEP AFTER A MISSION

COMPLETING A DUTY SHIFT

Conserve Energy

It's not unusual that a military mission or police operation takes some time to set up. However, because of the conditioned arousal of the mission/operation and the motivation "to get at it," arousal can be high at the start, though there can be a delay in the action. This "being stuck in neutral" with "your engine revving" can lead to a quick drain in energy before a lengthy mission even begins.

Say you are in the SWAT van or in a Humvee in a hurry-up-and-wait-status. Your ability to bring on relaxation can help conserve your energy. Use your command word as part of a routine to prep yourself for the action while monitoring and mastering your arousal and focus.

Manage Anger and Frustration

A more relaxed state helps prevent anger and frustration. If these destructive emotions are already present, relaxation can help reduce their intensity. Say you have been working in a specific forward area or on a particular police case for a while and you know the players or conditions better than anyone. However, your leaders are pressuring you to proceed in a manner that may lead to failure in the objective. You feel like exploding as you see your advice ignored and all your work about to go down the drain. TMR can help you manage that anger more effectively, so that you can effectively press your point without overreacting in a way that gets you written-off, escorted from the room, or worse.

Whether your anger or frustration is because of aspects of the mission, or with yourself for some reason, relaxation can reduce these feelings and help you refocus on the needs of the moment.

Help Re-energize, Re-charge: Personal Rehab and Recuperation

During those lengthy missions when you want a break or need to recharge, use relaxation for personal rehab and recuperation. Nowicki (1997) reports that Russian sport psychologists have, for some time, endorsed relaxation techniques as a way to speed recovery of ability during breaks in the competition. Relaxation promotes deeper breathing, greater muscle relaxation, decreased fatigue, and decreased pain or discomfort.

Nowicki provides a script to help train in such techniques. Engaging in active relaxation exercises can be more restorative and refreshing than just "hanging out" or resting (or getting a caffeine, nicotine or sugar fix!).

Co-author Christensen says that when he was a military policeman in Vietnam, he didn't know about the power of deep breathing and muscle relaxation. There were many times after a raid, a bombing or a violent arrest situation that his surge of adrenalin was so great that he could not sit still. "I was like a moth flickering around a light bulb," he says. "Then, when I'd tried to eat in the mess hall, my hands trembled so much I'd shake the food off my fork."

Years later, about half way through his police career, he would learn several relaxation techniques, a result of researching a book he was writing. He says that he particularly likes the progressive relaxation method he describes below because it works quickly and effectively to help him to relax, rest, recharge and be ready to "go out and get 'em" again. He has practiced the technique in a squad car, his personal car, a packed roll call room, in a park, and even while standing with others. He says that no one knows he is doing it since the procedure takes place inside the privacy of his head.

There were times, Loren recalls, when he was in a noisy, crowded office that he would pretend to be on the phone. Anyone looking his way just saw a cop sitting in a chair, leaning forward with both elbows on his desk, with one hand cupping his forehead and the other holding a phone to his ear. In reality, he was holding a dead phone as he performed progressive relaxation. (This experience is shared with you not necessarily because it's recommended, but to show the adaptability of relaxation techniques!)

A detailed approach to learning progressive muscle relaxation is presented in Appendix I.

Here is how Loren developed and adapted the technique:

- At first, find a quiet place, though with practice you can do this in a noisy crowd. Sit in a comfortable chair, back straight and hands folded in your lap. It's your choice whether to close your eyes, leave them open or close them part way.
- Begin by doing the 4-count breathing method also discussed in this chapter to induce a sense of calm to your mind and body. Repeat the cycle three or four times.

  > In through the nose, two, three, four
  > Hold, two, three, four
  > Out through the lips, two, three, four
  > Hold, two three four…

- Do not neglect to hold your breath in for a 4-count and then hold empty for a 4-count. This phase is critical to achieve a wonderful sense of relaxation washing over you.
- Follow your normal breathing for a few cycles just to enjoy the sense of relaxation you're already beginning to feel. Be aware of your breath as you inhale and be aware of it as you exhale. Don't think about the mission you just finished or the next task coming up. Just focus on your breath, in and out, in and out.
- The next step is to think about your face as you breathe in. Don't tense these muscles; just be aware of them. As the air passes in through your nostrils, mentally feel your forehead, your eyebrows, your eyes, your cheeks, and your jaw. Always include your jaw, as it's common to carry tension there.
- Hold the breath in for a couple of seconds and then slowly exhale as you let go of the muscles in your forehead, those around your eyes, in your cheeks and around your jaw. Allow them to sag as all the tension there oozes out. Repeat the procedure for your face three or four times, each time feeling the parts on your inhalation and then releasing the tension there as you exhale slowly.
- Now follow the same steps with your neck and shoulders. Don't tense the muscles, just feel them as you inhale slowly, then hold your breath for two seconds, and then relax the muscles as you exhale slowly. Repeat three or four times.
- Follow the same procedure for your chest.

- Follow the same procedure for your upper back, especially in the area of your shoulder blades.
- Follow the same procedure for your lower back.
- Follow the same procedure for your pelvic area.
- Follow the same procedure for your upper legs.
- Follow the same procedure for your calves and feet.

Loren says that should a loud noise from your environment or some other form of distraction penetrate your concentration, it can result in tension returning in your face or any other muscle group. No problem, just repeat the procedure to relax it again. Then go back to whatever body part you were about to do.

When you have progressively relaxed your entire body, spend a few minutes simply following your inhalation and exhalation as you enjoy the wonderful sensation and the resultant refreshed energy. When you have no other choice but to get up and go about your next task, you will be amazed at how good you feel and how ready you are for whatever might come your way.

Don't discard this technique if at first your results are not as good as described here. The more you practice the better you will get at this and the greater your results will be.

Surviving Injury

Relaxation is essential to surviving an injury. If you're injured and you need to wait for help, your survival will be promoted in a more focused state than in a panic mode that can easily result from seeing one's wounds, from feeling trapped or feeling in danger. Tactical self-control through relaxation techniques can help you avoid panic and maintain the survival attitude, allowing for needed decisions and actions. TMR can also help with managing and distracting yourself from pain.

Promoting Sleep and Completing a Duty Shift

While there is often a physical "crash" after a mission/operation from all the energy expended, you just might experience the opposite and feel charged with energy, especially after a successful high-stress response. This may make it difficult to get to sleep. Relaxation helps promote sleep more quickly in such situations, to get the rest you need before duty calls again. The same is true after a response when you need to "re-set" to get back and complete your shift.

Dr. Matt Hing is one of our brave and talented physicians serving in Afghanistan. Major Hing is a Flight Surgeon, Airborne Infantry Physician and General Medical Officer in the United States Army, currently serving as the Task Force Eagle surgeon. Senior military commanders and deployed physicians know the Major for his combat-focused approach to field medicine, as well as his aggressive patient advocacy. As a surgeon, he is engaged in his own form of high-stress and life and death situations. He describes how relaxation techniques can be highly effective in allowing him to do his job with continuing focus and expertise:

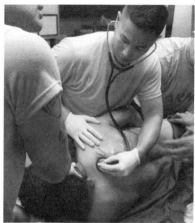

> You know, one of the best things about using relaxation techniques when practicing military medicine in austere settings is that you, the doc, find yourself calmer and more relaxed through the process of coaching a patient/casualty through their pain.

> One of my mentors once taught me that before you check the patient's vital signs in an emergency, you had best check your own, first. What he meant was that if you take just a second to scan your own physiologic and mental state before turning your attention to the patient, you will notice your own stress-reactions and can effectively deal with them by using tactical breathing. Then, and only then, will you be able to wield a scalpel or needles with the steady hand you need.

Tactical Breathing

This is another effective technique for managing mission stress. There are many names for self-control breathing techniques and many forms of it. The point is that tactical breathing is often quite useful in managing the arousal or stress of a mission. As we have discussed, slow rhythmic breathing shifts the body into a more relaxed state.

Siddle (1995) suggests:

> **We would argue that breath control should be a mandatory component of survival stress management.**

Dr. Hing provides two excellent examples of the effectiveness of tactical breathing as a tactical arousal control technique. Dr. Hing recounts:

> I have tried to coach patients through deep breathing many times in the operational setting. Most recently, I had a young private with minor blunt trauma to his knee when the HUMVEE he was driving struck an IED late one night on a patrol. He was so focused on the pain in his knee that all the other soldiers, including the NCO's in the patrol, started to freak out and assume that he was the most seriously injured patient when, in fact, there were multiple other soldiers with more serious penetrating wounds from the blast. This resulted in two outcomes.

> First, we ended up erroneously triaging the patient as the most seriously wounded and placing him on our trauma table reserved for such casualties. Second, we could not get a coherent history and perform a decent physical exam on the young man because he was screaming and writhing around in pain. In fact, he was in such exasperation that he was starting to hyperventilate. A medevac helicopter (called in haste by the leadership because they had panicked) was about to land at any moment, too, so I had to get all the patients assessed and packaged quickly so that the bird wouldn't present the enemy with another target while it waited on us at the HLZ.

> I got in really close to the young soldier's face and told him to take deep breaths. I had to repeat this three times, but he did take the deep breaths and finally calmed down enough for us to examine the knee and complete our search for any other, more occult wounds. By coaching him through the deep breathing, I was able to help him overcome his pain faster than even the most rapidly pushed intravenous injections of morphine or fentanyl. As a result of this simple measure, we were able to finish evaluating and stabilizing him and all the other casualties just in time to meet the medevac bird at the HLZ with no unnecessary loss of lives in a hostile environment.

The Eureka Effect: Relaxation Aids Problem Solving

The yelling of Eureka (which means "I found it") upon finding a solution to a problem, having a great insight, or discovering a desired object (as gold in California) can be traced back to the ancient Greek mathematician Archimedes (Alexander et al., 1990). After much intense concentration and thought as to how to solve the challenge given to him by his King — how to determine how much actual gold was in the king's crown without melting it down — he decided he needed a relaxing bath. Within minutes, he realized that gold would displace more water than other metals and jump from the tub and ran naked down the city streets yelling 'Eureka." This was an early instance of how relaxation after intense concentration can promote insight and problem solving.

The reason why deep breathing works faster than any other analgesic medications in the operational environment has to do with the fact that the pain has to be perceived and interpreted by the brain. As such, what one soldier might perceive as a pin prick, another soldier might liken to being struck by a train. The young soldier in this instance interpreted a minor trauma to his knee as show-stopping pain, even though on examination, the kneecap had not become dislocated, there were no open or exsanguinating fractures, and he was very much intact.

In his case, he had probably been terrified out of his mind by the entire milieu of the combat scenario that was so new, compared with his previous experiences in life. Deep breathing activates the parasympathetic nervous system by stimulating baroreceptors when the diaphragm contracts and relaxes. Patients instantly experience a soothing effect. At that point, you can insert the I.V. needle into them because they are not moving around. And if you can insert the I.V. needle, then you now have a conduit to administer a variety of powerful analgesic medications to further control their pain.

Dr. Hing also describes how to teach people who are associated with those injured to use tactical breathing to help manage the physical and psychological reactions in situations such as seeing a friend hurt or die. This gives these people a powerful tool to use whenever it's needed.

One of our Afghan interpreters watched my medical team perform extreme measures on his best friend in an attempt to save his life after he had fallen victim to a suicide bombing. The patient was riddled everywhere with penetrating wounds and his leg was shattered. There was blood everywhere including the floor. We applied tourniquets, thrust an intraosseus line into the bone marrow of his sternum, performed needle decompression, did rapid sequence intubation, initiated CPR, and finally hooked him up to electric defibrillations.

The interpreter watched tearfully as we performed all of these very invasive and, in some ways, violent measures on his best friend. Finally, he watched helplessly as his friend finally died on our trauma table. Unfortunately, at the time, we had a mass casualty incident on our hands, and I did not have adequate time to offer any comforting words or gestures to the grieving interpreter. Later on when the dust finally settled, I arranged for our combat psychologist, Dr. Ritschard, to speak with him.

We discovered that he had many symptoms of PTSD and depression resulting not only from this experience, but from many other instances in which he had watched his friends suffer and die in combat. He was having disturbing nightmares on a chronic basis, and it was beginning to show in his eyes, which had that classic thousand-mile stare so typical of combat fatigue. I then asked Dr. Ritschard to attempt a trial of hypnosis on him. So he set up a mat on the floor for the interpreter and began the process of guided hypnosis using deep breathing. After a few minutes, the man awoke looking far more peaceful and happy than we had ever seen him. The power of deep breathing had worked once again for us in the operational environment. It will probably continue to serve this interpreter quite well in the future whenever he is out on mission with us in the tactical setting.

Diaphragmatic Breathing

This method is called "diaphragmatic" because it involves breathing anchored at your diaphragm, those muscles and tendons about half way down your upper body that separate the chest and abdominal cavity. It's considered a "deep" breathing technique (Remsberg calls it "belly breathing.")

Try the following:
- Quickly count to 3 and then take a breath as quickly as you can.
- Hold it for about 2 seconds and then return to breathing normally.

What did you notice? If you're like most, you might be aware of several things. First, your breath (if inhaled quickly) probably was not deep. Further, if you remember your posture, you probably felt your chest and shoulders tense and lift towards your ears until you exhaled. What emotional state does this posture resemble? Most say it feels and looks like the state of being scared, surprised or shocked.

The Behavioral Physiology Institute in Boulder Colorado (www.bp.edu) focuses on enhancing breathing, health and performance and has many valuable views on stress and breathing. Rather than looking at shallow or deep breathing, the Institute suggests that problems occur from either underbreathing or overbreathing in stressful situations. Problems are the result, not only of changes in oxygen levels, but an imbalance of oxygen ($O2$) and carbon dioxide ($CO2$) chemistry. In fact, they propose that hypocapnia, or deficiencies in carbon dioxide levels, are the source of the unusual sensations (tingling, numbness, dizziness, etc) and impaired performance that occur with stressed breathing. (Behavioral Physiology Institute, 2008).

In their studies of dysfunctional breathing patterns, they found the following:
- There is a failure to breathe diaphragmatically.
- There is a failure to exhale completely.
- There is a failure to allow transition time between breaths.
- There is a failure to monitor breathing.
- There is the use of accessory muscles for breathing when not needed.

The Institute proposes that diaphragmatic breathing is superior to chest breathing. Chest breathing is described as inefficient, labor intensive, and makes breathing seem difficult and even exhausting. Chest breathing creates certain problems in addition to the characteristics (called dysponesis) described above. These include:
- It requires breathing faster leading to a sense of urgency or anxiety.
- It makes complete exhalation difficult leading to a sense of tightness.
- It can lead to feelings of being confined or trapped.
- It can create a sense of struggle with breathing rather than relaxation.

It is cautioned that "deep breathing" is not the unitary approach to managing stress-related breathing. The key is slow, quiet, individualized diaphragmatic breathing.

Here is a way to develop or improve your diaphragmatic breathing skills:
- Place one hand palm down on your stomach and the other hand palm down on your chest. If you're chest breathing (the less effective type), you will see the hand on your chest rise and fall.
- Now breathe slowly and low from your diaphragm. Notice your stomach distend and the hand on your stomach rise and fall.
- Purse your lips together like you're breathing through a straw. This helps produce diaphragmatic breathing, as well.

Diaphragmatic breathing tends to occur naturally when lying down on your back. From that position, look to see whether your stomach does indeed rise and fall more than your chest, an indication of diaphragmatic breathing. Singers use diaphragmatic breathing to enhance projection and endurance when performing.

In addition to the methods to train diaphragmatic breathing discussed above, the Behavioral Physiology Institute also offers these suggestions:
- Image breathing as an up & down, rather than in & out process.
- Breathe through your nose.
- Take quick sniffs of air to engage diaphragmatic breathing.
- Use productive self-talk like "The breath will come."

It is cautioned that "deep breathing" is not the unitary approach to managing stress-related breathing. The key is slow, quiet, individualized diaphragmatic breathing.

A Word on Posture and Correct Breathing

Co-author Loren Christensen says that sitting up straight and tall allows your diaphragm to be free. This is important because it allows you to better use your stomach muscles to breathe more deeply and more slowly. The average person breathes 12 to 15 times every 60 seconds. For an experienced meditator, however, breathing 12 to 15 times per minute would be as if they had just jogged up a set of stairs. For them, 8 to 10 times a minute is sufficient, as they have learned to breathe with their diaphragm and abdominal muscles.

Loren says that experienced meditators can go so deeply that they breathe only once a minute, or even less. He says that sometimes when he is meditating, he has to remind himself to breathe and it can almost feel like an effort to do so.

Breathing properly and deeply is of great benefit to the warrior. By breathing with the stomach, you release tension and experience a sense of calmness and confidence. Since you're using more of your lungs, you can adjust quickly to a sudden need for more air.

Diaphragmatic Breathing in Action

You can use this form of tactical breathing in several ways. Whenever you start to notice that you're becoming stressed, take one or two tactical breaths to help break the cycle of increasing stress (you do not need to do diaphragmatic breathing all the time; one or two breaths should work).

You can also develop a habit of taking one or two tactical (diaphragmatic) breaths at various intervals during a mission or a duty shift. This can help remind you to monitor your stress levels, as well as provide an "automatic reset" of any stress you might be experiencing. Tactical breathing techniques like diaphragmatic breathing are useful not only because of their effectiveness, but also because they are easy to do and can be done "covertly" in many different situations. In other words, you can control and relax yourself without anyone else being aware.

4- Count Method

Co-authors Grossman and Christensen describe another form of tactical breathing in *On Combat* called the "4-count method." You begin by breathing in through your nose to a slow count of 4. Hold the breath for a count of 4 and then exhale slowly for a count of 4. Then hold empty for another count of 4. The tactical self-talk (see the Chapter 8 "Personal Psy Ops") goes like this:

> **In through the nose, two, three. four**
> **Hold, two, three, four**
> **Out through the lips, two, three, four**
> **Hold, two, three, four...**

How long you hold each count is up to you: your comfort level and what works best. Like diaphragmatic breathing, use the 4-count technique to prevent stress or to reduce it. You can repeat as necessary, but you don't need to breathe diaphragmatically all the time.

Snipers frequently focus on their breathing and take a deep breath as part of a routine to prepare for a shot. Other warriors use a "ready breath" just before commencing action, such as breaching a door. Adapt breathing techniques to fit your tactical situations.

A SEAL breacher named Brian described (Drury, 2008) using breathing techniques while in Iraq and Afghanistan. Before blowing open any door, he would steady his hands with:

> **...four of the biggest, deepest gut-filling diaphragmatic breaths**
> **a human being can possibly take – to flood my body with as much**
> **oxygen as possible**

Centering

Centering is another breathing-related technique used to manage the stress of high-risk situations. It's well described by performance expert Dr. Robert Nideffer (1978, 1975) who learned it while studying the martial art of Aikido in Japan. The purpose of centering is to develop a controlled state of relaxed focus, which, to use the Japanese metaphor, is a "mind like still water."

Centering begins by taking a diaphragmatic breath, but adds a centering image.

Centering Yourself Using Traditional Asian Martial Arts Style

- Stand with one leg forward, your legs about shoulder width apart and knees slightly bent (a typical karate stance).
- Inhale slowly and deeply as in a diaphragmatic breath.
- Exhale and slowly let your eyes close.
- Let all of your attention and focus come to rest at your "center of gravity," which is located about two inches behind your belly button. This means that as you let your eyes close, let all your awareness focus on this point. Sometimes this is experienced as looking out from behind your belly button.
- Open your eyes and return to your regular breathing and activity.

If this is a little too mystical for you, try a more Western approach.

Centering Yourself Using a Western Style

- Stand with one leg forward and your legs about shoulder width apart and knees slightly bent.
- Inhale slowly and deeply as in a diaphragmatic breath.
- Exhale and slowly let your eyes close as you imagine a leaf or feather floating slowly, slowly drifting down… lower and lower… until it gently comes to rest, floating softly at your center of gravity (belly button).
- Open your eyes and return to your regular breathing and activity.

Initially, you should do this in a safe and quiet environment. However, like TMR, you will eventually develop the skill to do it quickly with your eyes open, in any position, focused but aware, even when all about you is chaotic. Adding a refocusing command as described in the next section "Attention Control Training" is critical in tactical situations.

Co-author Christensen teaches a simple variation of centering that can be done while sitting alone in a quiet place, in line at the grocery store, and moments before a dangerous mission. After a few weeks of regular practice, he says that you will find your center quickly and be able to bring on a powerful sense of calm and control.

To begin:

- Sit in a quiet place and get comfortable. Narrow your eyes a little and focus on something in front of you: a spot on the wall, the corner of a picture frame, a design on a lampshade.
- Perform three or four cycles of the above mentioned 4-count breathing method. Most experts say to breathe in through your nose and out through your nose. Others say to breathe in through your nose and out through your mouth. Find one method that you like and stick with it.
- Do your best to follow your breath by placing your complete attention on the 4-count inhalation, the 4-count hold and the 4-count exhalation. This is not a time to think about your bills or your annoying superior. All that exists in this moment is your breath: in… hold… out… hold…

Now that you're beginning to feel relaxed, you're more receptive to the centering phase of the exercise. Here is how it's done.

- Remain in your comfortable place, eyes partially closed. Direct your mind toward your center, that place a couple inches behind your belly button. (Some meditators pinch the spot hard enough at the beginning of their session so that they feel it for a few seconds after. This helps them to direct their breath there.)

- Inhale slowly through your nose, feeling your abdomen extend as you mentally focus on your center. Do this by mentally feeling the spot or by imagining that you're inhaling through it. Yes, the latter technique might seem strange at first (you don't have to tell anyone what you're doing) but it's a powerful way to maintain your focus on your center.
- Exhale through your nose or mouth as you continue to focus on your spot or as you imagine that you're exhaling out from it.

Continue to do this for five minutes. Add a minute each session until you're practicing for 10 to 15 minutes. Loren says that it will take only a few sessions before you're wondering why you have never practiced this before. You will enjoy the sense of focus it gives you, your enhanced ability to concentrate, your improved ability to listen to instruction, and the powerful sense of calm it gives you so as to carry our your duties well.

Loren says that once you feel comfortable with the seated centering exercise, you can do it standing, sitting and lying down, anywhere and anytime.

Do it when you got time to kill.
- Waiting in a line.
- Sitting in your patrol car waiting for a situation to unfold.
- Waiting to enter a dangerous environment.

Do it when you want to be especially alert and aware.
- Patrolling an Iraqi town.
- Working a guard post.
- Waiting for a suspect to show himself.

Do it when you want to collect yourself.
- After a violent resist arrest situation.
- After a foot chase.
- After a violent confrontation of any kind.

Loren further says that there is nothing mystical about these breathing exercises. They are all natural and easy-to-use tools that help you stay focused, help you maintain control of yourself, and help keep you calm so that you can function at your optimum no matter how extreme a situation.

Attention Control Training
Dr. Nideffer extends centering (Nideffer & Sharpe, 1978) into a technique called Attention Control Training. Attention Control Training is comprised of first completing the centering process: deep breath in, slow breath out and centering image. Then you give yourself a cue — a tactically relevant instruction or a tactical self-command —

to refocus on what you need to do. For example, after centering, you might instruct yourself or issue a tactical self-command to "lock and load" or "move to cover."

Use Attention Control Training:
> • to regain focus should an unexpected event occur that distracts you.
> • to regain focus and control when your stress increases to an uncomfortable level.
> • to regain focus when you have made a mistake and your inability to "shake it off" prevents you from reacting to the immediate challenge in front of you.

How to Do Attention Control Training
> • Stand with one leg forward, feet about shoulder width apart and knees slightly bent (a typical karate stance).
> • Inhale slowly and deeply as in a diaphragmatic breath.
> • Exhale and slowly let your eyes close.
> • Let all of your attention and focus come to rest at your center of gravity.
> • Open your eyes and give yourself a re-orienting command by thinking or saying a tactically oriented phrase, such as "lock and load....or...move to cover...or...power up..."
> • Return to your activity.

VISUO-MOTOR BEHAVIOR REHEARSAL

You can combine the above techniques into more structured and complex psychological training programs. For example, Suinn (1984) developed Visuo-Motor Behavior Rehearsal (VMBR), which combines relaxation and imagery techniques. It's been used extensively and effectively with athletes and I (Asken 1993) have written about its application to firefighting. (See Chapter 7 for a detailed discussion of tactical performance imagery and further evidence of the use and effectiveness of VMBR with other warrior skills).

It's best to learn VMBR with an expert trainer in a structured manner. However, generally speaking, VMBR begins by creating a tranquil state through relaxation techniques. Then the relaxation command word is "switched off" and the performance imagery of a specific skill or situation is "switched on." This process is alternated until the individual can go through the phases alone and quickly to prepare for a challenge.

Suinn used VMBR to help U.S. Olympic skiers prepare for competition by getting into a relaxed state and then skiing the race mentally, while reviewing critical points on the imaged course and the strategies to handle them. I've used the technique with firefighters to prepare for building searches, entrapments and other high-risk situations.

As another example, Suinn (1987) reported using relaxation techniques and imagery to improve performance in an Olympic athlete on the U.S. Modern Pentathalon Team, specifically with his pistol marksmanship skills. After relaxation training, the athlete would image being on the pistol range experiencing and controlling stresses, such as waiting for the announcement of his marks and ranking. Suinn reports that during one day's training, the athlete was able to learn to control his stress, shoot his best career score, apply the same mental toughness skills to his other events, and ultimately win the Pentathalon among a field of international competitors.

STRESS INOCULATION TRAINING (SIT)

Co-authors Grossman and Christensen noted in *On Combat* the value of Stress Inoculation Training (SIT) developed by Meichenbaum (1976). SIT builds resistance to specific stressful situations and integrates well with simulation exercises. As mentioned when discussing VMBR, the initial stress inoculation training typically needs the assistance of a psychologist skilled in the technique.

The Phases of SIT
The first phase is Cognitive Preparation, a point where the rationale and overview of SIT is presented, and then the problem, challenge, or stressful situation is analyzed. During Skill Acquisition and Rehearsal, specific tactical arousal control skills, such as relaxation training and self-talk, are learned and practiced. The last phase is Application, the implementation of the skills.

There are four steps to making the application of SIT skills to a stressful situation:

- **Preparation for Provocation:** You prepare mentally for the event and review the philosophy and strategy for meeting it.
- **Impact and Confrontation:** You prep for the way the event is likely to affect you and summon your practiced skills.
- **Coping and Arousal:** You apply the actual application of the tactical arousal control skills and SIT training to the challenge when it occurs.
- **Review and Adjustments:** You review the process for what worked and what did not, while behaviorally and emotionally managing the event. You make adjustments and practice them to prepare for the next situation.

Practice these in an imagery-based manner. They might even be part of role-playing and scenario training before applied in actual situations.

Say you want to enhance your skill at staying in control when receiving insulting, degrading, personally infuriating verbal abuse from a motorist you have pulled over or from a local civilian in an Iraqi town. Your goal is to remain calm, to manage the situation and not over-react, especially in a violent way.

- **Cognitive Preparation:** You review the rules of engagement, the purpose and responsibilities of your role, the importance of respectful reactions, possible reasons why the individual might be upset, and accept that you ultimately have control over your behavior.
- **Skill Acquisition:** This involves training in self-management skills, learning muscle relaxation techniques, refining tactical breathing skills, and creating self-talk (see Chapter 8).
- **Application:** This is about using your training in the actual encounter itself.

The four parts of the Application phase might look like this.

- **Preparing for Provocation:** You think about encountering angry motorists or angry civilians. You're alert as you approach the stopped vehicle or enter the town.
- **Impact and Confrontation:** You remind yourself how this might affect you and what you need to do to manage your response.
- **Coping and Arousal:** You remind yourself of your tactical arousal control skills and use them in the encounter.
- **Review and Adjustments:** You do a post-encounter review as to how you did. Did you remain in control? Were there points that were especially hard for you to manage or where you felt like you were losing control? What skills worked well and which did not? What do you need to work on and do differently next time?

Scenario training is an excellent opportunity to test out this process. It allows you to anticipate a situation, practice responses to it, apply those responses and review how you did. While the above example deals with controlling yourself and remaining calm, you can also use VMBR and SIT to prepare for situations where you might need to take more forceful action.

Thompson & McCreary (2006) have outlined three specific goals for SIT in military applications and reported three research-supported effects from its use:

- Improve your performance by changing problematic or sub-optimal. behavior in high-stress situations.
- Improve your ability to self-regulate behavior and responses.
- Increase your ability to cope with stressful situations.

They describe studies that show that SIT can decrease performance anxiety, decrease state (situational) anxiety and increase performance.

Driskell et. al., (2006) discuss a study by Inzana and colleagues in 1996 that looked at the effects of psychological preparation on confidence and performance. In the study, Naval personnel were put into a command and control decision-making task scenario under either high-stress or low-stress conditions, with or without psychological preparation.

The psychologically prepared group received:
- **Sensory information:** What they would likely feel physically during the challenge.
- **Procedural information:** Normal reactions and how these might negatively affect performance.
- **Instrumental information:** Suggestions on maximizing their response, such as matching their pace to the task.

Results showed that psychologically prepared people in high-stress conditions reported less anxiety, more confidence and made fewer performance errors than those who were not psychologically prepared.

The interested warrior might also read Anderson et al. (1995) who were early proponents of these more complex techniques. They describe how police officers can use these techniques to manage a domestic dispute involving threats with a baseball bat.

Remember, procedures such as VMBR and SIT typically need the guidance of an experienced trainer, at least initially. However, whatever the psychological approach, the techniques, like all psychological skills, need to be practiced and adapted to be used safely and effectively in any given situation.

Tactical self-control is an envied skill and ability recognized as a valuable edge in any military operation. Author Stephen Hunter makes the point well in his fictional, but militarily detailed, book *Point of Impact*. In describing the central figure, a former Marine sniper, he says:

> **Back in 'Nam, he was something of a legend for the nearly animal-like way he could will his body reactions down, stiller than death.**

Tactical Arousal Control Techniques can provide greater control over physical and psychological responses in military and police challenge situations.

6 On the Wall:
chapter   Concentration Skills and Mental Toughness

... concentration and mental toughness are the
margin of victory.

– Bill Russell

The ability to concentrate and focus is the most intuitively recognized essential skill for responding effectively in high-stress situations. Acknowledged as perhaps the greatest hockey player ever, Wayne Gretzky has been quoted by several bloggers and pundits as saying:

> **If you ask a fifty-goal scorer what the goalie looks like, he'll say the goalie's just a blur. But if you ask a five-goal scorer, he'll say the goalie looks like a huge glob of pads. A five-goal scorer can tell you the brand name of the pad of every goalie in the league. I'm seeing the net, he's seeing the pad.**

Wilson (2002) notes that at any given moment, your five senses take in 11 million pieces of information (based on the number of receptor cells and connections in the brain), but you can only process forty pieces at any given moment. While perhaps extreme for our purposes, these numbers nonetheless underscore the need to effectively focus and sort relevant information without being distracted by the irrelevant.

Navy SEAL Machover (2002) said that:

> **Combat requires the ability to focus like nothing else.**

Muth and colleagues (2006) emphasize that the complex battlefield environment demands that warriors perform simultaneous, complex tasks in extreme environments and do so with little room for error.

Janelle & Hatfield (2008) propose that:

> In the 21st century, soldiers face unprecedented challenges. In particular, the manner in which they manage information on the battlefield will be critical to both mission success and survival. The advances in weaponry systems that will likely occur in the U.S. military to aid the future warrior will place a premium on attention capacity, decision-making processes, and motor control to realize the advantages of these technologies.

CONCENTRATION IS CRITICAL

Concentration is perhaps the least understood and trained skill. As mentioned, knowing that it's essential to concentrate during a military mission or police operation is different from knowing *how* to do so.

The brain has incredible capability. For example, read the following:

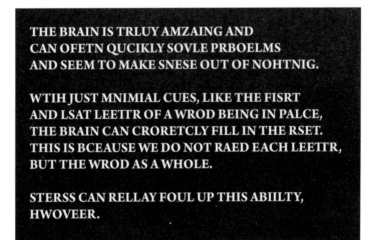

THE BRAIN IS TRLUY AMZAING AND
CAN OFETN QUCIKLY SOVLE PRBOELMS
AND SEEM TO MAKE SNESE OUT OF NOHTNIG.

WTIH JUST MNIMIAL CUES, LIKE THE FISRT
AND LSAT LEETTR OF A WROD BEING IN PALCE,
THE BRAIN CAN CRORETCLY FILL IN THE RSET.
THIS IS BCEAUSE WE DO NOT RAED EACH LEETTR,
BUT THE WROD AS A WHOLE.

STERSS CAN RELLAY FOUL UP THIS ABIILTY,
HWOVEER.

It's remarkable that we can make sense out of such scrambled and minimal information, but we can. Of course, this is often the very nature of police work and military assignments: You're given minimal evidence or intelligence, and you must quickly understand the meaning and significance of critical situations.

Unconscious Learning

While beyond the scope of this book, it's worth mentioning the fascinating and potentially groundbreaking research into the function and effects of the "adaptive unconscious." Wilson (2002) says that people possess a sophisticated, adaptive unconscious that is crucial for survival. He describes this as "mental processes that are inaccessible to consciousness but influence judgments, feelings, or behavior."

Many terms have been used to represent learning that occurs without active attention or even active intention to learn. These include "automatic learning," "implicit learning," "pre-attentive learning," "procedural learning" and "non-conscious learning."

One example of this type of learning is your ability to describe the decorations in the commander's office, though you didn't study them or plan on remembering the décor while you were there. Another is your knowledge of routes to certain locations on the base, or throughout the city, which developed without consciously trying to learn them. Such learning also includes terms and language you use without consciously making a decision to use them (like certain colorful words that might be a part of your speech!).

Non-conscious learning also occurs in other senses. For example, your ability to recognize and use certain keys by touch, and your ability to recognize objects, such as a pen, typically occurs without "studying" their feel (Hawkins, 2004). You recognize the grip or trigger pressure of your weapon while being aware of the different feel of another. Such abilities result from unconscious learning of sensations during training and practice.

The adaptive unconscious, however, may be even deeper and more inaccessible. There may be multiple forms of unconscious awareness that influence such behavior as judgments, feelings and motives. Cutting edge researchers, military trainers and police trainers are attempting to better understand these influences and how learning and training can affect the unconscious and enhance performance.

Stress Affects Thinking Skills

While the brain can be brilliant in function, it's also sensitive to disruption by stress. Driskell, Salas & Johnson (2006) describe the stress effects on combatants in World War II at Normandy. Soldiers at that time were (unfortunately and incorrectly) characterized as "slow-witted" because of their slowness to comprehend orders. They also exhibited memory defects, in that their ability to relay orders was not always accurate or consistent.

Other research (Baddely, 1972) supported the early observations made about the soldiers from that time. In one experiment, a group of military servicemen on a plane were told that one engine had failed and the landing gear was stuck. They were then asked to fill out a "possession disposition form" and "retention of emergency instructions form." The stressed group made many more errors processing the emergency instructions than the group that was not stressed in the same way.

In another similar experiment, a group of military recruits in a simulated tactical exercise were told that either (1) live fire was accidentally directed towards them or (2) they had accidentally entered a high radioactive environment. They were instructed to call headquarters for help but found that the radio was malfunctioning. They were then given complex instructions to fix it. The stressed group performed more poorly than the non-stressed group.

More recent studies (Lieberman et al., 2005) on the effects of stress on performance were conducted during combat simulation with Army Rangers and BUDS (Basic Underwater Demolition School) trainees. Compared to pre-stress levels, the studies found decrements in vigilance, reaction time, memory and logical reasoning.

Research (Harris et al., 2005) looked at the effects of extended stress on information processing. The study assessed cognitive function in participants undergoing Navy SERE (Survival, Evasion, Resistance and Escape) training. During the stress training there was:
- A significant deterioration in cognitive performance.
- An increase in subjective discomfort.
- An increase in simple reaction time.
- An increase in time to complete spatial processing tasks.
- A decrease in code substitution performance.
- A decrease in logical reasoning (this was the most susceptible skill to the weeklong stress training).

When the training was over, the participants' performance returned initially to pre-stress levels. However, unlike their performance in the pre-stress exposure (training) session, it declined as the testing session progressed. Thus, immediately following stress exposure, the participants were able to sustain normal performance, but only for a limited time.

Murray (2004) describes work on the "Jangle Effect," which says that fear creates difficulty with some forms of reasoning, especially verbal problem solving. It's said that the "internal dialogue" — thinking and talking to ourselves — (See Chapter 8 "Personal Psy Ops and Self-Talk") we use to think through and solve problems is especially sensitive to jangle effects.

Kavanagh (2005) summarizes considerable research that shows stress can produce a variety of negative effects on cognition:

- It might reduce your ability to analyze complex situations.
- It might reduce your ability to manipulate information.
- You might make decisions on incomplete information.
- You might fail to consider a range of alternatives.
- You might ignore long-term consequences.
- You might oversimplify assumptions and require more time to reach a solution.

Staal and colleagues (2008) reported that stress shifts attention to the "here and now" and may degrade memory.

Stress and the OODA Loop

Many readers are familiar with Boyd's OODA Loop of decision making and action, a four-phase process consisting of Observation, Orientation (processing of any information), Decision and Action. In the event the OODA Loop is new to you or you're rusty on the principle, here is what co-author Loren Christensen (2004) wrote about it in *Timing in the Fighting Arts*, cowritten with Wim Demeere.

> The late Colonel John Boyd, a United States Air Force Korean combat veteran and military tactics scholar, discovered several similarities in wars and in individual battles. His most striking discovery was that when Side A presented Side B with an unexpected and threatening situation, it allowed Side A time and opportunity to gain an advantage. If Side B couldn't adapt to the new situation, B would eventually be defeated since decisions and actions that are delayed are often rendered ineffective due to the constantly changing circumstances of a fight.
>
> This led Boyd to the conclusion that conflict is in essence a time-based problem. Whichever side is capable of being quicker at completing the OODA — Observation-Orientation-Decision-Action — loop is the one most likely to come out victorious. This cycle can be found in all manners of violent confrontations, whether it's all-out war or simple hand-to-hand combat.

A concern related to maximal performance is the effect of stress on the OODA Loop. According to Rahman (2007) stress can speed up the loop from a "trot" to a "gallop," which may negatively affect quality of performance, especially without training and psychological preparation.

While it's desirable to complete the OODA Loop as quickly as possible, stress can lead to a velocity differential (VEL-D). This means the Loop requires a faster response than the warrior can provide: he cannot "synch-up" with the dynamic event. Excessive negative emotional arousal can paralyze cognition, which the warrior often experiences as lost situational awareness or having an incorrect mental model of what is occurring (the fog of war).

Loren talks about the importance of experience in *Timing*, both real and manufactured:

> When you are somewhat conditioned to the stress and adrenaline rush of real violence, your brain takes less time to observe, orient and decide in the OODA loop because it's done it before under similar conditions. It draws on your previous experience to help provide you with fast solutions and then moves you quickly into the action phase for your fast response. It would be nice if you never had to face an attack that you hadn't trained for, but we all know that life doesn't work that way. Therefore, it's important to train for every possibility. Though there is no equivalent to actual, real fighting experience, good, realistic training is as close as you can get.

You & OODA

Loren notes in *Timing* that you need to cover two issues in your training. The first is to reduce the time you spend in the OODA loop, or minimize the number of loops needed before you achieve your goal. Know that the longer you spend in the loop, the more time your adversary has to aim his firearm or to ram a knife in your gut...It's only through sound training that you greatly reduce the chance of these things happening. On the flip side, you want to do everything you can to make your adversary waste time having to deal with his OODA loops.

Loren says that when practicing training scenarios, you want to continually strive to force your opponent into the OODA loop. He writes in *Timing*:

> When practicing scenario training, or any type of realistic drills, your objective is to reduce your time in Boyd's cycle, since the longer there, the slower you are to respond. Conversely, you want to do all that you can to make your opponent spend lots of time in the loop, to make it difficult, even impossible, for him to defend or attack you. If you can continue to force him into the cycle, he has to think about what he needs to do, all the while you are pressing forward with your attack. Your goal is to present him with numerous signals, all at once or in

succession. You want to continuously force him into the first stages of the loop. That way whatever action he does decide upon inevitably fails because his action will be based on information that is no longer current. He is forced continuously to try to catch up, but he can't because you remain in his face.

Actually, warriors have used OODA since an early caveman figured out that bashing Og in the head with a T-Rex bone was a good way to steal his food and get his woman. Move forward a few hundred thousand years and we are at Pearl Harbor and the Day of Infamy. Taken by total surprise, the American military was stuck in the observation, orientation and decision phases for what must have felt like ages before they began to return fire at the Japanese planes.

The principle of OODA Loop works to provide timing advantages in a fistfight, in mixed martial arts competition, in the game of basketball, in the dog-eat-dog world of big business, by the beat cop dealing with a volatile street thug, and by our military in the dangerous streets of any Iraqi town.

Autovigilance

High-stress situations can also affect thinking in what is called Autovigilance (Gray, 2004; Rahman, 2007). An example of this is when danger-induced arousal leads to all subsequent perception characterized as seeing threats everywhere and in everything.

But Awareness Leads to Enhanced Performance, Not Overreaction	Phenomena like autovigilance can raise a concern whether being primed and aware of possible danger leads to overreactions. Research by Mitchell and Flin (2007) suggests that this is not the case. In their study, British police officers were given either a threat awareness briefing or a neutral briefing prior to testing in a firearms training shoot or no-shoot scenario.
	The results showed that the average reaction time for the threat-briefed officers was nearly a half second faster than those who received a neutral briefing. Equally important was the finding that officers who received the threat briefing did not shoot at any subject in the no-shoot scenario, even when a gun was present.

Clearly, being more attuned to threat right after being exposed to danger can have survival benefits. However, with excessive arousal and limited experience or training, it can lead to overreactions.

Group Think

Of particular importance at the team, squad, platoon, company and all other levels is the phenomenon of stress-based "Group Think" (first discussed by Janis, 1973, and later by Kavanagh, 2005, Strentz, 2006). Group Think is a distortion of the creative potential for group problem solving that occurs when stress is not managed. The characteristics of Group Think include:

- An illusion of invincibility creating excessive optimism leading to extreme risks.
- Unquestioned belief in the group's morality.
- Stereotyped views of the adversary as weak or ignorant.
- Group members ignoring important intelligence.
- Group members being forced to adhere to a consensus opinion.
- Direct pressure on members to conform, especially those who express a counterview.

Strentz (2006) implicates Group Think in the failures of the British at Arnhem in September of 1944, and for the FBI shootings at Ruby Ridge, Idaho in 1992 and at Waco, Texas in 1993.

Mental Stalls

Siddle (1995) describes how stress affects reaction time and creates mental stalls. In summary:

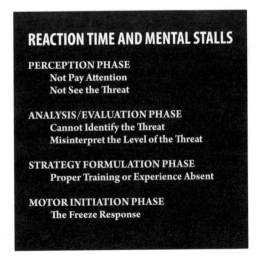

REACTION TIME AND MENTAL STALLS

PERCEPTION PHASE
  Not Pay Attention
  Not See the Threat

ANALYSIS/EVALUATION PHASE
  Cannot Identify the Threat
  Misinterpret the Level of the Threat

STRATEGY FORMULATION PHASE
  Proper Training or Experience Absent

MOTOR INITIATION PHASE
  The Freeze Response

Disruption can occur at any of several points.

- It can happen at the Perception Phase, where you're not paying attention and don't see the threat.
- It can occur at the Analysis/Evaluation Phase, where you cannot identify the threat or you misinterpret the level of it.
- It can occur at the Strategy Formulation Phase, where proper training or experience is absent or disrupted by stress.
- It can occur at the Motor Initiation Phase, where your stress causes a "freeze" or a slowness to start whatever the required action is. (There are similarities of this model to the OODA Loop and the impact of stress as discussed earlier).

Shalit (1988) proposed a similar schema called the Sequential Appraisal Model, or SAM. There are three aspects of appraising a potentially stressful or dangerous situation.

- **Cognitive Appraisal:** defining the overall and objective situation.
- **Affective Appraisal:** determining the emotional value of the situation (dangerousness, urgency, importance).
- **Instrumental Appraisal:** determining the possible acts and responses to the situation.

Cognitive Rubbernecking

Your Attention is drawn to (distracted by) stimuli that have a strong emotional aspect, especially of a negative nature (Rahman, 2007), i.e., guns, blood and motor vehicle accidents. This is often called "cognitive rubbernecking." While attention to such stimuli can be important to your function and survival, there can be problems when negative stimuli go from partial control of your attention to total control.

Concentration Skills

Concentration is an essential skill for optimal response in all military missions and police operations. Wegner (1989) underscores its importance:

> **Mental control thus precedes all other kinds of voluntary control — control over actions, our emotion, over thoughts themselves. To the degree that we can do anything at all on purpose, we do it by willfully moving our attention toward what it is we wish to do.**

Performance expert Dr. Robert Nideffer (1978) said this about concentration and attention:

> It's the ability to control attention under pressure and in response to changing demands that separates the average person from the super performer.

Janelle and Hatfield (2008) emphasize:

> Simply stated, the most critical factor in high-level performance is attention to the right thing at the right time.

Is Intuition a Magical Gift or a Trainable Skill?	It's also worth noting that components and skills called intuition in police and military work are not magical processes or rare abilities. As well-described by Dr. Laura Zimmerman (2008), a senior scientist at Applied Research Associates which specializes in critical incident decision-making issues, intuition "is really a package of cues, perceptual processes, situation recognition and action-choice evaluations…" which "can be decomposed, evaluated and enhanced, giving voice to the previously mysterious outcomes attributed to intuition." Integrating psychological and physical/tactical training can enhance the components and skills that are often called intuition.

Concentration is the ability to direct and maintain your thoughts and attention. Let me review five aspects of concentration I (MA) first addressed in *PsycheResponse* (1993). Are the following statements true or false?

TRUE OR FALSE?

Concentration is an automatic reflex.
Concentration cannot be learned.
Because we concentrate every day, practice is not needed.
Concentration requires little energy.
Our level of concentration always fits the situation.

All of the above statements are false.

Concentration abilities are not fully automatic; they can and need to be trained. Daily use does not create the type of intense concentration needed in high-stress military missions and police operations. Concentration takes a great deal of energy and can be quite tiring. There is often a mismatch between the degree of concentration needed in a situation and our ability to engage in it.

Wegner (1989) quotes the famous educator John Dewey to make this point:

> **…we can't just wish our minds to go in one direction or another, to concentrate or suppress, without the necessary practice, know-how and skill.**

Dewey called the development of effective means to control the mind, the development of "habits."

Excellence in concentration is a requirement for safe and successful missions and operations while a lack of concentration leads to disrupted performance or injury. Perry (2005) notes that once a skill is well learned or automated, it requires less conscious attention. However, pressure can shift attention away from relevant information or cues, and interfere with learned behavior. This is when choking occurs.

Stress creates changes in concentration. As an example, tunnel vision, which occurs with stress, affects vision and it has a cognitive and attentional component. When you hear a warrior say, "That was a stupid mistake," "Did that really happen?" or "I never saw it coming," what is really being described is a lapse in attention and concentration.

Siebert (1993) in discussing the survivor personality notes:

> **The more quickly a person grasps the total picture of what is happening, the better his or her chance of survival. Anger, fear and panic narrows what a person sees and reduces awareness.**

Warriors are not stupid (so "stupid mistakes" don't occur) but the ability to adequately control attention and concentration can be an issue, especially on difficult, protracted and tiring missions.

Test Your Concentration Skill: 1

To test your concentration and feel the "work" of concentrating, try the following drill:

Note the words **SMALL** and **LARGE** written in the columns. Beginning at the top of the first column, time yourself as you read down the list of words as fast as you can. Then immediately proceed to the second column and read down it, then the third, fourth and fifth until you reach the last word at the bottom of the last column. Then note your time.

Ready. Go!

SMALL	SMALL	SMALL	SMALL	LARGE
SMALL	LARGE	LARGE	SMALL	SMALL
LARGE	SMALL	SMALL	LARGE	LARGE
SMALL	SMALL	LARGE	SMALL	LARGE
LARGE	LARGE	LARGE	LARGE	LARGE
LARGE	LARGE	SMALL	LARGE	LARGE
LARGE	SMALL	LARGE	LARGE	SMALL
			SMALL	LARGE

How long did it take you?   TIME _____

Now do the same thing with the next block of words. But this time, do not read what the word says, but say whether it's printed in large or small font. On "go," time yourself or have someone time you as you proceed from the first word at the top of the first column and end with the last word at the bottom of the last column.

•

Ready. Go!

LARGE	SMALL	SMALL	SMALL	SMALL
SMALL	SMALL	LARGE	LARGE	SMALL
LARGE	LARGE	SMALL	SMALL	LARGE
LARGE	SMALL	LARGE	SMALL	SMALL
LARGE	LARGE	LARGE	LARGE	LARGE
LARGE	LARGE	SMALL	LARGE	LARGE
SMALL	LARGE	LARGE	SMALL	LARGE
LARGE	SMALL			

How long did it take you this time? TIME _____

The second exercise probably took longer because the task was harder and required more concentration. In fact, you probably felt your brain working at separating out the word cues from the size cues, a process much slower than just reading the words. This is based on the famous "Stroop Test," which demonstrates how difficult it can be to filter out irrelevant information. The result is that a failure to filter well impairs (slows) responding. You probably also found you made more mistakes and didn't perform as smoothly in this distracting situation.

Test Your Concentration Skill: 2
The next informal concentration test is located in Appendix II. This is from one of the pioneers in sport psychology, Dr. Dorothy Harris of Penn State University. Don't turn there yet. When you do, you will find a grid with randomly distributed numbers from 00 to 99. On "go," cross out as many in consecutive order as you can in one minute. Cross out like this: 00, 01, 02, 03 … 09, 10, 11 … 99 as quickly as you can.

Turn to Appendix II and … Go!

How high did you get in one minute? There is no hard and fast data on this, but generally, high-level performers score in the mid to upper twenties. When I (MA) taught a sport psychology class at a college, I often had much of the football team in my class (looking for an easy A, I assume). They typically scored in the high teens to low twenties; the highest was turned in by a professional soccer goalkeeper who scored 35 in one minute. Some very rough and unscientific data from my working with warriors finds that police officers generally score from 5 to 18 with an average score of about 8 on this exercise.

If you scored less than this, don't be concerned. This doesn't mean that you are eficient at concentrating; it simply means that you probably don't practice and use it the way that athletes do. More importantly, the purpose of the drill was to show concentration issues and the possibility of working to improve them.

ASPECTS OF CONCENTRATION

There are some aspects to concentration and attention that are important to understand to maximize your response in high-stress situations. The first is the width of concentration, attention or awareness. Attention can be broad, that is, it can have a wide perspective or, it can be narrow with a tight focus.

Circles of Attention

Nowicki (1994) says that Russian sport psychologists stress the importance of various "circles of attention."

- **Wide Circle of Attention:** you are aware of everything in your environment; a broad panorama of what is happening.
- **Middle Circle of Attention:** you are aware of what is happening in the general area where your responsibility lies.
- **Small Circle of Attention:** you are aware of what is going on in your personal space.
- **Internal Circle of Attention:** you are aware of what is happening in your body, what we describe later as the internal (versus external) focus.

High-Velocity Human Factors

High-Velocity Human Factors work describes three types of awareness of mission space (critical aspects of a challenge or mission) related to flexibility of attention.

- **Global Mission Space Awareness:** refers to strategic mission awareness and the broadest and most expansive in nature.
- **Local Mission Space Awareness:** refers to awareness within the operator's senses.
- **Glocal Mission Space Awareness:** refers to switching back and forth between global and local awareness.

Attention and Intention

Sonnon (2001) addresses the difference between "attention" and "intention." He says:

- Attention refers to the broad awareness typically needed in a combat situation.
- Intention relates to "intending" to engage in a specific act or execute a specific technique or tactic.

Sonnon cautions about mixing the two forms of attention and he especially cautions about excessive intention. While intention produces a focus on executing the skill, it can be so narrow that there is loss of awareness of other dangers present. For example, in extricating a subject from a car, your attention can be so focused on, say, a cross-face technique, that you fail to notice a weapon on the seat. This is a form of tunnel vision.

Ambient and Selective Attention

Mills (2005) uses the terms "ambient attention" for broad awareness and "selective attention" for a narrow focus.

Different Skills and Different Types of Attention

Just as with arousal, different tasks require or can tolerate different breadths of attention. Consider these sport skills and activities and decide whether each requires a broad/wide-range focus or a pinpoint/narrow focus. Write the skill under the appropriate column.

HOCKEY GOALKEEPING	BASKETBALL DEFENSE
ARCHERY	LINEBACKING
DIVING	PITCHING
WEIGHT LIFTING	PUTTING
PINPOINT/NARROW	BROAD/WIDE RANGE

Clearly, archery or putting requires a much narrower focus than linebacking, which requires scanning the broad field to read the play. Of course, many sport activities require (as do military and police skills) the ability to shift attention from narrow to broad, broad to narrow, and back and forth. A quarterback must first broadly read the defense, survey what is happening on the field and then zoom in on his targeted receiver. A baseball pitcher must focus on the signal from the catcher, and then check the statusof any base runners before returning to focus on the narrow strike zone. The next chart suggests where the skills might go.

HOCKEY GOALKEEPING	BASKETBALL DEFENSE
ARCHERY	LINEBACKING
DIVING	PITCHING
WEIGHT LIFTING	PUTTING
PINPOINT/NARROW	BROAD/WIDE RANGE
ARCHERY	BASKETBALL DEFENSE
DIVING	LINEBACKING
PITCHING	HOCKEY GOALKEEPING
WEIGHTLIFTING	
PUTTING	

Now do the same drill with the warrior skills listed here:

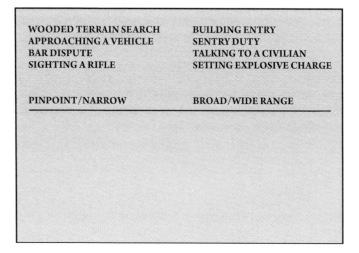

PINPOINT/NARROW	BROAD/WIDE RANGE

Here are some suggestions where these skills might fit.

WOODED TERRAIN SEARCH	BUILDING ENTRY
APPROACHING A VEHICLE	SENTRY DUTY
BAR DISPUTE	TALKING TO A CIVILIAN
SIGHTING A RIFLE	SETTING EXPLOSIVE CHARGE
PINPOINT/NARROW	BROAD/WIDE RANGE
SIGHTING A RIFLE	VEHICLE APPROACH
TALKING TO A CIVILIAN	BAR DISPUTE
SETTING EXPLOSIVE CHARGE	SENTRY DUTY
	BUILDING ENTRY
	TERRAIN SEARCH

There is general agreement that you can sight a rifle more successfully with a narrow focus. If you're an MP in a bar fight, you must focus broadly to watch what others are doing. Likewise, approaching a vehicle should include a broader awareness of other possible dangers at the scene, as would terrain search, sentry duty or building entry. Interviewing or helping a civilian will go better and the civilian will feel more attended to when you focus your attention on him. Again, many situations require the ability to shift attention from broad to narrow or narrow to broad, and back again. Assuring a match of attention to the requirements of the situation is the key to enhancing performance.

Locus of Focus

The other aspect of attention and concentration is called locus of focus, which refers to the location of your focus. Is your attention focused internally (inside yourself such as thoughts, feelings, physical sensations) or externally (outside yourself on what is going on around you)? Most often it's best to be externally focused — to be aware of what is going on around you - during a military mission or police operation. However, there are times when it's useful to be internally focused — to be aware of what is going on within your body and in your thinking - to assess your fatigue levels, to see if you need a break, or if you need to slow your pace during a response.

On the other hand, it would inhibit your responding properly if you were internally focused — attending to signs of anxiety, other discomforts, or worries — when you should be processing the events of the mission.

So, as noted, it's usually best to be externally focused, especially when you need to receive intelligence or orders. It's also important when you need to assess how others are doing and when you need to distract yourself from pain or fatigue to continue functioning.

It's a negative effect when you use an external focus to distract yourself from pain, fatigue or injury that requires attention and you can access help.

Solomon (1990) describes the nature of attention in high-stress shooting situations that illustrate the changing locus of attention. He says that when encountering unanticipated shooting incidents, a warrior can develop internal perceptions of vulnerability and lack of control. He says that if the attention remains internally "... focused on his vulnerability, further intensification of arousal, fear and distracting thoughts can develop and disrupt his ability to respond to the danger."

He suggests that to remain focused on stress and anxiety might cause the warrior to believe that the incident is more threatening than it is. Solomon says that this can create "a situation that may foster a panic reaction." He says that the warrior must transition to focus his response on surviving the situation:

> **...he must move away from an internal awareness of vulnerability with its negative emotional arousal to the external reality of the threat...**

Moran (1996) conducted research on the attentional skills of Canadian soldiers on a three-hour, weight-loaded endurance march. The soldiers used both an "associative" strategy of focusing on and monitoring how their bodies were doing as well as a "dissociative" strategy of distracting themselves from discomfort, fatigue and the like. The soldiers combined distraction from discomfort with a performance-related monitoring of the state of their body.

Another Form of Internal and External Focus

Research in the area of motor behavior and development suggests that another form of internal or external focus may affect quality of performance and has different effects depending on the skill level of the performer. The terms "internal" and "external" focus as used here are a little different from "locus of focus," where reference was made to attention to either one's internal physical and psychological feelings or external awareness of everything outside one's body in the performance environment.

For the motor behavior researchers, "internal focus" refers to paying attention to such things as the form of the skill, such as your grip on a golf club (Magill 2007; Wulf, 2007) and proper grip on a handgun. "External focus" refers to attention that is away from your body and on an object, such as focusing on the head of a golf club or the sights of your weapon. External orientation may refer to parts of your body. However, the focus is not on form or style (as in the internal focus above), but on the point of interaction for performance, such as your foot contacting a soccer ball. It can also refer to the "performance effect" of a skill, like the flight of a golf ball or a bullet striking the target.

In general, it's been found that experienced and skilled performers show enhanced performance with an external focus, while an internal focus may actually make performance worse. The opposite is true for less skilled performers.

For example, a less skilled baseball player's focus is internal: his grip on the bat. A skilled player's focus is external, such as on the movement of the bat or on its contact with the ball. Research (Castenada & Gray, 2007) shows that highly-skilled baseball batters perform better with an environmental/external focus, such as seeing the ball leave the bat and do worse with an internal focus such as the grip of their hands. The opposite is true for low-skill batters, who do better by focusing on their hands. For the skilled player, an internal focus might disrupt the flow of his skill.

Mental Imagery Focus	This raises the question as to the best way to focus when practicing tactical imagery (discussed in Chapter 7). Is it better to focus on form and skill or equipment and the result of performance (grip and squeeze or the bullet hitting a bullseye)? While there is no definitive research on this, it's generally suggested that tactical imagery should focus on the skill, the feel of the movement and the like. Further, other research has failed to find consistent effects on performance for internal versus external focus of attention.
	Therefore, since it's not clear what will work best, try various approaches to find what is most effective for you (Maurer & Munzert, 2005).

The point, as with arousal, is to begin to think about what type of attention you need for different skills and tasks during a given mission, and whether you're engaged in the appropriate type and if you can adjust focus as needed. There are three dimensions to concentration and three related questions to ask yourself about the quality of your attention and concentration.

DIMENSIONS OF CONCENTRATION & THE THREE ESSENTIAL QUESTIONS

INTENSITY	Can I concentrate hard enough?
DURATION	Can I concentrate long enough?
FLEXIBILITY	Can I shift attention as needed?

For **Intensity:** Ask yourself in any given situation: "Can I concentrate hard enough?"
For **Duration:** Ask yourself in any given situation: "Can I concentrate long enough?"
For **Flexibility:** Ask yourself in any given situation: "Can I shift attention as needed?"

If you cannot answer an emphatic "Yes" to each of these, you need to enhance your concentration and attention skills. This is essential, not only for excelling in performance, but also for avoiding performance decrements and mistakes.

In addition to the examples given before, Mills (2005) found that distracted concentration (for drivers) has two negative effects. The first is that it leads to missing important cues, like red lights. Secondly, distraction leads to more risky behavior. While this is sometimes related, as in trying to make up for mistakes, distraction can also lead to risky behavior on its own. For example, distracted drivers are willing to accept gaps that are more dangerous when merging and when following the car in front of them.

Finally, Navy Seal Richard Machowicz (2002) observes that:

> **Without a focused mind, results are happenstance, unreliable.**

Enhancing Attention and Concentration
It's possible and necessary to enhance concentration and attention skills. Mills (2005) notes:

> **What do professional drivers know that the rest of us don't? They have learned to discipline their attention through techniques that eliminate dangerous habits such as target fixation, tunnel vision and narrowed attention.**

There are a variety of ways to attempt to increase the effectiveness of concentration. As a basis, Perry (2005) reports that gaining an optimal level of arousal leads to optimal attentional skills. Actual training techniques for enhanced concentration range from simple exercises to the rather involved computer-driven training.

Reflections in a Tiger's Eyes
Wim Demeere, a multiple martial arts expert with national and international medals, author and international trainer offers an interesting approach (described here for interest, not necessarily a recommendation).

In training mental toughness for elite competitions he reports (Demeere, 2004) using a technique of which he became aware and purportedly was originally used by KGB recruits. The recruits were instructed to go to the zoo and study the stares of tigers and panthers. He states that the tiger is a natural warrior and when you stare into the eyes of a six-hundred pound animal that can "kill you with a casual swipe of its claws and deflesh you in a matter of seconds, it gives you a different perspective on the warrior mindset."

Video Games and Computerized Attention and Concentration Training

NASA looked at training astronauts in regulating their physiology as a way to control hazardous operator states, such as distracted attention (Prinzel, Pope & Freeman, 2001). To make it more interesting, NASA attempted to link playing video games to desired states of attention. Games are made accessible to the astronaut when he is in a desirable state of alertness (the games only turn on when the astronaut is in the target emotional psychological/physiological state). This leads to the astronaut's awareness of such optimal states being strengthened and the techniques to achieve such states being practiced more regularly.

Such research has also led to the development of commercially available attention/ concentration training devices, though the applications have been more about treating attention deficit disorder problems, rather than enhancing high levels of attention per se. However, Vernon & Gruzelier (2003) found preliminary data showing that a certain type of biofeedback, called neurofeedback (brain wave), may increase "working memory" capability (such as maintaining a phone number to be used shortly) by about 10 percent.

Recent research on video games (Dingfelder, 2007; Green et al., 2006) shows that regular players of certain games are exceptionally fast at visual searches, at monitoring a larger field of vision (attending simultaneously to the center of their vision and to their periphery), they may be more flexible in their attention, and they excel at target location. While it's known that training in search simulation can improve visual attention in air traffic controllers and fighter pilots, it's not clear if it transfers to other situations.

Attention-Fixation Training is among the simpler and more readily accessible techniques to train concentration. It initially involves sitting in a quiet place and choosing an object, usually duty-related (like your helmet, badge, insignia, or weapon) and concentrating on it. The idea is to learn to focus solely on the object (helmet) and nothing else. Here is how you do it:

- Select a safe quiet environment.
- Choose a duty-related object on which to focus, say, your helmet. Your task is to focus only on it and nothing else. Notice its shape, color and any scuffs or scratches. Hold only helmet-related thoughts in your mind.

- Maintain this attentional focus initially for 15 to 30 seconds and then slowly increase the duration to two minutes.
- The degree to which you can do this is a measure of your attentional discipline. If you find thoughts entering your awareness unrelated to your helmet — "Why am I doing this stupid crap," "I have other duties," "I'm bored," know that they represent thought drifting, distractibility and decreased attentional discipline. When it happens, and it will, don't get frustrated. Simply bring your focus back on the object.
- Slowly increase the time to about two minutes.
- Then introduce distractions after you have accomplished intense focus for the two-minute period. You might turn on the radio or CD player very low and see if you can ignore the music and maintain your attention on your helmet. Try the same thing with a talk radio program and strive to ignore the talk.
- Increase the distraction. When you're able to maintain focus successfully at a low volume, you should make the potential distraction a bit louder or more noticeable. Again, practice your focus at this level until it seems solid and then increase the distraction again.
- Use sounds from a real world setting in your concentration training. Focus on your helmet while listening to tapes of sirens, shouts, or sounds from a firing range. By training with sounds that mimic the type of settings in which you actually function, you more quickly transfer your skills to real-life situations.
- Train in the real world. It's also important to move your practice to "live" settings and train to maximize transfer to the real world. When it's safe to do so, practice concentration training in your cruiser, humvee or in the field.
- Broaden and alternate the distraction. Move beyond the distraction to become more aware of what is going on in the room you're in. Shift your attention from the narrow, to the broad, and back again.

Train Flexibility into Your Attention and Concentration

The above exercise strengthens your ability to focus your attention, which is often the hardest thing to do in highly charged distracting situations. But as noted before, too much narrowing can also occur, as represented by tunnel vision and auditory exclusion. Be sure to use the above exercise to train attention flexibility and broadening, as well.

Using the same approach to train your attention to focus as above, begin shifting your attention from the focus object to the distraction. For example, as described when using radio music as a distraction, shift your attention to listen to it and ignore the focus object (while still looking at it). Then become aware of other sounds and objects or activity in the room and then shift back to the focus object. Continue to train shifting your focus until it becomes a habit. It's easy practice, and the skill and the benefits develop quickly.

Other Suggestions for Training Attention and Concentration

When driving: Dr. Ken Mills' excellent book *Disciplined Attention: How to Improve Your Visual Attention When you Drive* (2005) provides several other techniques to exercise concentration. These include skills such as expanding the field of view, relevant movement, hazard awareness, anticipation and prediction. While he focuses on driving, there is certainly potential application to other types of skills.

Actually, driving is a good opportunity to work on training your broad attention and learning to control narrowing of focus. For a variety of reasons, from boredom to stress, your attention while driving can be narrowly focused or tunneled. In line with Mills' suggestion that drivers need to maintain awareness of multiple driving stimuli and events going on around them, make a conscious effort to broadly scan road and driving conditions to help you train and develop a habit of broad awareness.

When holstering: Though a bit controversial, conducting a visual scan of the scene before holstering a weapon after a high-stress situation or after shots have been fired, helps to counteract tunnel vision tendencies. Therefore, practicing such visual scanning every time before your weapon is holstered (even after range practice and after cleaning) can help train this habit.

In a noisy room: When you're in a noisy room, take the opportunity to practice auditory concentration, especially when there are multiple conversations occurring. We all have had the experience of trying to listen to someone talking to us in such a setting and being distracted by other ongoing (maybe more interesting!) conversations. Use the moment to strengthen your attention on the conversation in which you're engaged and block out others that are distracting. You can also work on broadening awareness by deliberately attending to the other conversations, while maintaining focus on your primary one. Then try shifting your attention among the conversations.

Training, Experience and Situational Awareness
Such training may be especially important for situational awareness. For not only is situational awareness affected by level of arousal, it may not readily transfer to other areas of performance without specific training (Endsley, 2006). Also, new and unfamiliar situations may hamper situational awareness due to of a lack of relevant (recognizable) cues or because of an opposite problem of pattern over-matching, applying well-trained but inappropriate interpretations and expectations to the situation.

This is critical as situational awareness has been said to provide "the foundation for military decision making and the framework within all plans and actions are conceived (Endsley, 2006)." And unlike pilots or others who receive their information from an engineered environment, platoon leaders function in an "embedded, natural and variable" world.

Endsley (2006) reports research by Strater and his colleagues (2001) on differences in situational awareness by more experienced versus less experienced platoon leaders. Situational awareness was defined as involving parameters of looking at enemy location, location of their own platoon, highest threat challenge, strongest enemy and strongest friendly.

Results showed that less experienced platoon leaders were less situationally aware in all areas except awareness of friendlies. The authors interpreted this as showing that experienced leaders had better situational awareness overall and were more attuned to threats and enemies than less experienced leaders. They note this is consistent with other research showing experienced leaders to be more aware of threats and enemies than friendly factors.

Specifically, the more experienced platoon leaders were better on situational awareness variables such as:

- Using assets to assess the environment.
- Using standard reporting procedures.
- Identifying key elements in the situation.
- Setting appropriate alert levels.
- Assessing information received.
- Gathering follow-up information as needed.
- Assessing key findings and unusual events.
- Communicating information.
- Focusing on the big picture.

The importance of critical decision-making under stress and the need for training and practice was reinforced (2008) by Drs. Audrey Honig & William Lewinski in their article on human factors in lethal force encounters:

> **Since cognition and critical decisionmaking under high stress is also typically the least practiced and yet critical skill an officer needs, the officer's ability to accurately perceive and process information in the heat of battle is therefore further impaired through this lack of practice.**

Strategic Vision:
chapter Tactical Performance Imagery and Mental Toughness

What the **mind** *can* **conceive** *and the* **heart** *can* **believe**,

you can achieve.

– **Cal Botterill, Canadian Sport Psychologist**

Mental Imagery, also called mental practice, is a natural process that can be one of the most powerful psychological skills for enhancing performance and mental toughness. You engage in mental imagery quite regularly when you anticipate your involvement in any situation, everything from a presentation, a mission scenario, or a party.

Although the use of mental performance imagery has a long history in human performance enhancement, it's perhaps best known and most widely used in high-level athletic compe-tition. Dr. Shane Murphy, former head of psychological training for the United States Olympic Committee says (2005):

> **Imagery… is the most important of the mental skills required for winning the mind game in sports.**

Ninety percent of the athletes and ninety-four percent of the coaches surveyed at the United States Olympic Training Center reported that they used imagery. Ninety-seven percent of the athletes and one hundred percent of the coaches agreed that imagery enhances performance.

TACTICAL PERFORMANCE IMAGERY AND THE WARRIOR

Remsberg (1986) may have been one of the first to discuss an imagery process for police work. He called it "crisis rehearsal," which was a good idea but perhaps not the best term, since it's not the crisis, but the response that should be the focus of imagery training. The use of imagery is now being recognized as useful in maximizing combat and other military, police and emergency skills (Murray, 2004).

Tactical Performance Imagery

Tactical Performance Imagery, as we will refer to it here, is the use of your imagination to improve specific military and police skills. Consider it as mental rehearsal of skills or missions.

Martin (2006) in his guide to succeeding in the selection process for Special Forces asks, "What does it take to be successful?" He answers:

> **Belief and commitment. Visualize yourself completing the various training events, the road marches, etc. Visualize yourself walking across the stage in your uniform with a Special Forces "Long Tab" on your shoulder and a Green Beret in your hand.**

In her study of mental readiness and performance excellence in police officers, McDonald (2006) found that about 40 percent of police officers used performance imagery. It was used most by officers with tactical experience (50 percent) and by those with college educations (50 percent). Eighty-seven 87 percent of officers used it on the way to a call, about 75 percent used it to rehearse possible responses and around 40 percent used it as a "mental checklist" for preparation readiness.

A Study of Lethal Encounters

The Force Science Research Center notes important research by Dr. Darrell Ross, Chairman of the Department of Law Enforcement and Justice Administration at Western Illinois University, on what promotes peak performance in lethal-force conflicts. The study was conducted on 121 male officers from 94 agencies who killed suspects in 94 percent of their encounters. All officers survived.

Among the factors that Dr. Ross found as influencing the outcomes of these encounters was that the officers "formulated flexible anticipations." This means that en route to the call, officers began to develop impressions of what they would likely encounter. Over one third had formal training in mental imagery and many others practiced on their own time. Dr. Ross says, "They mentally prepared themselves to recognize danger." They used performance imagery to develop flexible mental models (as described in Chapter 5) in preparation for the response. The study found that the other factors the officers had that contributed to their success in these encounters included possessing high situational awareness, the ability to screen out distractions, to draw reasonable inferences quickly, to act emphatically, to articulate well and, in a number of instances, they had participated in high-level weapons training beyond typical qualification.

Thus, imagery is often done naturally when we anticipate or think about what an upcoming mission or operation will be. What makes Tactical Performance Imagery more effective than everyday imagination is its application to military/police skills and the integration of scientific research on what, in fact, makes it effective.

Uses for Tactical Performance Imagery
Tactical Performance Imagery can be used to enhance military and police performance in several ways, including:

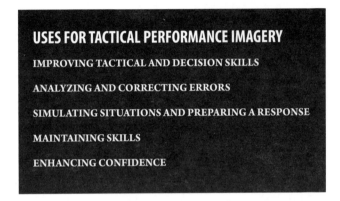

USES FOR TACTICAL PERFORMANCE IMAGERY

IMPROVING TACTICAL AND DECISION SKILLS

ANALYZING AND CORRECTING ERRORS

SIMULATING SITUATIONS AND PREPARING A RESPONSE

MAINTAINING SKILLS

ENHANCING CONFIDENCE

Skill Improvement
Tactical Performance Imagery is used to complement and enhance physical skills, such as weapon use, close-quarter combat, and even interactional skills. It can be particularly useful in skills that are sequenced, such as room clearing during a raid. By imaging the details of the mission, you not only "practice" the raid, but you can also check for any points of uncertainty or confusion about what should be done. If you cannot complete the mission smoothly in your imagery, you probably cannot execute it effectively in reality.

Moran (1996) provides an interesting cross-over on imagery training from sport to other complex motor skills. For example, imagery is a common performance technique used by professional golfers. Master's champion Nick Faldo, said this about his helicopter training:

> I took time off in the privacy of my room to spend ten minutes simulating in my mind how to land my helicopter. By the time the next lesson came around, I discovered not only was I an expert in landing it in theory, I could suddenly land it in reality, too. (p.209)

The particular form of performance imagery called VMBR (Visuo-Motor Behavior Rehearsal) has been shown to enhance performance in karate and pistol marksmanship, among other sport skills (Morris, Spittle & Watt, 2005). The same authors say that performance imagery for skill improvement can be effective for both novice and experienced individuals, a finding that is not without controversy (others say performance imagery is most appropriate for those with experience).

The Power of Negativity

Negative imagery — imagery of performance failure — can reduce the quality of performance. Just as we will see when we examine negative thinking, the impact of negative imagery is even more powerful than positive imagery (Murphy, 2005). In a study of the effect of positive and negative imagery on putting skills in golf (Morris, Spittle & Watt, 2005), it was found that performance was poorer in the negative performance imagery condition, with a mean putting error of 11.3 centimeters compared to other conditions. It's also been found that imagery of being overly relaxed hurts performance in strength-related skills.

Driskell, et al. (2006) found that mental imagery practice has three important applications. Use it to enhance performance in:

- Complex cognitive tasks.
- Physically dangerous tasks.
- Tasks where there is limited opportunity to practice required skills and tactics.

Error Analysis and Correction

In a training scenario or actual incident, use Tactical Performance Imagery to review the sequence of actions and define points of uncertainty, confusion, or mistakes. By imaging a more preferred or effective response, imaging helps "erase the old tape" of sub-optimal response and errors, to "reprogram" a more successful response to be stored in your brain.

Situation Simulation and Response Preparation

Tactical Performance Imagery is used to anticipate and rehearse different approaches or conditions in missions, such as multiple targets, different types of structures, and weather conditions. Use it to provide "experience" with situations that can't be recreated easily or frequently in physical simulation or live training.

Murray (2004) discusses work by Spick that shows that survivability in air combat is greatly increased after a pilot's first five engagements. However, getting to or through the first five engagements for a pilot or any soldier may take time and is certainly dangerous.

Imagery has the potential to speed the process and help succeed in those initial trials. It may help create "pre-battle veterans," as christened in *On Combat*. John Giduck offers (2008) that Russian special forces, Spetsnaz, believe only one thing is certain in combat; something will happen, but it will not be what you prepared for in training. As discussed shortly, simulation can reduce the surprise factor in an actual situation, thus resulting in a quicker response, a more sustained response, and a more effective response.

The situation simulation that can be accomplished through Tactical Performance Imagery seems especially important for developing expertise and elite level performance. The experts who study the experts (Feltovich, Prietula, & Ericsson, 2006) have reported the characteristics that comprise exceptional and expert performance. Among them are the following aspects to which tactical performance imagery in conjunction with designed and frequent practice and training can aid the process of elite development:

> ## How One Top Place Kicker Uses Imagery
>
> **Place kicker Morten Andersen is the leading scorer in the National Football League. In 2007, at age 47 and not having kicked for a while, he was brought in to perform once again. When asked how he prepares for pressure kicks, his answer shows how performance imagery helps him recognize and respond in critical situations:**
>
> *I do mental training throughout the week. I take myself through specific game situations, so when they come up I've rehearsed them.*

- *Expertise is Limited in Scope and Does Not Transfer to Other Areas of Performance*
  Although there is often a "halo effect" where we assume that people who excel in one area are accomplished in many or all areas, this is not the case. There can be some crossover, but this not guaranteed and caution is warranted. Expertise with marine assault craft does not translate to competence with tanks or, perhaps, even white-water rafting. Further, while expertise does not necessarily cross domains, it may also be limited within a domain, as well, without proper continued training.
- *Knowledge and Content Matter are Important to Expertise*
  Expertise and elite performance are not simply due to special learning, logical or thinking abilities or skills. The development of broad knowledge and deep content about an area or domain is needed.

- *Expertise Involves Larger and More Integrated Cognitive Units*
Experts have better pattern recognition of what they are looking
at and what it means. Based on experience and training, they are able
to see relationships between elements because of familiarity, and organize
them in meaningful ways. For example, the elements "t, a ,c" can been
seen as "cat" or "act." In addition to "amassing skill, knowledge and
mechanisms to monitor and control cognitive processes to perform
tasks efficiently and effectively," experts can "restructure, reorganize,
and refine" the knowledge and procedures for their environments.
- *Expertise Involves Selective Access to Relevant Information*
It is said that "one can not step into the same river twice." Elite
performers have a breadth and depth of experience which allows
accessing extensive, accurate, and appropriate information needed
in a given or changing situation.
- *Simple Experience is not Sufficient for Developing Expertise*
This is a critical point. More of the same does not lead to continued
improvement and elite skill levels. Simply additional time in a position/
role or repetitive training makes skill less effortful, but not necessarily
better. In order to develop expertise, training needs to focus (typically
under the guidance of an expert trainer) on:
  - Improving specific aspects of skills, tactics, knowledge.
  - Using reflection to consider, monitor, and adjust performance.
  - Providing and exploring alternatives to usual approaches.
  - Providing opportunities and challenges to problem solve.
  - Doing all of this within the context of repetition and feedback.

While it was once fully believed that a person's nature or raw talent was the limiting factor in the level of performance that could be attained, there is now growing acceptance that the key to expert and elite performance is extensive involvement in relevant practice activities (Ward et al., 2008). Tactical Performance Imagery integrated with training and practice can provide exposure for developing breadth and depth of knowledge and experience within a context of structured training, variable situations, repetition and feedback to practice accessing and applying skills in multiple challenges.

Skill Maintenance
Tactical Performance Imagery is used to keep skills fresh (Murphy, 2005). Use it as a countermeasure for those skills that deteriorate without use. Murray (2004) says:

> ...even when you don't have the resources to actually
> practice a skill, positive mental imagery is a tool that those
> who are at the top of their game use to maintain and
> improve proficiency.

Murphy (2005) tells the somewhat familiar legend of an American officer who was held as a prisoner of war. He is reported to have passed the time by playing a round of golf in his mind, shot by shot, on a daily basis. The legend goes that upon release from his years of captivity and playing his first round of golf at his home course, he shot par, despite the rigors of incarceration and not having ever actually practiced for that time.

Confidence Enhancement

While enhanced confidence is often a result of effective mental preparation for missions, it can be improved more directly by imaging needed emotional responses. Research shows that performance imagery can affect anxiety, motivation and feelings of effectiveness; in the earlier cited study of negative imagery, feelings of confidence were decreased, as well as performance (Morris, Spittle, & Watt, 2005). When someone tells you "I can see myself screwing this up," they are eroding their confidence, increasing their stress and programming themselves for failure. Conversely, Mastery Imagery has been shown to create feelings of confidence and control and Coping Imagery has been shown to enhance confidence in managing feelings of excessive arousal (Cumming, et al., 2007).

Imagery, Dreams, and Performance Anxiety

Performance anxiety dreams are a puzzling occurrence for many warriors. Discussed in some detail in *On Combat*, these dreams are neither unusual nor rare. Many individuals, even among the most elite units, have periodic dreams of weapon malfunction or an inability to fluidly execute a skill at a critical moment. While such dreams are more uncomfortable than problematic, a form of imagery called Imagery Rehearsal Therapy may have promise for reducing such dreams, as it has been shown to be effective in decreasing nightmares in individuals with post-traumatic stress disorder (Krakow, et al., 2001; Gibson, 2006). In short, imagery rehearsal treatment involves imaging different, more positive, or effective actions or endings to the dreams while awake; and the new action or endings are then rehearsed through imagery practice. The interested reader is encouraged to search out Krakow's and Gibson's work.

Martial arts expert, Win Demeere (2008), described his use of imagery in preparing to fight at the highest levels of international competition. In his words you will find many of the uses of tactical performance imagery including skill enhancement, error correction, situation simulation, and integration with other mental toughness techniques:

As I was now facing fighters on the international scene, men with knockout power in every technique, I could no longer afford to hold back. So I spent countless hours on mental programming, learning to invoke and then control a powerful mindset. I watched footage of my fights, mentally reliving each one, imagining going full power where I had held back.

My next step was to program my mind and practice deep meditation. I imagined highly detailed fights, each with a different opponent. I "fought" them like a demon, not letting up until they had been beaten unconscious. Though in my mental imagery I was a merciless animal, I made sure I was always in control of my physical actions. Since being out of control is a sure way to lose a fight, it was critical that my mental training included extreme aggression that was in harmony with the right mind-set to control it.

MAKING TACTICAL PERFORMANCE IMAGERY MAXIMALLY EFFECTIVE

As mentioned, it's the application of scientific findings to the imagery process that maximizes its effectiveness. Here are a few findings on how to make imagery maximally effective:

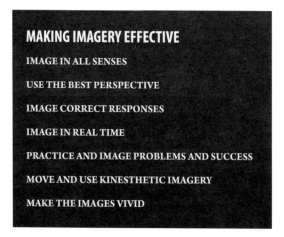

MAKING IMAGERY EFFECTIVE

IMAGE IN ALL SENSES

USE THE BEST PERSPECTIVE

IMAGE CORRECT RESPONSES

IMAGE IN REAL TIME

PRACTICE AND IMAGE PROBLEMS AND SUCCESS

MOVE AND USE KINESTHETIC IMAGERY

MAKE THE IMAGES VIVID

Image in All of Your Senses

Tactical Performance Imagery is sometimes called "visualization." We don't like or recommend this term because it implies you image only what you "see" or "visualize" during a mission or operation. On an actual mission, all of your senses are working, so the mental rehearsal with tactical performance imagery should include all of your sensory responses. It's crucial to think about:

- what you would See.
- what you would Hear.
- what you would Feel (both physical feelings and emotional feelings).
- what you would Smell.
- what you would Taste.

Using all of your senses promotes the best transference of imagery responses to the real situation.

Research has attempted to look at differences in visual imagery (imagining what you see) versus kinesthetic imagery (imagining what you physically feel). While a conclusion is not clear, it seems that kinesthetic imagery is crucial to maximizing the benefit of imagery training, if not preferable (Murphy, 2005).

Two other related factors that affect the impact of imagery training are the vividness and controllability of the images. The more vivid (intense, realistic) the image, the more effect it will have. Controlling the image, staying on the skill, switching to another focus, maintaining its vividness, and the like, also affect the impact of imagery training.

Try the following:

Sit in a comfortable chair, relax and close your eyes. (You may want to have someone read the following instructions to you). For each instruction, image the scene for a few moments, then open your eyes, clear your thoughts, and move on to the next scene. Make each one as vivid as possible, maintain your focus, and don't allow other thoughts to distract you.

- In your mind's vision, *SEE* the scene as you approach the location of a mission.
- In your mind's hearing, *HEAR* the issuing of orders; hear the intelligence provided to you as you travel to the location.
- In your mind's touch, *FEEL* the vibrations and rocking of the transport vehicle as you proceed to the location.
- In your mind's emotion, *FEEL* a sense of confidence as you interact effectively with your platoon or team members.

- In your mind's smell, *SMELL* the exhaust from the multiple vehicles that arrived at the staging area.
- In your mind's taste, *TASTE* warm, flavorful coffee during a cold damp mission.

Here is a more detailed script that incorporates multiple senses in tactical imagery training. Use it to image scenarios of missions in which you might be involved.

As you sit comfortably with your eyes closed, I'd like you to take a slow deep tactical breath. Hold it for a second or two and then just let it go and return to breathing lightly and normally. As you do, let pictures and images of a call-out develop in your mind. Let's say you're going to clear a building with an explosive entry. Use all of your senses. Think about what you see. Think about what you hear. Think about what you feel. And even think about what you taste and smell.

Feel the rocking and swaying of the van as it comes to a stop. Hear the creaking of the door and see streetlight flood in as the van door opens. Feel your feet hit the ground as you exit the van. See the other team members exiting and hear the muffled sounds as their feet hit the ground to move into position.

See the building's doors and windows as you approach. Feel yourself scanning the structure as you check for threats. See the team staging and feel the gentle shuffling and pushing as all of you get into position. Then focus quickly back to the staging of the entry.

See the charge being placed on the door. Feel your anticipation, confidence and readiness rise in your body. Hear the PA system with the announcement of identity, authority and purpose (for police warrants).

Hear the charge ignite, and see the flash of light and debris falling. Hear and feel windows breaking. Feel the push and thud of the overpressure from the charge.

Hear and feel the ringing in your ears from the charge until the sensation is replaced by your focus on commands from your team members. See the debris and door parts in the entryway. See, feel, taste and smell the dust and smoke in the air. See clutter and garbage in the residence. As you enter and turn the corner, see the subjects surrendering on their knees with hands and fingers interlaced behind their heads. See and feel yourself scanning the scene as you check for other suspects, weapons, contraband or threats.

Feel your continued vigilance until you are sure all is secure. Hear the shout of "clear" and feel the satisfaction as the subjects are led away. Taste some cool refreshing water as you stand down and prepare to leave.

Enjoy those good feelings of satisfaction and accomplishment for a few more moments until you open your eyes, feeling strong and confident.

This gives you an idea as to how to use performance imagery in all of your senses. Substitute other situations related to your particular duties as a way to practice and enhance imagery in all of your senses.

Strive To Make Your Imagery Vivid

While it has been said combat can never really be described or understood unless one has experienced it, a poignant sensory picture using descriptive (vivid) imagery was provided to co-author Dave Grossman by WWII Veteran Keith Kreitman:

> **It involves blurred vision from sweaty eyes, the acrid choking smell of layers of gunpowder smoke, ear bursting horrific noises, the kinetic nerve vibrations from exploding mortars, hand grenades and shells, the screams of humans, the cries of the wounded, the piercing whine of ricochets of bullets and shrapnel, hiding or stepping over bodies of perhaps someone you know. All at one time.**

Miller (2007) advocates using emotionally arousing imagery to train to prepare mentally for life and death situations. He describes an imagery scenario called "Loved-Ones-In-Danger" as a means of learning how to summon a response in a lethal situation. You would use it to train yourself to produce thoughts, feelings, and actions required in situations that are worth fighting for, dying for, but most importantly, living for.

Such emotionally intense imagery scenarios are probably best developed and initially trained with the help of expert guidance under safe and controlled conditions. Miller (2007) importantly cautions that the emotionally and physically intense violent imagery of such survival scenarios is not a means of training impulsive or uncontrolled violent behavior, but of summoning controlled emotion and power leading to survival action. Further, such intensity is not an indication to forget or forgo tactical training and skill. Indeed, just the opposite is true. Integrating mental and tactical training should allow ultimate control and maximal application of tactical skills.

Move with Your Imagery

While Tactical Performance Imagery is a psychological technique, it doesn't mean you have to be perfectly still or passive when practicing imagery. Just as it should include all your senses, it's ok and even better to move in motions that mimic the skills that you're imaging. This does not mean performing at full speed or intensity, but soft movements can integrate "feel" with the imagery.

Co-author Loren Christensen (2008) has made suggestions for schoolteachers and students on how to use imagery practice to better respond to a school shooter. He further describes how to employ minor movement to the practice. Loren writes:

> **While mental imagery is done in your mind, you don't have to always sit perfectly still when practicing. Just as you want to include all your senses, you should also practice from time to time using mini movements that mimic what you're imaging. You're not moving at full speed, full force or with full extension of your limbs, but simply using small, gentle movements to give you a sense of "feel" with your imagery.**

Here is how you can use mini-movements when imaging a traffic stop. Say you want to practice reacting to a motorist reaching quickly under his seat for something. In realty, the situation as presented here would take about 45 seconds. Therefore, your imagery should last just as long. Do it repetitiously for five minutes and you can easily perform five quality repetitions. Do it every other day and you add additional quality training time to your week. Here is how it's done:

Sit in a comfortable chair and bring on a sense of relaxation using the 4-count breathing technique or one of its variations.

Note: The below scenario has been presented in stages for clarity. However, you want to image it in one continuous action.

Image: Getting out of your vehicle and positioning yourself behind its open door for a moment as you scan the pickup you have just stopped. Image the sound of radio chatter, the feel of the sun on you, and the sound and rush of passing traffic. Image looking through the vehicle's back window and into the truck bed.
Physically: Straighten yourself in your chair to mimic standing and turn your head a little as if looking from the driver's side of the pickup to the passenger side. Let your eyes drop a little as if looking in the truck bed.

Image: Feel the energy in your legs as you move around your door and begin walking toward the truck. Hear the passing cars. Image watching the driver through his window and how he looks nervously into his rear view mirror.
Physically: Remain in your chair but alternate and mildly flex your legs muscles to mimic walking. Move your head slightly from left to right and then right to left as you pantomime scanning the inside of the truck on your approach.

Image: Stopping at the rear edge of the truck's driver's door. Look into the window and image the driver turn slightly to look at you. Feel controlled adrenaline surge through your body as all your senses tell you that something isn't right.
Physically: Stop flexing your leg muscles. Turn your head slightly to the right to mimic looking into the driver's window.

Image: Telling the driver to "Sir, put both of your hands out the window."
Physically: Mouth the words or even say them out loud, "Sir, put both of your hands out the window."

Image: Feeling your controlled arousal and awareness surge even more when he doesn't comply.
Physically: Deliberately accelerate your breathing and fill your body with energy.

Image: Leaning forward slightly to look inside the driver's window, being careful not to step into the path of the door.
Physically: Lean forward a little in your chair to mimic looking inside the truck.

Image: The driver leaning forward suddenly to get something under his seat. Feel yourself straighten and begin to reach toward your weapon.
Physically: Pull yourself up straight in your chair and make a mini-movement toward your imaginary holster.

Image: Moving backwards toward the rear of the truck, grasping your weapon and calling out, "Freeze! Don't' Move! Don't move!"
Physically: Remain in your chair but mildly flex your leg muscles to mimic scooting backwards. Pantomime a small motion with your hand of pulling your weapon. Mouth or actually call out, "Freeze! Don't' Move! Don't move!"

Image: Moving to the rear right corner of his truck where he can't back into you but you can see his movements through his window. Image extending your weapon as you lower yourself into shooting stance.
Physically: Turn your body slightly to mimic moving to the far side of the truck. Extend your gun hand partially and scrunch your body down a little to mimic a shooting stance.

From this place in your imagery, add any number of conclusions to the situation. With each one, add elements that involve as many of your senses as possible and as many mini-movements as you are able while remaining seated.

While sitting in a comfortable chair in a quiet place is a highly effective way to image, know that there are variations you can do that not only add variety to your practice but a level of realism as well. You can:

- stand in place and move your head, body and limbs slightly to correspond to your imaged scenario.
- stand and make larger movements: Turn your head all the way in a given direction, extend your arm all the way, and physically take a step or two to the front, rear or side.
- stand and wear your uniform and gear when you practice your imagery.
- stand and practice in different environments: the cluttered basement in your home with a radio playing or at work in your vehicle compound.
- stand conjure your optimum arousal performance state instead of inducing deep relaxation.
- vary the perspective you use in your imagery between the Third-Person External View and the First Person-Internal View (see the next section for more information on this); vary between imagery of watching yourself react and imagery of what you see (hear, feel, taste & smell) when you are reacting.

Imagery practice is a powerful training tool that can be done comfortably in an easy chair, standing in the middle of a room or while being jostled in the back of a noisy transport vehicle. It's easy to do and the benefits are many.

Use the Best Perspective

There are at least two perspectives for tactical performance imagery:

- **The External or Third Person perspective:** You image as if watching yourself on a videotape; being outside yourself, like a spectator at a game.
- **The Internal or First Person perspective:** You image what you actually experience during a response; you are doing the action, not watching yourself perform. You see (hear, feel, taste, smell) what you actually experience during a mission or response.

The above graphic shows the difference between the two types of perspectives for sighting a rifle. When using tactical imagery in the third person or external perspective, you might see yourself as the above officer sighting the weapon. However, if you use first person or internal imagery, you would image a view like that through the scope; you actually experience the situation rather than seeing yourself acting.

Neurolinguistic programming or NLP is a performance enhancement approach that grew from combining computer science and linguistics. It seeks to maximize performance by observing elite and expert behavior and translating it into training techniques. Its proponents (Andreas & Faulkner, 1994) suggest three perspectives for imagery: Self, Observer and Other. Self is the first person perspective and Observer is the third person perspective. The interesting addition is the perspective of the Other, which is how your adversary will view you and your actions. Robert Dilts one of the developers of NLP is reported to have stated that:

> "Excellence is passionate commitment to something from the self position. Wisdom is the ability to consciously move back and forth between self, other and observer positions."

Police and military training innovator Chris Ghannam (2008) emphasizes a fourth imagery perspective. He calls it the Top-Down view; imaging as if you were observing from above your actions, much like a sky-cam or the Goodyear Blimp at a football game. While this is a third person or external view, it is a unique perspective that allows evaluation of strategy, performance and anticipation of tactics and responses. It also allows you to step out of the action for analysis. Like the coaches seated high in the stands at a football game that communicate observations to the players on the field who then translate the information into action and adjustments, the top-down perspective enhances your feedback and refining of skill during training and mission.

There are no firm conclusions about which perspective is best for enhancing performance. Initial reports indicated that elite athletes tended to use internal/first person imagery; this made sense as this perspective is most like a real-life situation. However, later research found that the perspective used did not correlate with performance and being selected for elite teams. Further, more recent reports from Olympic athletes note that 17 to 35 percent use internal/first person imagery; 30 to 39 percent use external/third person imagery and 34 to 44 percent use both (Morris, Spittle, & Watt, 2005).

Personal experience in working with athletes, police, and in other areas of human performance has engendered our preference for the internal/first person perspective. We believe the more realistic view is ultimately important. Research has shown that international elite-level pistol/rifle marksmen tend to use the internal/first person perspective more frequently than state and junior level marksmen. Individuals who were predominantly internal imagers but also used external imagery at times ("switching" internals) did better on learning a kata (a choreographed set of fighting moves) in their karate training (Morris, Spittle & Watt, 2005).

Since both perspectives can be effective, you should use the view that is most comfortable and works the best in terms of performance. That said, using both can also be effective. A good place to start is with the external perspective, one that is like watching a demonstration of the skill. Then follow by imaging the execution of the skill operation from the internal perspective.

Neurolinguistic Programmimg (NLP) calls the internal/first person view the *associated* perspective and suggests it is effective in allowing the performer to "step into" the imaged scenario and fully experience it. The external/third person view is called the *dissociated* perspective and NLP suggests that it is very effective in observing and critiquing the quality of performance and gaining emotional distance (Andreas & Faulkner, 1994). Use the associated perspective when you really want to experience or be in the imaged scenario. Use the dissociated perspective to review how you are performing or when you want to have distance from the emotional impact of the imaged scenario. Perhaps most important is to be sure to include kinesthetic and not just visual imagery.

Image Correct Responses

Performance Imagery is like physical practice: When you mentally rehearse a response sloppily or incorrectly, you will perform sloppily or incorrectly. It's essential to not be sloppy, lazy, or incorrect in your images. There is an important lesson in the adage that "Practice does not make perfect; perfect practice makes perfect."

It's also our experience (or bias) that the focus of imagery should be on the "process" rather than the "outcome." Since maximal performance comes from executing skills or plans as flawlessly as possible, then this should be the focus of tactical performance imagery. Imaging the execution of a successful leg trip (the process) is more likely to result in taking down your adversary than imaging him surrendering on the ground (the outcome). Dr. Mike Mahoney, a pioneer in sport psychology and avid weight-lifter, often counseled that if you focus on the process, the outcome takes care of itself.

Image in Real Time
Just as with physical practice, it may be useful to begin imaging a skill or tactic in slow-motion. However, ultimately the skill or tactic should be imaged in real time speed for the best effect.

Practice and Image Problems and Success
It's useful and important to image difficult or even negative situations, such as someone pointing a weapon at you, having your weapon jam, entering a building that is structured differently from the intelligence you received, or someone in your squad getting injured. There should be preparation for handling unanticipated and critical situations by tactical performance imagery.

The critical point is to never stop with the problem image but always go to a success image of how that problem will be handled.

Scott Sonnon, an expert martial arts training coach, teaches that in a real assault, mistakes happen and unexpected events occur (Lepp, 2004). It may not be a perfect execution of skill that is necessary to be victorious, but rather a matter of making the fewest mistakes, or recovering most quickly from them, that is the margin of victory. He further suggests that psychological training can create an emotional archetype, that is, an imprint or blueprint for perseverance and action, to manage mistakes and surprise.

Just like physical training, Tactical Performance Imagery must be practiced repeat-edly to be effective. Smith (2006) suggests the acronym PETTLEP for the factors that make performance imagery effective.

P for Physical: Your imagery should be as similar to the actual physical skill as possible.

E for environment: Your imagery should be practiced in the environment where the actual application will occur.

T for Task: Your attention during imagery should be focused on the same things as during actual execution of the skill.

T for timing: The effects of your imagery will be enhanced if the skill is imaged in real time, at the actual speed needed.

L for Learning: Your imagery should incorporate changes in feelings and techniques as your skill improves.

E for Emotion: Your imagery should include emotions associated with the event.

P for Perspective: You should use the perspective, external or internal, that works best for you.

An excellent approach to integrating physical and imagery practice is described by co-author Loren Christensen in his book, *The Mental Edge Revised* (1999). He suggests a sequence of first imaging a skill, then doing the skill in pantomime. Finally, the skill should be tried live. This type of sequence nicely integrates the physical and psychological and can be applied to many training situations.

Loren writes that martial arts icon Chuck Norris would observe his opponents at a tournament in their earlier matches, and then retire to privacy to image his fight with them. He would image their attacks, his blocks and his dynamic counters. Then he would go to compete. Norris said that this process gave him the advantage of having fought these opponents before (albeit in his mind), though they had not previously fought him.

Loren is a longtime advocate of imagery practice in martial arts training, in particular with movement. He said it's also a valuable tool for firearms training, first aid, defensive tactics and a host of other warrior-related activities. He recently suggested it to a U.S. Army medical surgeon serving in Afghanistan. The surgeon already practiced pantomiming various emergency medical procedures and was enthused to learn this simple procedure to improve his mental training even more.

Here is how to do it with military and police defensive tactics in hand-to-hand training.

The first stage is to practice a technique — let's make it a foot sweep out of a clinch — with a live partner. But instead of just going through the motions, your task is to see and feel as many details as you can.

Clinch with your opponent and:

- Feel his arms entangled in yours.
- Feel how his weight leans against you one moment and then leans away the next.
- Feel his hot breath in your face.
- Feel your body move in concert with his as you jostle for a dominant position.
- Feel his heaviness one moment and his lightness the next.
- See and feel the opportunity to sweep his left leg as his weight begins to shift off of it.
- Feel the muscles in your right leg contract and your grip on his arms tighten.
- Feel your right leg move forward quickly as the inside of your foot makes contact with the outside of his.
- Feel the sudden weight shift of his body as his left leg is removed from his foundation.
- Feel your right foot set back onto the floor quickly as you pull his left shoulder down in the direction he is beginning to tilt.
- Feel and see his body fall as you push his shoulders downward.

Loren says that your objective is to be cognizant of every minute aspect of the move so that you ingrain the sight and feel of it into your mind, and then take that into your solo mental imagery practice. The more detail, the more real your practice becomes, all of which adds up to greater results. (This is much in accord with the advanced training techniques of elite trainer Chris Sarkis Ghannam who advocates sensory deprivation as a way to train in every sensory modality. The interested reader is encouraged to review his work.).

After executing a technique with a live partner a few times, step away from him and pantomime the exact steps you just did. As if practicing tai chi, that slow moving, dance-like exercise that is hugely popular in China, proceed through the stages of the foot sweep, seeing and feeling every nuance as you move.

- See and Feel your arms entangle with the imagined opponent's arms.
- Feel how the imagined opponent's weight leans against you one moment and then leans away the next.
- Feel the imagined opponent's hot breath in your face.
- Feel how your body moves in concert with your imaginary opponent as you jostle for a dominant position.
- And so on…

So often we just mindlessly practice hand-to-hand or other warrior skills. Not only is this an inferior way to train at anything, it doesn't provide us with sufficient detail to use in our seated and moving imagery practice. However, by engaging in the moving imagery phase as soon as possible after executing the technique on a live opponent, all that you saw and felt is still fresh in your mind. That is greatly beneficial to your solo moving imagery practice. Then later, when you practice mental imagery while sitting relaxed in your easy chair, you can more easily incorporate into it that same detail.

Loren says to think of it this way. Say you did 10 reps with an opponent, 10 moving imagery reps in the air and 10 mental imagery reps in your easy chair. When you train with attention to every small facet and include that into all three training methods, your mind and body believe that you actually performed all 30 reps with a partner.

And in a way, you did.

Thus, the message is that you don't have to be perfectly still when engaging in Tactical Performance Imagery. It's allowable, and at times helpful, to move a bit, mimicking the physical skills that are being imaged. While not performed at full force, these partial physical movements can help make imagery more vivid and enhance the kinesthetic effects.

It's important to again stress that imagery can be adapted to your needs and preferences. For example, in a study (Silbernagel & Short, 2006) of Division I athletes involved in weight training, it was found that imagery of their appearance was used most frequently, followed by imagery of technique and then imagery of energy. While our advice would likely be to try technique or energy imagery first, it's apparent that there was a preference for a results-oriented focus ("lookin' good") among this group. Use what works for you.

CONVERGING EVIDENCE ON THE POWER OF PERFORMANCE IMAGERY

Smith (2006) claims that using mental imagery can produce gains of fifty-percent of that from physical training. While, it's tempting (and of some value) to rely on comments from individuals who use imagery as proof of benefits, research makes a stronger case. At this writing, most of the research has been done in the area of sports performance.

Sports Examples

The most often cited piece of evidence is an early sport psychology study of foul shooting improvement by basketball players (Clark, 1960). Half the team physically practiced foul shots as usual for two weeks while the other half never shot fouls but just imaged shooting them. After two weeks, it was found that for experienced players, both physical practice and imagery practice improved their foul shooting percentages equally.

For new players, the group that practiced physically improved their foul shots by 47 percent. The imagery group, which didn't shoot any fouls, improved 26 percent. So even for new players, while the gains were less than for physical practice, performance imagery yielded a significant improvement in their skill.

Improvement in free throw shooting with imagery training was again found in a more recent study (Peynircioglu, 2000). For the interested reader, it should be noted that the sport psychology literature contains multiple studies of the use of performance imagery on multiple skills in multiple sports.

An Example with Emergency Skills

A second study is important because it showed how psychological training can significantly improve emergency medical skills. While the study was done with civilians, the relevance to military and police personnel is clear.

Two concerns typically arise with civilian CPR training: 1) though trained, individuals are hesitant to use their skills and, 2) their retention of correct skills fades quickly over time. Starr (1987) incorporated performance imagery and psychological skills training with standard CPR training. The point of his study was to try to assess the effects of imagery and psychological skills-enhanced CPR training compared to standard CPR training on confidence and willingness to use learned skills. Additionally, the study assessed the drop-off in correct responses in doing CPR that occurs over time and as training becomes more distant. The results are summarized in the following:

PSYCHOLOGICAL SKILLS TRAINING IN CPR

		6 MONTHS	12 MONTHS
RESPONSE TIME (secs)	S-CPR	18.70	50.10
	IE-CPR	6.55	19.00

		6 MONTHS	12 MONTHS
CORRECT RESPONSES (%)	S-CPR	75.56	53.33
	IE-CPR	93.33	88.00

The study compared performance between individuals trained by the standard CPR (S-CPR) training methods versus imagery enhanced CPR (IE-CPR) that used psychological skills and imagery added to the traditional training. The study measured how long it took individuals who were "surprised" by an emergency situation to actually begin to administer CPR. The table shows that six months post-training, the imagery enhanced group (IE-CPR) began emergency care in an average of only 6.5 seconds compared to an average response time of 18.7 seconds for those trained in the standard manner (S-CPR). When tested at twelve months post-training, the IE-CPR group again responded much faster at an average of 19.0 seconds compared to the S-CPR group that took an average of 50.1 seconds to respond.

The second part of the study looked at whether psychological skills training could help people to better remember how to do CPR correctly and effectively even when they hadn't used or practiced it for a long time. It was found that, six months post-training, the IE-CPR group (psychologically trained) averaged 93.3 percent correct CPR skills compared to 75.6 percent correct for the ST-CPR (standard training) group. At twelve months post-training, the IE-CPR group averaged 88.0 percent correct CPR skills compared to only 53.3 percent correct and effective skills for the ST-CPR group. Thus, psychological skills training did help individuals maintain a higher quality of physical skills even over long periods.

Some Examples with Warrior Skills

Shooting skills study:
Whetstone (1996) demonstrated the effectiveness of imagery training on shooting skills with group of police cadets. Seventy-two cadets were split into two groups: one receiving imagery training/mental practice and the other group not receiving it.

The imagery training began after the first four hours on the range. It consisted of an initial two-hour session on mental rehearsal concepts and techniques followed by ten, five-minute sessions to reinforce the original training. Cadets in this group were also asked to practice imagery on their own for at least five minutes every night during the three weeks of training.

The control group was trained as usual at the academy. However, to counteract any expectations, they were given extra time on the range, where they didn't shoot any more practice rounds but were lectured on performance and technique.

The end results showed a significant difference in performance between the two groups of cadets.

The group trained in typical manner had an initial average score of 119.5 points and final average score of 170.1 points for an increase of 50.61 points.

The imagery-trained group had an initial average score of 111.50 points and a final average score of 194.97 points for an increase of 83.47 points.

Therefore the imagery-trained group showed greater gains in performance (32.86 more points) and a higher final average score. It should be noted that there was no difference in performance between cadets who had stronger versus weaker imagery skills: Both benefited from imagery training. However, time spent practicing the imagery did make a difference. Those who practiced more consistently performed better, besting those who did not practice as much by 55.09 points.

Simunitions Study

Shipley and Baranski (2002) conducted a study of a more dynamic and stressful situation. They looked at the impact of the form of imagery/relaxation training called Visuo-Motor Behavior Rehearsal (VMBR) on performance in a simunitions-based scenario. Fifty-four police recruits were divided into two groups, one that received the VMBR training and one that did not, the control group.

The VMBR group was told to report one hour early for an evening session of scenario training. They then underwent relaxation and imagery training for approximately thirty minutes based on the VMBR protocol.

The control group simply arrived a half hour before the scenario training and was unaware of the VMBR experience given to the experimental group.

The scenario training consisted of a routine traffic stop that quickly turned into a deadly force situation. Each recruit was shot at multiple times with simunition rounds by suspects who didn't give up, though some were wounded. To add to the stress, each recruit carried only two magazines with two rounds in each. They were not told of the limited ammunition.

The results showed that the recruits who underwent VMBR training:
- reported significantly less cognitive anxiety (worry, negative thoughts) than the control group.
- managed significantly more simunition hits to the assailants than the control group.
- were hit less than the control group, though the difference was not statistically significant.

It's important to note that these important performance advantages were gained after only one 30-minutes session of VMBR training, as opposed to full training and practice. Other measures, such as somatic anxiety or instructor evaluation of performance didn't show a difference between the two groups.

Elite Level Shooters Study
Studies of expert pistol marksmen who were wired to biofeedback machines (Deschaumes-Molinaro, et al., 1992; Guillot et al., 2004) compared physiological variables like heart rate, skin temperature, and skin blood flow in three conditions: concentration and focus before firing, actual firing and mental imagery of firing. It was found that the body's responses were similar in all three conditions. The mental imagery practice produced realistic body reactions. Further, the similarities between the mental imagery conditions and the actual fire conditions were greatest for the best shooters.

HOW DOES IMAGERY WORK?

There are several mechanisms that explain how mental practice improves physical performance (Suinn, 1985).

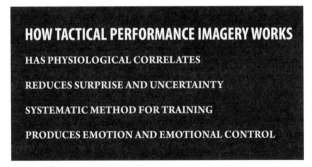

HOW TACTICAL PERFORMANCE IMAGERY WORKS

HAS PHYSIOLOGICAL CORRELATES

REDUCES SURPRISE AND UNCERTAINTY

SYSTEMATIC METHOD FOR TRAINING

PRODUCES EMOTION AND EMOTIONAL CONTROL

The first involves measuring responses to it in the body, the physiological correlates of tactical performance imagery.

Advances in physiological monitoring have provided the most dramatic and convincing evidence of how and why tactical performance imagery is effective. There are several sources:

Biofeedback: When athletes were attached to biofeedback monitors and imaged a skill, very small electrical signals could be detected in muscles of the same body parts involved when the skill is actually executed. This suggested that performance imagery strengthens the connections between the brain and the body parts involved in actually doing the skill.

Brain Scans: The next source of evidence is found in various forms of brain scans during imagery. Many of the same parts of the brain activated are also activated when the same skill is actually performed.

Near-Infrared Spectroscopy: The third source of evidence comes from measurements by near-infrared spectroscopy, which shows that when a skill is imaged, blood flow is increased to that part of the body involved in that skill.

The second explanation of the power of tactical performance imagery is that it reduces surprise and uncertainty. When you image various scenarios, similar real ones are no longer new or surprising. You benefit by experiencing a more rapid pattern recognition that leads to a more rapid response.

Tactical performance imagery also works because it's a systematic method of training. It provides a logical approach and packages the various aspects of imagery to allow them to integrate and enhance performance.

Lastly, tactical performance imagery is effective because it not only trains and rehearses the skills of a mission or response, it also produces emotions and then trains you to control them should they be activated in a real situation.

Note: If you're interested in more complex details about why tactical performance works, read the next sections. If you're not, simply skip to the section on "Cautions when practicing Tactical Performance Imagery."

More on the Physiological Correlates of Imagery

It has been demonstrated that when a skill like throwing a ball is imaged, very small, but measurable neuro-electric signals are sent from the brain to the body part involved (the arm), just as occurs in physical practice. Training physically increases the link between the brain and the involved body parts by strengthening nerve connections. Like physical practice, imagery seems to "grease" the neural tracts from the brain to the body. The more greased these tracts become through repetition, the more quickly and accurately you respond.

Most of the early and more recent research used EMG (electromyographic) measures and feedback (indications of electrical activity in the muscles) and has been well summarized by Morris, Spittle & Watt (2005). Work by Jacobson in the 1930's showed that mental imagery of forearm bends, biceps curl, sweeping, and rope climbing produced more muscle activity in those used in the imagery than were used when the same muscles were at rest.

Jacobson also showed that when subjects were asked to *visualize* performing a biceps curl (just "seeing" the curl), eye-related activity increased. But when they were asked to *imagine* experiencing a biceps curl (which involved all of their senses to experience the motion), it was actual localized biceps muscle activity that increased. (This is another reason to use the word "imagery" rather than "visualization" for mental practice).

Work by Dr. Richard Suinn of Colorado State University (1980) demonstrated similar results. He did EMG readings of the leg muscles of U.S. Olympic skiers who imaged their race while at rest. He found that the electrical activity in their legs and the activation of the activity reflected their description of where they were on the course.

Perhaps most fascinating is the recent research on imagery that has been enhanced by the advent of brain scanning technology that allows us to "watch" a live brain in action.

We can now document that practice creates changes in the brain. Typically, the changes represent less brain activation or effort in doing the task over time and with practice. In the first twenty minutes of learning, many areas of the brain are active. With every ten minutes, brain activity decreases, with a total reduction of about 85 pecent of activity after the first hour. Decreased activity can be seen in brain areas that problem solve, control tasks, use working memory, and involve attentional control. However, perceptual and motor areas of the brain involved in making actual responses remain more activated (Hill & Schneider, 2006).

The technology and use of brain scans with imagery has resulted in the Theory of Functional Equivalence, which means that research shows that the same areas of the brain used in seeing things (visual perception) are used during imagining (visual imagery). Said another way, imagery shares some of the same brain processes and pathways as visual perception (Murphy, 2005).

The same mechanism, or functional equivalence, may be present for motor skills, as well (Morris, Spittle, & Watt, 2005). These authors describe the work of Ingvar & Philpson in 1997 who asked subjects to either imagine or actually clench their hands into fists. The researchers found that both methods changed the blood flow in the motor areas of the brain that control such movements. Other researchers are reported to have measured brain blood flow when golfers of various handicap levels imaged a golf swing. With imagery, increases in blood flow were found in areas of the brain that are associated with motor control, execution of motor skills, action planning and error detection.

Advances in a technique called Near-Infrared Spectroscopy (NIRS) has provided further evidence of how tactical imagery exerts an effect on performance. NIRS allows measurements of oxygenation and hemodynamic (amount of oxygen and nature of blood flow) parameters. A study (Griffin & Cooper, 2006) was done using NIRS measurements while an individual either rehearsed (imaged) squeezing a ball or actually did squeeze the ball. It was found that imaging the squeeze (but not actually squeezing he ball) resulted in increased blood flow in the wrist (carpi radialis muscle).

Smith (2006) also emphasizes the importance of kinesthetic imagery that involves bodily feelings to make imagery effective, especially for strength skills. He reports research with EEG (brain wave) readings of "late contingent negative variation," which is a measure correlated with messages from the cortex of the brain to the muscles to enable contraction of those muscles. The research shows that imagery that emphasizes bodily feelings has more of this effect than imagery that is just visual in nature.

The idea that imagery causes the same nerve firings (neuro-electric signals) in the body as does physical practice is called Psychoneuromuscular Theory. However, research from Arizona State University (Slade, Landers & Martin, 2002) has raised some questions about the ability of Psychoneuromuscular Theory to explain the enhancing effects of performance imagery. The researchers used EMG to monitor muscle effects in actual and imaged biceps and triceps movement. They did find increased EMG activity when muscle movement was imaged and they found that expectancy effects (that is, expecting to show EMG changes) didn't account for the activity. However, they found that the pattern of EMG activation during imagery did not exactly mirror the pattern of EMG activation during actual muscle movement.

The authors feel that this research gives more validity to Functional Equivalence Theory, which suggests that similarity in what happens in the brain activation during both real and imagined skill execution accounts for the performance-enhancing effects of imagery. They note the evidence showing that the similarity in the amount and location of brain activity during real and imagined activity is much more consistent than data for Psychoneuromuscular Theory.

The Reduction of Surprise and Uncertainty
By having practiced various scenarios, at least mentally, the situations and your responses to them become familiar, thus reducing any surprise factor. You're able to process a situation quickly because you recognize it. Although surprise or inexperience might delay your response for only fractions of a second (as you interpret a situation and determine a course of action), it's time that can be crucial. With imagery training, you respond more quickly and effectively because you

recognize the situation (you have seen it in your imagery). It reduces the surprise, disbelief and "What do I do now?" reactions that delay effective responses in new situations.

Pattern Recognition is important for speeding thought and action. It involves instantly evaluating the emerging pattern of an event by comparing it with a mental model. The mental model is typically developed by training and/or experience (Rahman, 2007), including proper tactical imagery training.

Pattern Recognition

Hawkins (2004) also suggests that much of performance is reliant on pattern recognition, that is, the ability to put meaning and action to characteristics of a situation. Through what is called auto-associative memory, we can recognize a whole picture from its parts and recognize complex patterns from only partial or distorted inputs.

For example, by seeing feet under a curtain, we know "see" that there is a whole person present. Or, we can read a book whether sitting, standing, reclining, or in any position despite how this changes lighting, shadows, and perspective of the pages and print.

Pattern recognition abilities can be limiting, however. Without flexibility or broad training, patterns available to us can inhibit or misdirect our responses. For example, you can say the alphabet quickly and flawlessly when progressing forward from A to Z. But how smooth are you at saying it backwards from Z to A? Even though it's the same letters we have said and seen thousands of times, we learned them in a sequence that limits our reciting them backwards. Consider a story you have told with ease many times. But should you begin the tale in the middle or recount the events backward, it will likely slow the recounting.

Thus, it's essential that you train and practice your actions in varied and changing conditions. Tactical imagery can expand these variations and consequently expand your library of patterns and inputs to be used in recognition reactions.

Gavin DeBecker and his colleagues (2008) provide important insight on the "moment of recognition" in responding to a threat. As executive protection experts, they emphasize the critical nature of the moment of recognition as the point where they "get their heads around" what is happening between an assailant and their protectee.

They are describing pattern recognition, a process that allows pieces to form the whole, which gives them the advantage of expediting their action to stop a threat. DeBecker and his colleagues are absolutely correct in stating that if the moment of recognition can be moved forward by even a fraction of a second, the odds of success increase greatly.

Tactical imagery can provide a mental model or *multiple mental models* of various situations and responses to promote more effective pattern recognition.

It's well accepted that in many situations self-defensive techniques are reactive in nature. This means that the enemy or bad guy has the distinct speed advantage. Wisecarver & Tucker (2007) summarized research from the Force Science Research Center on the time it takes to draw a weapon and the time it takes to react to it defensively.

The authors note that:

- a suspect can draw a firearm from a waistband and fire from the hip in an average of .23 seconds.
- a suspect in a vehicle driver's seat and a weapon by his right thigh can draw, bring the weapon across his body, and fire over his left shoulder in an average of .25 seconds.

Upon seeing the suspect's action and reacting to it, the authors note that:

- an officer with his firearm in an unsnapped holstered can draw his weapon, get on target and fire in an average of 1.61 seconds.
- an officer with his weapon securely holstered can draw his weapon, get on target and fire in an average of 1.71 seconds.

The discrepancy in times and the advantage to the bad guys are clear. It should also be clear that anything that can speed up pattern recognition time (recognizing that a gun is being drawn) can create a faster response. Tactical performance imagery can aid in speeding recognition of situational threats.

Tactical Performance Imagery training can essentially make someone "more experienced." Solomon (1990) found that in life-threatening shooting situations, "automatic," tactical responses are more likely to occur among those who have used mental rehearsal in their training and preparation. W.E. Hicks conducted research in the 1950's that showed that uncertainty or unfamiliarity and multiple possible responses slow reaction time. He found that as response options increased from one to two, reaction time increased 58 percent.

It has been cautioned (Hochheim, 2008) that Hick's Law should not be misinterpreted to mean that all techniques and training should be simple or limited, or that the brain is incapable of speedy processing of information. Indeed, the brain can process multiple bits of information and brain processes can occur in fractions of a second (milliseconds). The point is that reaction time is enhanced and can occur quickly with proper training that increases pattern recognition and choice selection. In other words, having to make an unpracticed choice between two options takes more time and slows the speed of reaction.

Mills (2005) makes his point as it relates to driving skills, but it has broader relevance. He says that drivers react more quickly to familiar targets. For example, the average response time to a vehicle changing one lane in daylight is about one second. However, the response time to someone or something unfamiliar blocking the path after starting a turn with a green turning signal is about three seconds.

He goes on to say that most drivers are not trained for the unexpected. Because basic driving skills are so well-learned and because emergencies are rare, we become overconfident about our skills to handle them. Research shows that emergency attention skills do not improve automatically and, in fact, degrade without practice or reinforcement. Having well-practiced responses for a variety of situations can reduce the need for this processing of choices, thus increasing the speed of response. Tactical performance imagery can provide greater awareness and more immediate choice of response for many different situations and their possible variations.

The Systematic Method of Training

Logical systematic methods work best and allow for focusing on areas that need work. The various forms of imagery training, such as Visuo-Motor Behavior Rehearsal and Stress Inoculation Training present a structured approach to learning and applying imagery. They have been constructed and refined based on experience and research.

The Production and Practice of Emotion and Emotional Control

Tactical performance imagery provides for practice of emotions found in high-stress situations and the focus and emotional control needed in typically emotion-charged ones. Rehearsal of these situations reduces the emotional impact.

Holton (1995) quotes General U.S. Grant as saying:

> **There is no great sport in having bullets flying about me in every direction, but I find they have less horror when among them than when in anticipation.**

Tactical performance imagery can reduce negative anticipation and fill the ti
a mission with more productive anticipation.

Since imagery can produce physical changes in the body (muscle activity and brain-blood flow, for example) as well as autonomic changes (such as heart rate, skin temperature and skin-blood flow), as found in the Descahumes-Molinaro et al. study (1992) and Guillot's (2004) study of shooters, it can help you anticipate, get used to and learn to control these responses.

Other research also found that imagery could affect physiological responses (Cumming, at al., 2007). Individuals who engaged in anxiety-related imagery showed increased heart rates and reported increased mental and physical anxiety. When individuals used imagery to "psych up," increased heart rates, indicating increased arousal were found.

This research further demonstrated that imagery is effective in helping individuals cope with feelings of increased arousal. In the study, Cumming and her colleagues (2007) compared the effects of several different types of motivational general imagery.
- **Mastery Imagery:** feeling confident and in control.
- **Psyching-up Imagery:** done to increase performance arousal.
- **Anxiety Imagery:** used to create uncomfortable feelings.
- **Relaxation Imagery:** used to produce calmness.
- **Coping Imagery:** used to create feelings of being able to handle higher arousal, such as increased heart rate.

The results showed that Coping Imagery did allow individuals to experience increased heart rates but also feel good and in control. Thus, imagery can also be part of training for complex and stressful situations by integrating it with relaxation and desensitization.

Performance imagery has shown its usefulness in many areas of application. Tactical Performance Imagery is a reasonable extension that many military and police warriors have happily discovered aids the performance of their skills. Although warriors may vary in their ability to image, this should not be seen as a deficit or a problem. Murphy (2005) observes that almost everyone can generate imagery, though there are differences in how easily and effectively it can be done. He also suggests that it can be enhanced with practice, especially when you describe in detail what you're experiencing through your senses, and by using vivid and highly descriptive words in the images.

There is no definitive answer as to how much imagery practice is needed for maximum performance. Murphy (2005) found that among Olympic athletes, 20 percent used imagery every day and 40 percent used it three to five days per week. Morris, Spittle & Watt (2005) notes research suggesting that to obtain the best results one should practice imagery for either a period of one to three minutes or ten to fifteen minutes. The key, as demonstrated by Whetstone (1996) as described above in his study of marksmanship, appears to be to practice imagery, sharpen it as a skill and integrate it with the practice and performance of physical skills.

Cautions when practicing Tactical Performance Imagery

There are also some cautions associated with the use of imagery (Morris, Spittle & Watts, 2005 and Murphy, 2005). First, remember that effective tactical performance imagery is not as effective as actual practice. However, combining imagery and physical training can transfer well to physical skills, even to those that are not specifically practiced. For example, training on a bicycle ergometer (stationary bike) combined with imagery practice of a race, resulted in improvements in performance in a 40-meter sprint, even without actual track training.

Warriors need some hands on experience with the skills or situations they want to image. Actual exposure and initial practice is best for this, although it can be approximated by vivid descriptions from instructors. Performance imagery must be based on the realities of the skills and situations, not solely on the warrior's "fantasy" of them.

Be aware that imagery can cause anxiety, although this really reflects untrained imagery or inadequate practice. For example, this could occur when the psychologically undisciplined mind engages in images of failure or when the warrior doesn't confront the stressful situation in imagery often enough (inadequate practice) to reduce the anxiety. The point of tactical imagery training is to provide control and focus to promote quality and successful performance.

Another caution is that imagery may be distracting, meaning that it may consist of irrelevant actions or details. An example might be imagining one's R&R while still engaged in a mission. Again, this is more likely to represent untrained imagery. Trained imagery should direct and keep attention on the critical aspects of a skill or mission.

While rare, it has been cautioned that imagery can lead to overconfidence. Ramsey, Cumming, and their colleagues (2006) note that one of the cautions in using imagery may be feelings of confidence about performance that exceed actual ability. This is known as "imagination inflation."

In their study, individuals watched a demonstration of a stabilometer, a device on which one stands and works to stay balanced to avoid falling off. After seeing the demonstration, one group physically practiced with the device, another group practiced via imagery and a third group spent their time doing crossword puzzles. Afterward, the three groups were tested on the stabilometer, which revealed that the physical practice group performed best. While the imagery group was most confident prior to the testing, they did not perform better than the physical practice group, which was less confident, perhaps because of having had some experience with the new and difficult task.

There are two lessons here to re-emphasize. The first is that psychological techniques are not a substitute for physical training and practice; they should be integrated with other training. Secondly, tactical imagery is best performed and will be most effective when you already have some physical experience with the skill or situation. Imagination inflation will occur when the imagery is fantasy and not experienced-based.

Superficial imaging solely of successful outcomes and celebrations rather than the specific skills needed to achieve success and victory may create a diverted focus and false confidence.

To summarize, keep in mind these key cautions about Tactical Performance Imagery:
- It's not a substitute for scenario, tactical or other skills training.
- The key is to integrate simultaneously live training with imagery training.
- Effective tactical imagery requires some level of experience with the skill or operation through physical training, practice and/or briefing. It's unlikely that realistic and relevant images of skill or operations can be successfully developed without having engaged in actual experience.
- Using imagery within the context of trained mental toughness skills should actually reinforce the practice of all skills and the importance of constant appropriate vigilance.

Co-author Dave Grossman has previously noted that the important goals of military training are to take the surprise out of combat, raise the sense of confidence, and cognitively prepare the warrior for battle. Tactical Performance Imagery, like other psychological performance techniques, when integrated with other physical skill training, contributes to reaching these goals. Imagery should be adapted and applied as the individual warrior sees fit and each situation warrants.

Personal Psy Ops:
chapter Tactical Self-Talk and Mental Toughness

A warrior has only **one true friend.** *Only one man he can rely on.* **Himself.**
*So he feeds his body well; he trains it; works on it. Where he lacks skill,
he practices. Where he lacks knowledge, he studies. But* **above all he must
believe.** *He must believe in his strength of will, of purpose, of heart and soul.*

Do not speak badly of yourself, for the warrior that is inside you hears your words and is lessened by them.

You are **strong** *and you are* **brave.** *There is a nobility of spirit within you.
Let it grow-you will do well enough.*

> – David Gemmel's character, Chareos,
> speaking to a young apprentice warrior,
> in *Quest for Lost Heroes*

Warrior excellence is not just about action. Commitment, passion and thought are also central to the warriors' existence. How and what warriors think, as well as, how and what their leaders think all have a profound effect on performance during a mission.

COGNITION

How we think about things is termed cognition, a subject on which there has been much research as to its nature in human beings. This work and the performance applications of cognitive techniques have shown that our thoughts have a strong effect on our emotions, behavior and, therefore, the quality of our performance.

Self-Talk

Most people experience thinking as "talking to themselves." While we often make jokes about people who walk around talking to themselves, all of us do it "internally" much of the time. (While there are some people who think predominantly in pictures, most of us experience thinking as having a conversation with ourselves). This is called self-talk and it's a powerful process that affects your behavior and a powerful tool to maximize your performance. Performance and sport psychology expert Dr. James Afremow (2008) of Arizona State University labels the nature of self-talk as either being your internal enemy (negative self-talk) or your internal ally (performance-related self-talk). He asks "what channel is your self-talk on?"

To use self-talk to your advantage, there are several important aspects to understand:
- Self-talk always occurs before you say anything, do anything, or feel any emotion.
- Self-talk is fast and though you are often unaware of it, it's there.
- The more well-practiced a skill, the quicker and "quieter" the self-talk.
- You can become aware of your self-talk.
- You can change your self-talk.
- Changing your self-talk can modify your response and performance.

The Power of Words and Expectations

WORDS
The importance of self-talk is not surprising when you recognize the profound influence of words ("The pen is mightier than the sword"). The emotional, behavioral and performance impact of words are powerful, as any songwriter, advertising executive, salesperson, or attorney will concur. A couple of examples:

When a group of individuals were asked "Do you get headaches *occasionally*, and if so, how often?" the average number reported was 0.7 per week. However, when a group of individuals were asked "Do you get headaches *frequently*, and if so, how often?" the average number was 2.2 per week.

Consider the following:
- How fast and how much damage do you think occurred when you hear that a car was *hit* in an accident?
- How fast and how much damage occurred when you hear the car was *smashed* in the accident.

Did you have the same picture of the damaged car in your mind in both situations? Probably not.

Other research highlights how much influential words and expectations can affect our responses and performance. For example, individuals were asked to rate the pleasantness or unpleasantness of an odor. In one case, the odor was labeled as "cheese" and in the other, the same odor was labeled "body odor." The odor labeled "cheese" was given an average rating of negative .10, but the same odor labeled "body odor" was rated a negative .86. Even when smelling clean air, the air "labeled" body odor was rated a negative .40.

EXPECTATION

One area where the power of expectation is clearly demonstrated is in the phenomenon of the placebo effect in medical treatment. The placebo effect refers to the situation where people react to or have the effects expected from a medicine when they were actually given an inert or "fake" one. While traditionally this was seen as a curiosity, nuisance or negative, medicine is now starting to look at how and why this works and how this effect might be harnassed for positive change.

Dramatic examples of the placebo response are found in what are called sham surgeries. This is where a patient believes a surgical procedure was performed, but in actuality, at most, an incision was made but nothing else done. Especially with surgeries designed to reduce chronic pain, positive results and relief of pain are often found even with such sham procedures.

A recent study showing this effect and the power of expectation was reported by Moseley, et al. (2002). One hundred and sixty-five patients with osteoarithitis underwent one of three types of arthroscopy (having their knee scoped): debridement where the knee was cleaned out; lavage where it was cleansed, or placebo where incisions were made just like the other procedures, but there was no insertion of the scope. Patients who had the placebo procedure (but didn't know it) responded as well or better in terms of lessened pain complaints and improved walking than the other actual procedures. Expectation and belief are very powerful.

The Power of Expectation and Belief

Dr. William Collins would go on to become chief of surgery at Yale University. But in the 1950's he was a military surgeon in Korea working day and night tending to our country's wounded. He developed appendicitis himself and underwent surgery. With typical warrior spirit, he wanted to re-enter the operating room and get back to work only hours after his own procedure, but the pain was too great.

He asked the nurse for a pain shot but was informed that he had reached his allowed limit. Unhappy with the answer, as surgeons have been known to do, he raised his voice and insisted (and threatened) that he receive a pain shot. He did and shortly thereafter returned to OR duty for his shift. The next day he reviewed his medical record to find that he did not receive any real pain medicine in the shot but merely inert saline ! Desire and expectation are powerful influences (Carey, 2004)

Warrior Words

The importance of the impact of the words and phrases we use on our behavior has also found its way into military and police literature. Duran & Nasci (2000) talk about "tactical terminology," defining it as: "Terminology that instills the proper attitude necessary for safe completion of a law enforcement task." Examples include replacing the term "officer safety" with "officer survival" or "routine traffic stop" with the term or (even better) "unknown risk" traffic stop.

Willis (2005) echoes this important concept and further suggests that the concept of the "survival" mind-set should be replaced with that of the "winning" mind-set to avoid conveying a weakened or dominated condition. Likewise, he suggests replacing "strong hand-weak-hand" with "dominant-non-dominant hand" to avoid conveying an attitude of weakness.

The nature of our self-talk affects our performance as well. Duran, in *Developing the Survival Attitude* (1999), says:

> **But you should understand that a relationship between words and actions does exist and that words can have a direct positive or negative impact…**

Toughening Tactical Terminology

The emphasis on tactical terminology has changed the way some training is framed. Instead of working on what to do "if" a situation occurs, training is provided on what to do "when" a situation occurs. There is also an emphasis on having each individual think in terms of responding *when*, rather than *if* a situation occurs. This seems additionally poignant as General U.S. Grant is often quoted :

> **Ifs defeated the Confederates…**

Martin (2006) explains why the word "try" is not part of the Special Forces vocabulary:

> **I did not say TRY. TRY is a WEAK WORD. In Special Forces we don't give you a mission and tell you to try. In Special Forces, you will be handed a mission that seems impossible and be told <u>DO YOUR BEST</u>. It may seem like a small change, but the implications are huge.**

All this becomes important when we consider the role of self-talk in the performance of our duties, especially in high-stress missions. Here are several areas where self-talk and focus can be directed during a mission or operation:

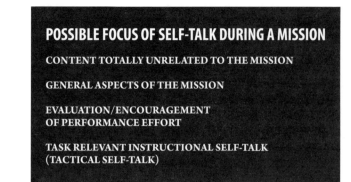

POSSIBLE FOCUS OF SELF-TALK DURING A MISSION

CONTENT TOTALLY UNRELATED TO THE MISSION

GENERAL ASPECTS OF THE MISSION

EVALUATION/ENCOURAGEMENT
OF PERFORMANCE EFFORT

TASK RELEVANT INSTRUCTIONAL SELF-TALK
(TACTICAL SELF-TALK)

- **Totally unrelated:** Your thoughts are focused on getting home, your hunger, or the golf game you would rather be playing.
- **General aspects of the mission:** Your thoughts are focused on the location, such as the terrain, and on others involved.
- **Encourage yourself:** Your thoughts are focused on giving a pep talk to yourself to do well, or to not screw up.
- **Tactical "task-relevant instructional" self-talk:** Your thoughts are focused on the challenge at hand, your mission or your response; phrases that tell you specifically how to react and respond.

Which one of the above do you think will have the greatest positive impact on your performance?

The answer is "task-relevant instructional self-talk (Asken, 1993)." This is the main focus that will enhance your performance and, therefore, your success. It's even more important than that of encouragement and pep talks. While encouragement may have an effect on motivating you to do a good job, it does not tell you how to do a good job.

In *On Killing*, co-author Dave Grossman noted that shooting another person is not a natural act for soldiers. Many thoughts may speed through their heads at such a choice point. Likewise, Remsberg (1986) writes on thought distraction for police officers during a high-stress situation of having to shoot someone. He describes typical distracting thoughts as:

Can I really shoot this guy?
If I shoot him, I'll be sued.
If I take him out, I'll be writing reports for a week.
I can see the headlines about this incident.
I'm going to get into trouble for this.
Why am I thinking this NOW?

Obviously, none of these thoughts promote the best vigilance, decision-making, or quickest response. That is why tactical training and self-talk training become so important.

Sonnon (2001) differentiates between "declarative" and "procedural" self-statements. Examples of declarative self-statements are thoughts that urge you on, or urge you to react to, say, a punch with: "That really hurts." Or "Hell, he was faster than me." Procedural self-statements thoughts tell you what to do to deal with the situation: "Shake it off and look for an opening." Or "Counter his speed with surprise."

STEPPING-UP

We like to call developing and using task-relevant self-talk as being able to **STEP-UP** which stands for Self-Talk for Enhanced Performance–Under Pressure. Being able to STEP-UP (or STEPPING-UP) is like having your instructor, coach or your DI sitting on your shoulder and "whispering" what you need to do at each given point in the mission. This type of self-talk is often a series of short cues.

Machowicz (2002) recognizes the importance of self-talk and of task-focused or tactical self-talk. He writes:

> **Thought precedes every action, so in order to focus the mind, you need a way to streamline your thinking.**

Officers "Hear" Their Instructors

Pinizzotto and his colleagues (2006) make an interesting observation in their landmark study of felonious assaults on law enforcement officers. They indicate that many officers reported that during their critical incident their instructors' voices, and some-times their faces, came back to them in the form of issuing various commands, such as "Tap, rack and go," "Stay calm, you'll get through it," "Concentrate on breathing, not on the injury," "Never give up," and "I'm always going to win no matter what." This was despite these officers not recognizing the importance of the training at the time.

An Oklahoma State Trooper (Plunkett, 2008) reported he uses "out loud" self-talk to maximize performance on patrol. "I talk out loud about what I observe, what might occur and what my response might be." He feels this is especially helpful when running "hot" by helping him maintain steady breathing, maintain focus, react more quickly, bring events to his conscious mind and make better decisions. He credits this for thirty safe and successful years on the job and for his reputation for "calmness."

In her account of U.S. female soldiers in Iraq, *Band of Sisters* author Holmstedt (2007) describes the experience of Army Captain Robin Brown, co-piloting a Kiowa Warrior helicopter. Note the importance of self-talk, the initial negative self-talk, and how it changes to task-relevant self-talk that focuses on what to do in a crisis situation.

For a split second, as the helicopter dropped, Brown thought, *This could be it. This could be bad.* However, she didn't really think she would die and she wouldn't let herself be captured. She knew in the back of her mind that to not be captured she had to do certain things. She would rely on her instincts and her Army training when she hit the ground, if she got out alive.

As the aircraft hit the ground, Brown focused on the positive. *This might work out.* She considered all the steps as they were happening. It felt like the action was occurring in slow motion and very deliberately. While she thought through each step, she felt calm and detached.

She didn't have time to think about anything else. Only, *What's my next step?*

An example of self-talk, STEPPING-UP, using the acronym BRASS for a specific skill like target shooting, includes:

BREATHE
RELAX
AIM
SIGHT
SQUEEZE

Co-author Loren Christensen believes strongly in the power of words when training. These can be onomatopoeia words, those that imitate the sound they are describing, such as "pop" and "buzz." Or they can be words that have a general meaning, but to you they mean a little more. For example, Loren says that as a person who has read much about the samurai warrior and watched many classic movies on the subject, "samurai" connotes a special feeling in him that he likes to translate into different aspects of his martial arts practice.

He says that interpreting words is especially effective when you're training alone and have total control over you performance. It can be done with a partner, but it requires good communication so that you both agree on the meaning of the word. Here is how you can use words when training with the baton or with hand-to-hand techniques.

Baton training on an impact target: heavy bag, a post, or a rolled mattress.

Define:
- Onomatopoeia: Explode (*EKS-SPLODE!*)
- Onomatopoeia: Quick (*KWIK!*)
- Onomatopoeia: Bam (*BAAAM!*)
- Onomatopoeia: Soft (*SOFFFFT*)
- Onomatopoeia: Slow (*SSLOOOW*)

Pantomiming hand-to-hand movements.

Define:
- Onomatopoeia: Slow (*SSLOOOW*)
- Onomatopoeia: Flow (*FFFLOOOOW*)
- Onomatopoeia: Snap (*SSSNAPP!*) Maybe not the best word for wristlock practice!
- Bring up from inside you and define in your movements: Confidence
- Bring up from inside you and define in your movements: Precision

To reiterate, it does not matter what the word is as long as it means something to you that you can interpret through movement. It's a dynamic way to link your mind and body, one that can be applied to a variety of training exercises. The more vivid and meaningful are the words, the greater the impact on your performance.

The Armed Services Survival, Evasion and Recovery Manual uses an acronym (BLISS) for shelter construction. This is essentially an acronym for self-talk cues on what to do to erect effective shelter for survival:

> **B = Blend**
> **L = Low Silhouette**
> **I = Irregular Shape**
> **S = Small**
> **S = Secluded Location**

The same approach can be seen in the 5 A's of responsibilities as the first person in a rescue raft.

AIR -	**Assure all chambers are inflated**
ASSISTANCE -	**Assist others; remove puncture articles**
ANCHOR -	**Assure properly deployed**
ACCESSORY BAG -	**Locate it**
ASSESSMENT -	**Assess situation and keep a positive mental attitude**

The Department of the Army Field Manual 3-05.70 also uses this approach. The acronym SURVIVAL suggests the tasks on which to focus:

> **S -** **Size up the situation**
> **U -** **Use all your senses**
> **R -** **Remember where you are**
> **V -** **Vanquish fear and panic**
> **I -** **Improvise**
> **V -** **Value living**
> **A -** **Act like the natives**
> **L -** **Live by your wits**

Self-Talk and Survival

It's striking, that when one reviews or hears the stories of police officers who have survived a potentially lethal encounter, there is similarity in the self-talk used in those situations. Whether to themselves, or whether out loud, officers have used self-talk to coach themselves to survival and victory. For example, Wilkison (2005) reports the story of a wounded police officer and how a winning mindset and "calming self-talk saved his life after a terrifying ambush." After receiving multiple wounds in an unanticipated ambush, the officer reflected:

> **"I remember saying out loud 'I ain't f… … dying here. Then I heard another shot." After being wounded again, he reacted: "I was prepared to die, but I knew at that point that if I died, they would get away and that was not an option." He went on to reflect: "I remember talking to myself, out loud, telling myself to 'calm down. I've got to do this. I've got to stay alive.' I told myself that over and over."**

The officer did survive.

Stinkin' Thinkin'

The use of task-related self-talk is important in that it also blocks negative self-talk. When things are not going well it's easy to get into a negative thinking cycle, sometimes called "Stinkin' Thinkin.'" We discuss this more later. For now realize that negative self-talk gets in the way of performance; so avoid it. STEPPING-UP can help you do that.

How to STEP-UP (Self-Talk for Enhanced Performance - Under Pressure)

There are several ways to train to STEP-UP more effectively.

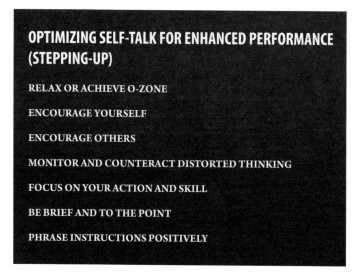

OPTIMIZING SELF-TALK FOR ENHANCED PERFORMANCE (STEPPING-UP)

RELAX OR ACHIEVE O-ZONE

ENCOURAGE YOURSELF

ENCOURAGE OTHERS

MONITOR AND COUNTERACT DISTORTED THINKING

FOCUS ON YOUR ACTION AND SKILL

BE BRIEF AND TO THE POINT

PHRASE INSTRUCTIONS POSITIVELY

Get Into Your O-ZONE (Optimal Zone of Natural Excellence)

STEPPING-UP can be improved by first achieving your optimal arousal level, as performance and learning are maximized in this state. Understand the level of arousal that works best for you and know how to create it (Chapter Three). Use the techniques we discussed earlier to create your O-ZONE.

Encourage Yourself

This is critical. If you're a leader, believe that what you do is incredibly important, difficult and skilled work. Using words like "stupid" and "idiot" to describe yourself when you screw up, or when things are not going well, is never appropriate or accurate and should be avoided. These terms can only serve to interfere with focus and erode concentration and confidence.

Encourage Others

The same awareness and courtesy should extend to your fellow warriors because encouraging others yields positive benefits. It's well-recognized that military and police humor can be dark, sarcastic and strange. However, excessive use, especially in the absence of encouragement and focus, can become a detrimental habit. Not only can it influence the reactions of others, but habitual sarcasm and negativism can make it more difficult to be encouraging to yourself.

Monitor and Change Self-talk

The key to being able to STEP-UP is to monitor and change self-talk to promote performance. One way to do this is use a STEP-UP Monitoring chart like this one:

STEP-UP MONITORING CHART

SITUATION	AUTOMATIC OR NEGATIVE SELF-TALK	SELF-TALK FOR ENHANCED PERFORMANCE (STEP-UP)

It's important to look for situations where you might engage in automatic negative and non-productive self-talk. Write the situation and the "automatic" negative self-talk in the first two columns. You might be able to do this by thinking about past situations where you became frustrated, upset or stressed. Or, do it after a current response when memories and emotions are still fresh.

The crucial point is to then STEP-UP, create and enter in the third column Self-Talk for Enhanced Performance (under pressure) that will facilitate more effective performance.

The following chart illustrates an example of a potentially critical and stressful situation involving serious injury during a training exercise. By recognizing and charting the automatic negative self-talk that creates dysfunction and distraction, the officer-in-charge becomes aware of his negativity and the source of further frustration. Also note the STEP-UP effort by self-talk used to replace the automatic negative one the next time a similar situation occurs.

STEP-UP MONITORING CHART

SITUATION	AUTOMATIC OR NEGATIVE SELF-TALK	SELF-TALK FOR ENHANCED PERFORMANCE (STEP-UP)
BAD INJURIES ON A TRAINING EXERCISE	HOW COULD THIS HAPPEN? WHO'S GETTING BLAMED? THIS IS GONNA BE BAD WHAT IF I SCREW UP? WHAT IF HE DIES?	FOCUS AND ACT USE THE SKILL YOU HAVE RADIO FOR HELP STABILIZE FOR MEDICS

Look at the STEP-UP column and see (feel) how these words have a less upsetting effect and actually direct the officer-in-charge to a more productive focus and action.

The next chart outlines a situation that could be frustrating and problematic for you: being yelled at by the drill instructor, trainer, or superior. Write in the appropriate column what your automatic negative self-talk might be. Then think about and write in the STEP-UP column the self-talk you would use to prevent increasing stress and to focus on how to manage this change in the situation.

STEP-UP MONITORING CHART

SITUATION	AUTOMATIC OR NEGATIVE SELF-TALK	SELF-TALK ENHANCED PERFORMANCE (STEP-UP)
YELLED AT BY D.I. TRAINER OR SUPERIOR		

An example might be the following:

STEP-UP MONITORING CHART

SITUATION	AUTOMATIC OR NEGATIVE SELF-TALK	SELF-TALK ENHANCED PERFORMANCE (STEP-UP)
YELLED AT BY D.I. TRAINER OR SUPERIOR	WHO DOES HE THINK HE IS? WHAT A FREAKING JACKASS I CAN'T STAND THIS I'M GONNA DECK HIM	HEY, IT'S PART OF THE DRILL USE THIS TO TOUGHEN UP I CAN GET THROUGH THIS HE WON'T GET ME

Try the same process with this situation: During building entry for a search, you can't get the ram to break open the door after several tries:

STEP-UP MONITORING CHART

SITUATION	AUTOMATIC OR NEGATIVE SELF-TALK	SELF-TALK ENHANCED PERFORMANCE (STEP-UP)
RAM FAILS TO BREACH DOOR		

An example might be:

STEP-UP MONITORING CHART

SITUATION	AUTOMATIC OR NEGATIVE SELF-TALK	SELF-TALK ENHANCED PERFORMANCE (STEP-UP)
RAM FAILS TO BREACH DOOR	PIECE OF SH-T C'MON YOU FRE-KING BA-TARD THE GUYS ARE PIS-ED	ADJUST ANGLE ADJUST TARGET POWER FOCUS

Try one more exercise, this time dealing with a weapon jam:

STEP-UP MONITORING CHART

SITUATION	AUTOMATIC OR NEGATIVE SELF-TALK	SELF-TALK ENHANCED PERFORMANCE (STEP-UP)
WEAPON JAMS		

An example might be:

STEP-UP MONITORING CHART

SITUATION	AUTOMATIC OR NEGATIVE SELF-TALK	SELF-TALK ENHANCED PERFORMANCE (STEP-UP)
WEAPON JAMS	HELL, I DON'T BELIEVE IT WHAT NOW? I'M REALLY SCREWED	TAP, RACK & GO COVER, RETREAT, REGROUP IMPROVISE A WEAPON OUTFOX HIM

Notice that instead of engaging in anxiety-arousing, angry or frustrating statements, STEP-UP provides focus and suggestions of what to try.

Use an Action Focus

Self-talk should be focused on the behavior and action you need to take to accomplish your goal. Murphy (1996) calls this an "Action Focus" rather than a "Results Focus." The action focus in self-talk is more useful since it tells you how to get the result. If you perform the actions, the result should follow.

Be Brief

Too much self-talk, or self-talk that is too complicated, may be detrimental. Several studies (Mummert & Furley, 2007) now suggest that too much instruction can be a problem, especially for skilled performers, as it can interfere with smooth performance. Too much coaching and too much thinking lead to a narrowing of attention, which may be a cause of decreased performance. This is an example of the caution "analysis leads to paralysis."

Research shows that *experienced* performers who try to use a "set of rules" to self-coach maximal performance in high-stress situations are more likely to "choke" than those who are less rigid and let their practiced "automatic" skill drive performance (Svoboda, 2009).

Self-talk should be relevant and accurate reminders of the keys to needed performance, but should be brief, creating a focus to set into action the well-learned automatic skills.

Make it Positive

A final approach to maximizing self-talk for enhanced performance is to always phrase your self-talk positively in terms of what you should do, not what you should not do. Telling yourself not to do something puts the focus on what you want to avoid doing.

As an example, for the next two seconds don't think of a tree. What did you just think of? Most likely, a tree. This is because of the six words in the statement that is supposed to tell you not to think of a tree, five of them refer to the tree. A better STEP-UP for not thinking of a tree would be "Think of the ocean."

Wegner (1989) says that an early anecdote that illustrates this comes from Leo Tolstoy, author of the classic *War and Peace*, who as a child was ordered by his older brother to stand in a corner until he could stop thinking of a white bear! He goes on to note that the human brain isn't built to "not think of something." Phrasing it in the negative still puts the focus on what is to be ignored. Neurolinguistic Programming offers that our brains "simply do not know how to put things into negative language." In order to know what not to think of, you must first think of it (Andreas & Faulkner, 1994).

This is an important concept since instructions are frequently phrased negatively. For example, the *Armed Services Survival, Evasion and Recovery Procedures Manual* states:

DO NOT APPROACH A RECOVERY VEHICLE UNTIL INSTRUCTED

Again, most of this instruction is focused on what should be avoided: approaching the vehicle before cleared to do so. Better instructions would be:

WAIT FOR INSTRUCTIONS BEFORE APPROACHING A RECOVERY VEHICLE

or

STAY UNDER COVER UNTIL SIGNALLED TO APPROACH THE VEHICLE

The manual also provides excellent instructions for map use without compromising information, though all are phrased negatively:

DO NOT WRITE ON THE MAP
DO NOT SOIL THE MAP BY TOUCHING THE DESTINATION
DO NOT FOLD THE MAP IN A MANNER SHOWING TRAVEL PLANS

Better instructions would be:

KEEP INTEL, PLANS AND NOTES SEPARATE FROM THE MAP
KEEP MAP CLEAN; TOUCHING MAY LEAVE INDICATIONS
   OF PLANS
FOLD MAP IN MANNER THAT DISGUISES TRAVEL PLANS

Becoming aware of and managing self-talk can provide additional control for enhanced performance in high-stress situations.

Critical situations may not seem to allow time to "think" or construct self-talk, especially since too much lengthy or complicated thinking can get in the way of executing skills effectively. While this is true, it does not negate the impact of self-talk on performance. It really argues for the importance of training and practice prior to critical situations, so that your self-talk is focused, direct, to the point and so powerful that it promotes excellence and appropriate action. It should be response-oriented. Self-talk is both the trigger and trajectory for the "automatic" actions and responses you train.

Your "automatic" self-talk should be immediately performance-enhancing, not of a negative nature — ever.

The practice and training of integrating mental and physical skills promotes their merging together into a more automatic and seamless response. By planning and practice, self-talk should become second nature, occurring automatically when needed. Whether you step it up or it tears you down depends on your mental preparation and practice.

Cognitive Counter Response:

chapter

Negative Thought Stopping and Mental Toughness

When **speech** *is* **corrupted,**
the mind is also.

– Seneca

There are many names for it: "Toxic Thinking," "Stinkin' Thinkin,'" "Defeatist Thinking" and "Negative Thinking." Call it what you want, these negative cognitive states degrade mental toughness and performance. Understanding this process and, importantly, developing an effective counter response to combat negative thinking is essential for maximizing mental toughness and performance. Let's examine what it's about and how to master it.

NEGATIVE THINKING IMPACTS PERFORMANCE

It was said earlier that negative thinking or negative self-talk can interfere with optimal performance in military missions and police calls. Here is how:

MISSION PERFORMANCE EFFECTS OF NEGATIVE THINKING

CREATES STRESS AND ANXIETY

DEGRADES SELF-CONFIDENCE

DISTRACTS AND IMPEDES CONCENTRATION

**PROGRAMS SELF-DOUBT AND FAILURE
(SELF-FULFILLING PROPHECY)**

INFECTS OTHER PERSONNEL

INFLUENCES OTHER AREAS OF YOUR LIFE

Anxiety and Worry

Negative thinking or negative self-talk creates anxiety, worry, erodes confidence and distracts you from the task at hand by putting your attention on an irrelevant but disruptive focus. As a result, your concentration and creativity suffer.

Negative thinking and negative self-talk affects your physiology, as well. Tennenbaum and his colleagues (2008) report research where subjects were exposed to a noxious traffic noise broadcast. Stress responses were evident in fast heart rates (tachycardia) and narrowing of the blood vessels (vasoconstriction). These effects were most pronounced in individuals who responded to the stressor with thoughts like "I can't handle this" or "this is making me crazy."

Self-Doubt and Degraded Confidence

Negative thinking is at the root of self-doubt. The concept of self-fulfilling prophecy says that our expectations about success or failure greatly influence our efforts and performance on a task. Expectations are indeed powerful.

Thomas Jefferson said:

> **Nothing can stop the man with the right mental attitude from achieving his goal; nothing on earth can help the man with the wrong mental attitude.**

A study was done on competitors at a national arm wrestling championship (arm wrestling is taken very seriously in some circles). Each pair of finalists was tested for arm strength and each member was then given false feedback. The objectively stronger member of the pair was told he was weaker and the objectively weaker competitor was told he was stronger. In a majority of the final matches, the objectively weaker competitor won the event.

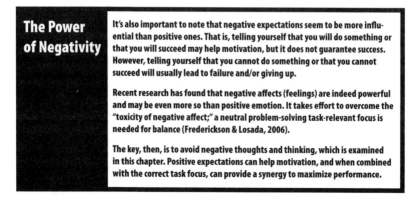

The Power of Negativity

It's also important to note that negative expectations seem to be more influential than positive ones. That is, telling yourself that you will do something or that you will succeed may help motivation, but it does not guarantee success. However, telling yourself that you cannot do something or that you cannot succeed will usually lead to failure and/or giving up.

Recent research has found that negative affects (feelings) are indeed powerful and may be even more so than positive emotion. It takes effort to overcome the "toxicity of negative affect;" a neutral problem-solving task-relevant focus is needed for balance (Frederickson & Losada, 2006).

The key, then, is to avoid negative thoughts and thinking, which is examined in this chapter. Positive expectations can help motivation, and when combined with the correct task focus, can provide a synergy to maximize performance.

Spreading Negativity
Negative thinking is contagious; it easily spreads to others. You might have had the experience in which one person drags down a whole group. This is because negativity spreads more easily than does confidence. Maxwell (2001) calls this "The Law of the Bad Apple." Negativity easily spreads to others and to other areas of your life. Negative self-talk can become a destructive habit.

Martin (2006) says that Special Forces members hate to hear someone whining or complaining. This is not because they don't think the complaints are not valid, but because they believe whining means the person is not thinking about the right things to be successful; their focus and concentration are off. If continuous whining is not addressed, it can hurt morale and ultimately lead to mission failure.

NEGATIVE THOUGHT STOPPING

Understand that we are not suggesting that you always be positive and sunny. It would be unrealistic and artificial to be overly optimistic. What is being suggested is that you stay in an instructional, problem-solving mindset: thinking about *what needs to be done to achieve the outcome*. Your self-talk should give you guidance as to how to act.

However, it's likely that even with the best attempts to step-up and focus on tactical self-talk, you will still have negative thoughts from time to time. Therefore, a skill called Negative Thought Stopping can be helpful in managing performance in high-stress situations. The skill is one of several techniques originally developed by Dr. Joseph Cautela at Boston University to help individuals gain greater control over negative thinking. Although it's rather simple it's easier to demonstrate than to explain.

Demonstration of Negative Thought Stopping
Here is how I (MA) demonstrate Negative Thought Stopping in training. After discussing the toxic nature of negative thoughts, I ask everyone to close their eyes and think a negative or critical thought about themselves related to a mission or a call. After they have concentrated on the thought for about five seconds, I suddenly bang my hand on the desk and yell as loudly as I can, "Stop it!"

Everyone's eyes pop wide open as they sit bolt upright and refocus their attention on me. The point I'm making with them, and confirmed when the students are asked, is that the negative thought was completely ejected from their thinking. (I always check to see that everyone is heart-healthy before I do this demonstration!)

Here is the procedure for Negative Thought Stopping. As outlined below, whenever a negative thought enters your thinking, forcefully think (or "yell" to yourself), "No" or "Stop it!" Then immediately give yourself a Step-Up cue like "Focus, Smooth, Engage" to get to the skill you need to do at the moment.

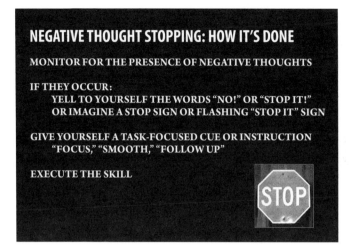

NEGATIVE THOUGHT STOPPING: HOW IT'S DONE

MONITOR FOR THE PRESENCE OF NEGATIVE THOUGHTS

IF THEY OCCUR:
    YELL TO YOURSELF THE WORDS "NO!" OR "STOP IT!"
    OR IMAGINE A STOP SIGN OR FLASHING "STOP IT" SIGN

GIVE YOURSELF A TASK-FOCUSED CUE OR INSTRUCTION
    "FOCUS," "SMOOTH," "FOLLOW UP"

EXECUTE THE SKILL

Make it Work for You

There are several ways you can modify Negative Thought Stopping. For some warriors, imaging a STOP sign or a flashing neon sign that says "NO" may be more effective than thinking the word STOP.

Here is another variation when safety and time allows. You can add performance imagery to enhance your actions, cue your behavior and help you refocus on the challenge. For example, after thinking "NO" or "STOP IT," immediately think a task-focused cue, such as "SECURE THE SCENE" and then image yourself, say, scanning the area for unanticipated dangers. Then cue yourself to return to actual action. The use of reorienting commands like "Secure the scene," or "Scan" or even just "Focus" after thought stopping is essential for effectiveness and safety.

Negative Thought Stopping helps return your focus in a more effective manner. As with all psychological performance techniques, practice and use enhances this skill.

Distraction for Enhanced Focus and Coping

Wegner (1989) has contributed much to our understanding of what makes the control of thinking effective. He notes that just trying to "directly suppress" a thought is not effective, as it is much like trying to, as he says, "not think of the color white." Remember, your mind is not built to "not think of something."

In fact, trying directly to suppress a thought:
- can cause you to focus on it even more.
- can cause a "rebound effect" where you think about the banished thought even more frequently after the suppression attempt is stopped.
- can, if you are not effective in suppressing the thought, cause an "intrusion reaction" in which the thought recurs, bringing with it a strong emotional response (usually negative).
- may not alter your body's reaction to it (you will still react with a physiological response, usually negative stress-type reactions).

The great Japanese Zen Master and swordsman, Takuan (1573-1645) described the paradox of trying not to think of something this way:

> **To think that I am not going**
> **To think of you anymore**
> **Is still thinking of you**
> **Let me then try not to think**
> **That I am not going to think of you**

The use of distraction is much more effective. Distraction is thinking about something else, or replacing the unwanted thought with one or more others. Use a single thought or multiple thoughts as distractors (in fact, most people distract by using more than one thought). This works well when the thoughts are of great interest and significance to you.

There is the story of an elite Olympic swimmer who spent hours every morning swimming thousands of yards in a pool. Rather than trying to not think about the boredom, fatigue and pain, he would picture a beautiful woman standing on the pool deck at the end of each lane beckoning to him.

Holmstedt (2007) provides a dramatic example of using active distraction rather than suppression to cope with a potentially overwhelming situation. Army Captain Tammy Duckworth was co-piloting a UH-60 Blackhawk helicopter when Iraqi insurgents hit it with an RPG. Captain Duckworth lost both her legs and her right arm was broken in three places.

Captain Duckworth shared:

> **In my first week at Walter Reed, I was in so much pain that
> I found myself counting to sixty over and over again. I didn't
> have the strength to survive the day, but I was pretty sure I
> could survive sixty seconds. So I counted the minutes away,
> one at a time.**

Rather than trying to "not think about" the pain, she used limited and achievable periods of distraction. Captain Duckworth survived and was awarded the Purple Heart, Air Medal, Army Commendation Medal and was promoted to Major at Walter Reed Army Medical Center.

Practice before You Need it
Having considered, planned, developed, and practiced negative thought stopping and distracting thoughts/self-statements prior to needing them makes them more effective at a critical moment.

chapter 10

Personal Briefings:
Attitude, Affirmations and Mental Toughness

The empires of the future
are the empires of the mind.

– Sir Winston Churchill

S elf-talk and negative thought-stopping intersect in the concept of attitude, making for two major ingredients in its quality. They are the answer as how to create and maintain a successful attitude. Maxwell (2001) captures its essential role with this:

> **Attitude is the advance man of our true selves.**
> **Its roots are inward, but its fruit outward.**
> **It is our best friend and our worst enemy.**
> **It is more honest and more consistent than our words.**
> **It is an outward look based on past experiences.**
> **It is a thing that draws people to us or repels them.**
> **It is never content until it is expressed.**
> **It is the librarian of our past.**
> **It is the speaker of our present.**
> **It is the prophet of our future.**

Attitude is the essence of the survival mindset, the winning mindset. Warriors have always known this.

In the fourth century, the Greek General Xenophon said:

> **I am sure that not numbers or strength bring victory**
> **in war; but whichever army goes into battle stronger**
> **in soul, their enemies generally can not withstand them.**

Lord Moran said it this way:

> **It is not the number of soldiers but their will to win**
> **that decides battle**s.

Military strategist Carl von Clausewitz believed:

> **Psychological factors exert a decisive influence on the elements involved in war.**
>
> (Cited by Rouse, 2008)

Affirmations and Positive Thinking

There is one other approach to maximizing attitude in addition to self-talk and negative thought stopping that is worth discussing briefly. This is the use of affirmations and positive thinking. As mentioned earlier, you must be cautious when using positive thinking, encouragement or affirmations because while there may be some effect on attitude, they do not provide direction and focus on *how* to maximize performance. However, with proper training and integration of the mental toughness psychological skills discussed earlier in the book, affirmations and positive thinking can contribute to the quality of performance by bolstering motivation and attitude. Perhaps the best source of effective attitude is your confidence in your ability to perform physically and psychologically, both of which come from the mental toughness techniques describe earlier in this book.

Affirmations and their related positive thinking can affect your motivation. Let's examine them briefly since they are commonly offered in other resources and training as a way to foster survival mindset and winning attitude components of mental toughness.

What are Affirmations?

The nature and characteristics of affirmations are:

- they are positive statements about ourselves that we make to ourselves.
- they are truthful, not trash talk or boasts that create unrealistic expectations or hopes.
- they are statements that remind us of our strengths, talents, skills and goals.
- they work best when they are in the form of an "I" statement.
  - they are also most effective when stated in the present tense.
  - they are to be reviewed, stated, or meditated upon on a daily basis.

Ben Franklin Affirmed

Ben Franklin wrote affirmations of his 13 values and kept them in his pocket watch case. This way he carried his affirmations with him at all times and frequently reviewed them whenever he checked the time (Andreas & Faulkner, 1994)

Andreas and Faulkner (1994) suggest that if an affirmation is not yet true, you can change the wording to promote its potential. For example you can replace "I am...:" with the phrasing *"I can learn to be... or I will strive to develop..."*

There are three typical categories of affirmations.

Personal Affirmations: These statements recognize your unique qualities, such as:

> **I trust myself.**
> **I am committed to excellence.**
> **I always seek to improve myself.**

Professional Affirmations: These statements recognize your unique qualities as a warrior; they may also reflect qualities of your unit, such as:

> **I am a dedicated warrior.**
> **My unit demonstrates readiness and determination.**
> **I am mentally tough.**

Performance Affirmations: These statements recognize unique aspects of your skills and performance efforts, such as:

> **In all duties and responsibilities, I take pride in my preparation.**
> **I strive to maintain integrity at all times in my actions.**
> **I look out for my teammates at all times.**

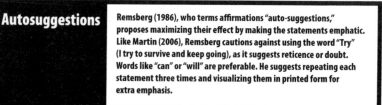

Autosuggestions

Remsberg (1986), who terms affirmations "auto-suggestions," proposes maximizing their effect by making the statements emphatic. Like Martin (2006), Remsberg cautions against using the word "Try" (I try to survive and keep going), as it suggests reticence or doubt. Words like "can" or "will" are preferable. He suggests repeating each statement three times and visualizing them in printed form for extra emphasis.

Ruge (2005) presents a detailed and highly instructive description of the nature and use of affirmations in his excellent book *The Warrior's Mantra*. He defines an affirmation or mantra as a formula of invocation, a short phrase repeated until it's ingrained in your consciousness.

Examples of affirmations given by Ruge include:

> **I will maintain my equipment in proper working order
> and train with it until I have achieved mastery.**

> **I will stay focused on my mission and complete my assignment.**

> **I will overcome any threat with courage.**

The Soldier's Creed is an inspirational collection of affirmations:

SOLDIER'S CREED

I am an American Soldier.

I am a warrior and a member of a team.

I serve the people of the United States and live the Army Values.

I will always place the mission first.

I will never accept defeat.

I will never quit.

I will never leave a fallen comrade.

**I am disciplined, physically and mentally tough, trained
and proficient in my warrior tasks and skills.**

**I always maintain my arms, my equipment, and myself.
I am an expert and I am a professional.**

**I stand ready to deploy, engage, and destroy the enemies of the
United States of America in close combat.**

I am a guardian of freedom and the American way of life.

I am an American soldier.

Notice some of the demands of the Creed are stated in the negative! Might they be better stated in the positive, e.g. "I will only accept victory."

The power and impact of affirmations and affirmation-like statements can also be seen in the U.S. Navy's Core Values Charter.

U.S. NAVY'S CORE VALUES CHARTER

Honor

I am accountable for my professional and personal behavior.

I will be mindful of the privilege I have to serve my fellow Americans.

I will:

> Abide by an uncompromising code of integrity,
> taking full responsibility for my actions and keeping my word.

> Conduct myself in the highest ethical manner in relationships
> with seniors, peers and subordinates.

> Be honest and truthful in my dealings within and outside the
> Department of the Navy.

> Make honest recommendations to my seniors and peers and
> seek honest recommendations from junior personnel.

> Encourage new ideas and deliver bad news forthrightly.

> Fulfill my legal and ethical responsibilities in my public
> and personal life.

Courage

Courage is the value that gives me the moral and mental strength
to do what is right, with confidence and resolution, even in the face
of temptation or adversity.

I will:

> Have the courage to meet the demands of my profession and
> the mission entrusted to me.

> Make decisions and act in the best interest of the Department of the
> Navy and the Nation, without regard to personal consequences.

> Overcome all challenges while adhering to the standards of
> personal conduct and decency.

> Be loyal to my nation while ensuring the resources entrusted to me
> are used in an honest, careful and efficient way.

Commitment

The day-to-day duty of every man and woman in the Department of the Navy is to join together as a team to improve the quality of our work, our people, and ourselves.

I will:

> Foster respect up and down the chain of command.
>
> Care for the professional, personal, and spiritual well-being of my people.
>
> Show respect toward all people without regard to race, religion, or gender.
>
> Always strive for positive change and personal improvement.
>
> Exhibit the highest degree of moral character, professional excellence, quality, and competence in all that I do.
> (Carlson, 2000)

Remsberg (1986) provides an example of affirmations used by an officer for high-risk calls:

> On any high-risk call, I will survive.
> I have succeeded on dangerous calls before.
> I know the tactics I need.
> I know how to make the physical moves I need.
> I am skilled with my firearms.
> I can stay focused on what I have to do.
> I can take care of myself.
> I have options for controlling any problem.
> I can take each call step by step without rushing.
> I can breathe deeply to control stress any time I start feeling tense.
> I can keep any situation within limits I can handle.
> I can decide not to be afraid.
> I can defeat any threat against me.
> I can use deadly force to save my life or the life of someone else.
> I can survive and keep going, no matter what, even if I am hit.

As we discuss the value of reflecting on developing and using specific performance-oriented affirmations, it may be well to notice that the "direct" and "in your face" credos used by many in the military are essentially affirmations. They are even found in tattoos.

Mansfield (2005) describes Lance Corporal Darrin McKay as "thickly muscled and plastered with tattoos," a "smaller, meaner-looking version of Arnold Schwarzenegger." He goes on to say: "His credo adorns his left arm: 'Though I walk through the valley of the shadow of death, I shall fear no evil, for I am the baddest warrior in the valley.'"

With alternative content, but still representing the nature and impact of affirmations, Mansfield writes of soldiers given a "shield of strength," which is similar in appearance to a dog tag. One side of the shield has a picture of the American Flag with the words "One Nation Under God" and, on the reverse, modified words from Joshua 1:9, which reads: "I will be strong and courageous. I will not be terrified, or discouraged; for the Lord, my God, is with me wherever I go."

Because attitude is so essential to all aspects of your life, we close by asking you to reflect on the words of two others. Soccer pro David Bascome said:

> **I believe that attitude more than anything else determines what you make of yourself.**
>
> **Attitude is the foundation on which you build your professional success and your personal accomplishments, your relationships with others and the quality of your life.**
>
> **Attitude is not just how you speak. It is how you walk, work, present yourself to others, react to situations and approach life. It reflects the true core of who you are and what you believe.**

Renowned social psychologist and Stanford University professor emeritus Philip Zimbardo observed (2007):

> **We have erred in making heroes mythical creatures. Most heroic acts are acts by ordinary people... The way to oppose evil is planting this heroic imagination in little kids and saying... "You are going to have the chance, once in your lifetime, to do a heroic act on the behalf of other people. When that time comes, if you don't take the opportunity, it may never come again."**

May you be staunch and strong, decisive and determined, when your opportunity comes.

PROGRESSIVE MUSCLE RELAXATION INSTRUCTIONS

Overview

Initially, practice Progressive Muscle Relaxation in an environment that is quiet, comfortable and free from distraction. It should be a place where you can safely close your eyes and relax. Sitting in a comfortable recliner is an excellent approach.

PMR involves first tensing and then relaxing different groups of muscles in your body. For example, start by clenching your left hand into a fist, strongly enough to feel the muscles working but not so strenuously that it's uncomfortable. Then slowly relax your fist and open your hand. Your objective is to do this progressively with all your muscle groups so that you teach them to loosen and relax. Spend only a few seconds on any muscle group, and if you need to skip one that is injured, that is okay.

People experience their relaxation in different ways. Some feel it as a deep heaviness, as if it would be difficult to get up from the chair. Others feel a light floating sensation, as if lying on an air mattress on a lake. Still others feel a light tingling. When you feel any one of these sensations during PMR, you know the relaxation is beginning to work. Most people find this comfortable and pleasurable but if for any reason you find it uncomfortable, discontinue the process. Consult with your physician first should you have a medical problem, although relaxation is a helpful adjunct treatment for many medical conditions.

Control Word

Before beginning, think of a control word to enhance your relaxation and to be your cue for future relaxation. This is a word to "condition" your feelings of relaxation. When you say the control word to yourself when experiencing feelings of deep relaxation, you condition an association (remember the earlier discussion about Pavlov's dogs) between your word and the relaxed state. Then any time in the future, you can bring on relaxation by thinking your control word and not having to do the full tension-relaxation procedure. Choose any control word you like, though it's best if it suggests a focused relaxation that fits with the demands of responding during a call like "Steady," "Easy," "Focus," "Smooth," or the like.

Before You Begin

Rate how tense you're feeling right now. Pick a number between 1 and 10, where 1 represents feeling as relaxed and good as you have ever felt and 10 represents as much tension or anxiety as you have ever felt. Write your rating here:

My level of tension right now is _____ (1 to 10)

You might have someone read the following instructions to you or, even better, read them into a tape recorder. It is best to read and record the instructions yourself. Recording your voice allows you to instruct yourself at a pace and in a manner that is comfortable for you. Additionally, it's your own voice that you "hear" when you relax yourself in situations in the field.

Note: If you make your own tape (or have someone read the directions to you), simply ignore the headings, bullets and bold words below. If you (or your reader) simply read the text in italics, it should flow for you.

Begin Now

- **Relax** *Settle back in the chair and get as comfortable as you can. If you're comfortable closing your eyes during this exercise, do that now as you take a slow, deep breath. Hold it for a second or two, and then slowly exhale and return to breathing lightly and normally. When you're ready, take another slow deep, breath, hold it for a second or two, and then exhale. Return to breathing lightly and normally.*

- **Left Hand** *Begin by focusing on your left hand. Make a fist just hard enough so you can feel the muscles working; don't strain. Hold it for a second or two. Now relax by letting go as your fingers slowly open. Allow your hand to rest lightly on the arm of the chair, and notice the difference between the tension that was there and the relaxation you're beginning to feel.*

- *When you're ready, repeat the procedure. Make your left hand into a fist. Study it to experience the tension. Hold it for a second or two… then relax as you slowly and smoothly let your fingers open to release all the tension you can. Notice the difference between the tension that was there and the relaxation you're beginning to create.*

- **Right Hand** *Begin by focusing on your right hand. Make a fist just hard enough that you can feel the muscles working; don't strain. Hold it for a second or two. Now relax by letting go as your fingers slowly open. Allow your hand to rest lightly on the arm of the chair, and notice the difference between the tension that was there and the relaxation you're beginning to feel.*

- When you're ready, repeat the procedure. Make your right hand into a fist. Study it to experience the tension. Hold it for a second or two... then relax as you slowly and smoothly let your fingers open to release all the tension you can Notice the difference between the tension that was there and the relaxation you're beginning to create.

- **Both Forearms** Begin with your palms down on the arms of your chair. Keep your forearms on the chair as you bend both wrists back so that your fingers point toward the ceiling. You will feel tension in your forearm muscles. Hold it for a second or two... and now steadily relax the tension in your forearms as you slowly let your hands lower to the arms of the chair. Let your hands rest comfortably without tension. Notice the difference between the tension and relaxation.

- Once again, point your fingers toward the ceiling to bring tension into your forearms. Study it, hold it for a second or two... and now relax as you lower your hands slowly to the arms of the chair. Notice the difference between the tension that was there and the relaxation you can create for yourself.

- **Biceps** Bring both your hands up toward your shoulders and tense your biceps muscles, the big muscles in your upper arm. Hold for a second or two, study the tension... and now relax. Slowly, smoothly, let your arms come forward and down, releasing all the tension. Let your arms rest comfortably on the chair. Note the difference between the tension that was there and the relaxation you're beginning to create.

- Repeat by bending both arms at the elbows and curl your fists to your shoulders, tensing your biceps muscles. Study it... hold it... and now relax. Let your arms come forward and down, and notice the difference between the tension and relaxation.

- **Shoulders** Shrug your shoulders as if trying to touch your ears. Study the tension in your shoulders and neck, hold it for a second or two... and now relax. Allow your shoulders to come down as your relaxed body sinks into the softness of the chair. Let the chair do all the work; there is no need to have any tension in your shoulders at all.

- When you're ready, do it again. Raise your shoulders up, as if trying to touch your ears with them, and feel the tension in your neck and shoulders. Study it... and now relax. Let go of the tension. Sink into the chair... let it do all the work... no need to have any tension in your neck and shoulders at all. Notice the difference between the tension that was in your neck and shoulders and the relaxation you can begin to create for yourself.

- **Face** It's also possible, and important to relax the various muscles of your face To begin, keep your eyes closed as you raise your eyebrows to bring tension into your forehead and brow. Study and hold it for a second or two... now let it go.

Lower your eyebrows and notice the difference between the tension that was in your forehead and the relaxation you can begin to create for yourself.

- *Do it again. Lift your eyebrows, and feel the tension in your forehead and brow… and now relax. Let your eyebrows come down and notice the difference between the tension and relaxation.*

- **Eyes** *Shut your eyes tightly to create tension around them. Hold that for a second or two… and now relax. Just let your eyes remain gently and comfortably closed. Notice the difference between the tension and the relaxation.*

- *Do it again. Shut your eyes tightly, notice the tension… and now relax. Release all the tension you can, and allow your eyes to remain lightly and comfortably closed.*

- **Mouth** *Press your lips together to create tension around your mouth. Study it, hold it… and now relax. Just let your lips remain lightly and comfortably closed. Notice the difference between the tension and the relaxation you can begin to create for yourself.*

- *Once again, press your lips together, feel the tension… and now relax. Just let your lips remain lightly and comfortably closed.*

- **Chest** *When you're ready, take a slow deep breath to fill your lungs. Hold it for a second or two to feel the muscles of your chest working…and now relax. Exhale and return to breathing lightly and normally. As you do, notice the difference between the tension that was in your chest muscles and the relaxation you can begin to create.*

- *When you're ready, take another slow deep breath, filling your lungs, and feeling the muscles in your chest working… and now relax. Exhale and return to breathing lightly and normally. Notice the difference between the tension that was in your chest and the relaxation you can create.*

- **Stomach** *Tighten your stomach muscles and hold them that way for a second or two, study it… and now relax. Feel your muscles unwind and notice the difference between the tension and the relaxation.*

- *Once again, tighten your stomach muscles, hold it, study it… and now relax. Send a message to the stomach muscles to relax. Notice the difference between the tension that was there and the relaxation you can begin to create.*

- **Thighs** *Stretch your legs out in front of you and feel the tension in your thighs. Study it, hold it… and now relax. Let the chair do all the work to support your legs so that there is no tension in your thighs at all.*

- *Once again, stretch your legs and feel the tension in your thighs… and now relax. Notice the difference between the tension that was in your thighs and the relaxation you can begin to create.*

- **Calves**   *Point your toes back toward your head until you feel pulling and tension in your calf muscles. Study it, hold it… and now relax. Allow your feet to drop slowly back down to a comfortable position. Notice the difference between the tension and the relaxation.*
- *Once again, draw your toes back toward your head and feel the tension in your calves. Study it, hold it… and now relax. Let your feet slowly lower back to the floor. Notice the difference between the tension that was there and the relaxation you can create for yourself.*

Scanning Your Body for Residual Tension

Just as you have been directing your muscles to tighten, you have also been teaching them to loosen and relax. Now, scan your body for any muscle tension that might remain. If you find tension in a muscle, send a message to it to loosen and relax. You don't need to tense the muscle first. If you think about relaxing it, you can do so, even if it's just a little more.

Begin by scanning and relaxing your toes, feet and calves. Relax all the muscles of your lower legs from your knees to the tips of your toes.

Relax your thighs and hips. Relax all the muscles of your lower body...relax your hips and thighs… knees and calves… feet and toes.

Relax the muscles of your stomach and the muscles of your chest. Beginning now, every time you breathe out, think your control word. Every time you exhale… so gently...so easily… so calmly… focus on your control word. If your mind wanders… that is okay. Do not fight it. Just bring your thoughts back and refocus on your control word… as often as you need to.

Every time you breathe out… think your control word. Every time you breathe out… so gently… so easily… so calmly. Every time you breathe out. Use your control word to help you relax further and further, and feel better and better.

As you focus on your control word, continue to relax… the muscles in your shoulders and in your neck. Relax the muscles of your face. Relax your forehead and brow. Your eyes are so lightly and comfortably closed. Relax your jaws and cheeks and mouth. Feel the relaxation down your neck and shoulders. Feel the relaxation in your upper arms, forearms and hands, right down to your fingertips.

You may continue relaxing like this for a few more moments or as long as you like. Focus on your control word… use it to help yourself relax and feel better and better. Practice relaxing like this as often as you like, so that it works better and better each time you do. That means each time you practice relaxing, you relax yourself faster and faster to help yourself feel better and better… as relaxed and good as you need. Whenever you think your control word, your body will remember these good feelings of calmness and relaxation. Whenever you think your control word, you will be able to create the feelings of calmness and relaxation that you need.

Now, when you're ready, open your eyes, stretch, be wide wake, feel good, comfortable, relaxed and refreshed.

Don't forget to rate how tense you feel now on the scale of 1 (very little tension) to 10 (the most tension you have ever felt).

My level of tension right now is _____ (1 to 10)

How does this rating compare to the rating you made just before starting the relaxation? If you experienced any decrease in your tension level, it suggests that you have an ability to manage it. If you did not experience change, it means you need a bit more practice. If you do not like this method or find that it does not work for you, that is okay. It does not mean that you have a problem or that something is wrong. Remember, individuals are different in how their bodies function. There-fore, try one of the many other forms of relaxation and self-control that are available until you find one that works well for you.

PROGRESSIVE MUSCLE RELAXATION "LETTING GO" INSTRUCTIONS

Overview
"Letting Go" is a more advanced form of Progressive Muscle Relaxation that allows a faster creation of a relaxed state. Practice it after the full PMR procedure has been mastered.

Just as with full PMR, you should practice Letting Go initially in a quiet, comfortable environment that is free from distraction and interruption. It should be an environment where you can safely close your eyes and relax. Sitting in a comfortable recliner is an excellent approach.

People feel their relaxation in different ways. Some experience it as a deep heaviness, as if it would be difficult to get up from the chair. Others feel it as a light floating sensation as if lying on an air mattress on a lake. Still others feel a light tingling. When you feel any one of these sensations during Letting Go, you know the relaxation is beginning to work. Most people find this comfortable and pleasurable but if for any reason you find it uncomfortable, discontinue the process. Consult with your physician first should you have a medical problem, although relaxation is a helpful adjunct treatment for many medical conditions.

Control Word

As with the full PMR, think of a control word to use during the training to enhance your relaxation and serve as cue for future relaxation. This should be the same control word you used for the full PMR training.

Your control word "conditions" your feelings of relaxation. When you say it to yourself while experiencing feelings of deep relaxation, you condition an association (remember the earlier discussion about Pavlov's dogs) between the control word and a state of controlled relaxation. Then any time in the future, you can bring on relaxation by thinking your control word and not having to do the full tension-relaxation procedure. Choose any control word you like, though it's best if it suggests a focused relaxation that fits with the demands of responding during a call.

Before You Begin

Rate how tense you're feeling right now before doing the Letting Go exercise. Pick a number between 1 and 10, where 1 represents feeling as relaxed and good as you have ever felt and 10 represents as much tension or anxiety as you have ever felt. Write your rating here:

My level of tension right now is _____ (1 to 10)

You might have someone read the following instructions to you or, even better, read them into a tape recorder. It is best to read and record the instructions in your own voice. Recording your voice allows you to instruct yourself at a pace and in a manner that is comfortable for you. Additionally, it's your own voice that you will "hear" when relaxing yourself in situations in the field.

Begin Now

- **Relax** *Settle back in the chair and get as comfortable as you can. If you're comfortable closing your eyes during this exercise, do that now as you take a slow, deep breath. Hold it for a second or two and then slowly exhale and return to breathing lightly and normally. When you're ready, take another slow, deep, breath, hold it for a second or two, and then exhale. Return to breathing lightly and normally.*
- **Left Hand** *Send a message to the muscles in your left hand to loosen and relax. Think about letting go of all the tension that you can in your hand. Just let it rest comfortably on the arm of the chair…. no need to have any tension there at all.*
- **Right Hand** *Send a message to the muscles in your right hand to loosen and relax… no need to have any tension there at all. Let your hand rest comfortably on the arm of the chair… let the chair do all the work.*

- **Forearms** *Now relax… the muscles in your forearms. Send a message to them to loosen and relax… get rid of all the tension that you can… now relax… the muscles in your forearms.*

- **Biceps** *Think about relaxing your biceps muscles, the big muscles in your upper arms… send a message to those muscles to loosen and relax.*

- **Shoulders** *Now relax… the muscles in your shoulders and neck… let go of all the tension as best you can. Sink into your chair. Let the chair do all the work… no need to have any tension there at all.*

- **Face** *It's possible and important to relax the various muscles of your face. Relax the muscles of your forehead. Send a message to those muscles to loosen and relax. Perhaps you can feel ridges of tension smoothing out, relaxing, and dissolving into soft, silky relaxation. Now relax the muscles around your eyes. Just let your eyes remain so lightly and comfortably closed. Relax… the muscles in your jaws… and cheeks… and lips. Send a message to those muscles to loosen and relax as best you're able. Let go of all the tension.*

- **Chest** *Relax the muscles of your chest. Every time you breathe out, send a message to those muscles to loosen and unwind. Every time you breathe out, relax those muscles.*

If you haven't already, begin focusing on your control word now. Every time you breathe out, think your control word. Every time you exhale… so gently...so easily… so calmly… focus on your control word. If your mind wanders a bit… that's okay. Don't fight it. Just bring your thoughts back and refocus on your control word… as often as you need to. Every time you breathe out, think your control word to yourself. Every time you breathe out… so gently… so easily… so calmly. Every time you breathe out. Use your control word to help you relax further and further, and feel better and better.

- **Stomach** *Relax the muscles of your stomach. Send a message to them to loosen and relax. Perhaps you can feel any knots of tension, loosening, unraveling, unwinding, dissolving… into a soft silky relaxation.*

- **Hips and Thighs** *Relax… the muscles of your hips and upper legs. Send a message to the muscles in your hips and thighs to loosen and unwind. Let go of all the tension.*

- **Calves, Feet, Toes** *Relax… your calf muscles. Send a message to them to loosen and unwind. Use your control word to get rid of all the tension that you can. Relax… the muscles in your feet. Send a message to those muscles to loosen and unwind. Let go of all the tension right down to the tips of your toes.*

Scanning Your Body for Residual Tension

You have been teaching your body and muscles to loosen and relax. Now scan your body for any muscle tension that remains. If you find tension in a muscle, send a message to it to loosen and relax. If you think about relaxing that muscle you will be able to do so, even if it's just a little more.

Begin by scanning and relaxing your toes, feet and calves. Relax all the muscles of your lower legs from your knees to the tips of your toes.

Relax your thighs and hips. Relax all the muscles of your lower body. Relax your hips and thighs... knees and calves... feet and toes.

Relax the muscles of your stomach and the muscles of your chest. Every time you breathe out, think your control word. Every time you breathe out... so gently... so easily... so calmly. Every time you breathe out, use your control word to help you relax further and further, and feel better and better.

As you focus on your control word, continue to relax... the muscles in your shoulders and in your neck. Relax the muscles of your face. Relax your forehead and brow. Your eyes are so lightly and comfortably closed. Relax your jaws and cheeks and mouth. Feel the relaxation in your upper arms, forearms and hands, right down to your fingertips.

You may continue relaxing like this for a few more moments or as long as you like. Focus on your control word... use it to help yourself relax and feel better and better. Practice relaxing like this as often as you like, so that it works better and better each time you do. That means each time you practice relaxing, you relax yourself faster and faster to help yourself feel better and better... as relaxed and good as you need. Whenever you think your control word, your body will remember these good feelings of calmness and relaxation. Whenever you think your control word, you will be able to create the feelings of calmness and relaxation that you need.

Now, when you're ready, open your eyes, stretch, be wide wake, feel good, comfortable, relaxed and refreshed.

Don't forget to rate how tense you feel now on the scale of 1 (very little tension) to 10 (the most tension you have ever felt).

> ***My level of tension right now is*** _____ (1 to 10)

appendix

NUMBER GRID CONCENTRATION TASK

23	12	07	15	62	93	82	36	21	37
31	50	59	28	46	30	25	48	69	76
45	49	73	19	02	67	04	77	41	64
26	29	88	03	34	13	91	38	56	86
87	83	98	35	43	44	24	39	40	20
90	96	89	80	42	94	53	05	55	57
61	75	65	32	22	11	08	10	27	09
00	99	95	85	14	01	74	60	92	31
18	51	71	54	63	17	79	33	70	52
97	78	58	84	06	16	66	72	47	68

References

Adelson, R. (2005). The Power of Potent Steroids. APA Monitor, 36, (7), 20-22.

Afremow, James (2008). Personal communication. Health and Sport Psychology Clinic, Arizona State University.

Air, Land, Sea Application Center. (2003). Survival, Evasion, Recovery: Multi-service Procedures for Survival, Evasion, Recovery – Army, Marine Corps, Navy, Air Force. Army Knowledge Online. www.usarmy.mil.

Alexander, J., Groller, R., & Morris, J. (1990). The Warrior's Edge. NY: William Morrow.

Anderson,W., Swenson, D. & Clay, D. (1995). Stress Management for Law Enforcement Officers. Englewood Cliffs, NJ: Prentice Hall.

Andreas, S., & Faulkner, C. (1994). NLP: The New Technology of Achievement. New York: Harper

Anthes, E. (2008). Six ways to boost brainpower. Scientific American Mind, 20, (1), 6-63

Artwohl, A., & Christensen, L. (1997). Deadly Force Encounters: What Cops Need to Know to Mentally and Physically Prepare For and Survive a Gunfight. Boulder: Paladin Press.

Asken, M. (2006). Mindsighting: Training psychological skills for maximal shooting performance. The Firearms Instructor, 40, 53-55.

Asken, M. (2006). Tactical performance imagery: What you see (hear, feel, taste and smell) is what you get. The Tactical Edge, (24 (1), 45-48.

Asken, M. (2006). Avoiding the "Stale Beer Effect": Psychological Techniques to aid the Retention of Learned Skills. The FireArms Instructor, 40, 15-17.

Asken, M. (2005). MindSighting: Mental Toughness Skills for Police Officers in High Stress Situations. Camp Hill, PA: www.mindsighting.com.

Asken, M. (1993). PsycheResponse: Psychological Skills for Optimal Performance by Emergency Responders. Englewood Cliffs, NJ: Brady-Prentice-Hall.

Asken, M. (1990). Dying to Win: Preventing Drug Abuse in Sport. Minneapolis, MN: Community Interventios, Inc.

Asken, M., Murphy, E., Banis, G., & Colon, E. (2008) Does scenario training for police negotiators create the stress and realism of reality. The Crisis Negotiator, In Press

Asken, M, & Yunk, J. (2006), Study suggests need for psychological skills/ mental toughness training as part of undercover narcotics training scenarios. Vice News, Spring, Eastern States Vice Investigators Association, Pine Grove Mills, PA.

Asken, M. & Bascome, D. (2000). PsychKicks: Sport Psychology Skills for Super Soccer. Camp Hill, Pa: Next Level Consulting.

Asken, M., & Goodling, M. (1986). The use of sport psychology techniques in rehabilitation medicine: A Pilot Study – Case Report. *International Journal of Sport
Psychology*, 17, 156-161.

Asken, M., Vonk, K., & Sterland, T. (2009). Heart rate variability and police performance: The next evolution in training? www.policeone.com. 03-05-09

Baddely, A. (1972). Selective attention and performance in dangerous environments. British Journal of Psychiatry, 63, 537-546.

Barnard, J., et al., (1973). Response to sudden strenuous exercise in healthy men. Circulation, 48, 936-942.

Beckett, A. (2008).The thoughts of Marcus Wynne. Dennis Martin Forums www.self-potection.com.

Begley, S. (2007). What the Beatles gave science. Newsweek, November, 19, p.59.

Behavioral Physiology Institute (2008). CapnoLearningTM. Boulder, CO: www.bp.edu.

Warrior Mindset

Benson, H. (1975). The Relaxation Response. New York: Morrow

Billet, E., et al. (2001). British Journal of Sports Medicine, 35, 342. Cited by www.psychiatrymatters.com. Chemical behind exercise lift discovered.

Blum, L. (2004) Force under Pressure. New York, NY: Lantern Books.

Brady, J. (2007). Why Marines Fight. New York: Thomas Dunne.

Carey, C. (2004). The neurobiology of the placebo effect: A review. http://staff.washington.edu/ccarey/placebo

Carlson, T. (2000). Leadership and Management: Naval Reserve Officer Training Corps. Boston: Pearson Custom Publishing.

Carlstedt, R. (2004). Critical Moments During Competition. NY: Psychology Press, Taylor & Francis.

Carmichael, M. (2007). Stronger, faster, smarter. Newsweek, March 26, 38-46.

Castenada, B., & Gray, R. (2007). Effect of focus of attention in baseball batting performance in players of different skills levels. Journal of Sport and Exercise Psychology, 29, 60-77.

Castro, C. (2007). 8 Tough Facts About Combat and What Soldiers Can Do to Help Themselves and Their Buddies. Land Combat Team, Walter Reed Army Institute of Research (WRAIR) www.battlemind.org.

Castro, C. (2006). Military courage. In T. Britt, C. Castro, & A. Adler (Eds.). Military Life: The Psychology of Serving in Peace and Combat. Volume IV: Military Culture, 60-78.

Christensen, L. (2008). Surviving a School Shooting: A Plan of Action for Parents, Teachers, and Students. Boulder, CO: Paladin Press, In Press.

Christensen, L. (2004) Timing in the Martial Arts: Your guide to Winning in the Street and in the Ring. Santa Fe, NM: Turtle Press.

Christensen, L. (Ed.) (2004). Warriors: On Living with Courage, Discipline and Honor. Boulder, CO: Paladin Press.

Christensen, L. (2002) Crouching Tiger: Taming the Warrior Within. Santa Fe, NM: Turtle Press.

Christensen, L. (1999). The Mental Edge Revised. El Dorado, AZ: Desert Publications.

Clark, L. (1960). Effects of mental practice on the development of a certain motor skill. Research Quarterly, 31, 560-569.

Cohen, W. (1998). The Stuff of Heroes: The Eight Universal Laws of Leadership. Atlanta: Longstreet.

Cole, B., & Seaman, R. (2009). Mental toughness the Navy way. www.mentalgamecoach.com/articles/MentalTougnesstheNavyWay.html. Retrieved 01-28-09.

Coombs, J. (2008). Functional conditioning: Part 2. The Firearms Instructor, 43, 10-12.

Cromie, W. (2002). Meditation changes temperatures: Mind controls body in extreme experiments. Harvard University Gazette, April 18, www.hno.harvard.edu/gazette/2002/04.18/09-tummo.html

Csikszentmihalyi, M. (1990). Flow: The Psychology of Optimal Experience. New York: Harper.

Cumming, J., Olphin, T., et al., (2007). Self-reported psychological states and physiological responses to different types of motivational general imagery. Journal of Sport and Exercise Psychology, 29, 629-644.

DeBecker, G., Taylor, & Marquart, J.(In press, 2008). Just Two Seconds: Using Time and Space to Defeat Assassins.

DeBecker, G. (1997). The Gift of Fear. New York: Dell Publishing.

De Los Rios (2007). Sweat Spot. ESPN, The Magazine, March 26, 2007.

Department of the Army (2002). Field Manual 3-05.70. Washington, D.C.

Deschaumes-Molinaro, C., Dittmar, A., & Vernet-Maury, E. (1992). Autonomic nervous system response patterns correlate with mental imagery. Physiological Behavior, 51 (5), 1021-1027

Dingfelder, S. (2007). Your brain on video games. Monitor on Psychology, 38, (2), 20-21.

DiNasio, J. (2006). The law of exercise specificity: Is your workout really going to help you in the field? Retrieved 07-25-2006 from www.policeone.com.

Dixon, N. (1976). On the Psychology of Military Incompetence. NY: Basic Books.

Doss, W. (1994). Train to Win. 1st Books Library.

Driskell, J., ...as, E., & Johnston, J. (2006). Decision making and performance under stress. In T. Britt, C. Castro, & A. Adler (Eds.). Military Life: The Psychology of Serving in Peace and Combat. Volume I: Military Performance, 128-154.

Drury, R. (2008). Navy SEALS strength and courage: Bravery (and how to master it). Men's Health, www.menshealth.com, 03-15-08.

Drury, R. (1979). My Secret War. Fallbrook, CA: Aero Publishers, Inc.

Endsley, M. (2006). Expertise and situation awareness. In K. Ericsson, N. Charness, P. Feltovich, &. R. Hoffman, (Eds.). The Cambridge Handbook of Expertise and Expert Performance. Cambridge, England: Cambridge University Press.

Epstein, M. (1980). The relationship of mental imagery and mental rehearsal to a motor task. Journal of Sport Psychology, 2, 211-220.

Etter, D.A., personal communication, November, 2007.

Etter, D.A. (2007) The worst and best 18 months. American Legion Magazine, Nov., 26-32.

Farley, K. & Curry, S. (1994). Get Motivated! Daily Psych-Ups. New York: Fireside.

Feigley, D. (1989). Coping with fear in high-level gymnastics. Technique, Apr/June, 4-9.

Feltovich, P., Prietula, M., & Ericsson, K. (2006). Studies of expertise from psychological perspectives. In K. Ericsson, N. Charness, P. Feltovich, &. R. Hoffman, (Eds.). The Cambridge Handbook of Expertise and Expert Performance. Cambridge, England: Cambridge University Press.

Fenz, W., & Epstein, S. (1967). Gradients of physiological arousal in parachutists as a function of an approaching jump. Psychosomatic Medicine, 29 (1), 33-51.

Ferrell, M., Beach, R., Szeverneyi, N. (2006). An fMRI analysis of neural activity during perceived zone-state performance. Journal of Sport and Exercise Psychology, 28, 421-433.

Fiore, S., & Salas, E. (Eds.), (2008). Special issue: Cognition, Competition and Coordination: Understanding Expertise in Sports and its Relevance to Learning and Performance in the Military. Military Psychology, 20 (Supplement 1).

Force Science News (2008). An officer's down in a kill zone that's still hot. What should you do? PoliceOne.com News, www.policeone.com., 11-13-2008.

Force Science Research Center (2006). Cops give weaker commands in violent Encounters, ground-breaking new FSRC studies reveal. Retrieved 09-26-2006, www.policeone.com.

Force Science Research Center (2007). What promotes peak performance in lethal-force conflicts? Force Science News Transmission # 75, 06-26-2007, info@forcesciencenew.com.

Frederickson, B., & Losada, M. (2006). Positive affect and the complex dynamics of human flourishing. *American Psychologist.* 60 (7), 678-686.

Frick, Nathaniel (2005). One Bullet Away: The Making of a Marine Officer. Boston: Houghton Mifflin.

Friedl, K., & Penetar, D. (2008).Resilience and survival in extreme environments. In Lukey, B., & Tepe, V. (eds.) Biobehavioral Resilience to Stress. Boca Raton, FL: CRC Press.

Garcia, R. (1989). Field study of side handle baton techniques. PPCT Research Publications, Millstadt, Il.

Gauron, E. (1984). Mental Training for Peak Performance. Lansing, NY: Sport Science Assoc.

Ghannam, C. (2007, 2008). Personal Communication. www.sarksecurities.com.

Giduck, J. (2008). The reality of hand to hand combat II: Psychological aspect and benefit. SWAT Digest, 1st Edition 2008, 34-38.

Giduck, J. (2005). Terror at Beslan: A Russian Tragedy With Lessons for America's Schools. Golden, CO: Archangel Group.

Gladwell, M. (2000). The Tipping Point. Boston: Little, Brown & Company.

Gibson, L. (2006). Nightmares: A national center for PTSD fact sheet. www.ncptsd.va.gov.

Goldfried, M., & Davison, G. (1976). Clinical Behavior Therapy. NY: Holt, Rinehart & Winston.

Goleman, D. (1997). Emotional Intelligence. New York: Bantam.

Gonzales, L. (2003). Deep Survival: Who Lives, Who Dies, and Why. NY: W.W. Norton.

Gray, J. (2004). Integration of emotion and cognitive control. Current Directions in Psychological Science, 13.

Green, S., & Bavelier, D. (2006). Effect of action video games on the spatial distribution of visual attention. Journal of Experimental Psychology: Human perception and performance, 32,(6), 1465-1478.

Greist, J., Eischens, R., Klein, M., & Faris, J. (1979). Anti-depressant running. Psychiatric Annals, 9 (3), 23-33.

Griffin, M, & Cooper, C. (2006). Using near-infrared spectroscopy to "measure" imagery. NASPSPA Abstracts 2006, Journal of Sport and Exercise Psychology, 28, 576-577.

Grillon, C., Ameli, R., et al. (1993). Measuring the time course of anticipatory anxiety using the fear potentiated startle reflex. Psychophysiology, 30, (4), 340-346.

Grossman, D., & Degaetano, G. (1999). Stop Teaching Our Kids to Kill: A Call to Action Against TV, Movie and Video Game Violence. New York: Crown.

Grossman, D. (1995). On Killing: The Psychological Cost of Learning to Kill in War and Society. New York: Little, Brown & Company.

Grossman, D. (2004). On Combat: The Psychology and Physiology of Deadly Conflict in War and Peace. Millstadt, Il: PPCT Publications.

Grossman, D. www.killology.com

Grossman, D. (2005). Personal Communication.

Grunow, C. (2006). Advising Iraqis: Building the Iraqi Army. Military Review, July-August, 8-17.

Guillot, A. Collet, C., Molinaro, CV. & Dittmar, A. (2004). Expertise and peripheral autonomic activity during the preparation phase in shooting events. Perceptual and Motor Skills, 98 (2), 371-381.

Hancock, P. (2009). Performance on the very edge. Military Psychology, 21 (Suppl. I), S68-S64.

Hancock, P., & Szalma, J. (2008). Stress and performance. In P. hancock & J. Szalma (Eds.). Performance Under Stress. Hampshire, England: Ashgate Publishing Limited.

Harris, W., Hancock,P., & Harris, S. (2005). Information processing changes following extended stress. Military Psychology, 7, (2), 115-127.

Hasnain, Q. (1967). Psychology for the Fighting Man. Dehra Dun: EBD Publishing.

Hawkins, J. (2004). On Intelligence. New York: Henry Holt and Company

Heim, C. & Schmidtbleicher, D. (2003). The risk of unintentional firearm discharge. Book of Abstracts for the ECSS Congress, 197.

Heim, C., Schmidtbleicher, D. & Niebergall, E. (In Press, 2006). Towards an understanding of involuntary firearms discharges – possible risks and implications for training. Policing: An International Journal of Police Strategies and Management.

Heim, C., Niebergall, E., & Schmidtbleicher, D. (2008). Involuntary firearms discharge –Does the finger obey the brain? The Firearms Instructor, 43, 34-39.

Helin, P., Sihvonen, T., & Hanninen, O. (1987). Timing of the triggering action of shooting in relation to the cardiac Cycle. British Journal of Sports Medicine, 21 (1), 33-36.

Hill, N., and Schneider, W. (2006). Brain changes in the development of expertise: Neuroanatomical and neurophysiological evidence about skill-based adaptations. In K. Ericsson, N. Charness, P. Feltovich, &. R. Hoffman, (Eds.). The Cambridge Handbook of Expertise and Expert Performance. Cambridge, England: Cambridge University Press.

Hochheim, W. (2008). Combative applications. ILEETA Use of Force Journal, 8, (1), January-March, 3-5.

Hoiberg, A. (1985). Cardiovascular disease among U.S. Navy pilots. Aviation, Space and Environmental Medicine, 56, (5), 397-402.

Holmstedt, K. (2007). Band of Sisters: American Women at War in Iraq. Mechanicsburg, PA: Stackpole Books.

Holton, B. (1995). Leadership Lessons of Ulysses S. Grant. New York: Grammercy.

Honig, A., & Lewinski, W. (2008). A survey of the research on human factors related to lethal force encounters: Implications for law enforcement training, tactics and testimony. Law Enforcement Executive Forum, 8, (4), 129-151.

Honig, A. & Sultan, S. (2004). Reactions and resilience under fire: What an officer can expect. The Police Chief, 71, (12). www.policechief.org.

Hunter, S. (1993). Point of Impact. New York: Bantam.

Jadick, R. (2007). On Call In Hell: A Doctor's Iraq War Story. New York: NAL.

Janelle, C., & Hatfield, B. (2008). Visual attention and brain processes that underlie expert performance: Implications for sport and military psychology. Military Psychology, 20 (Suppl. 1), S39-S69.

Janelle, C., Hillman, C. et al. (2000) Expertise differences in cortical activation and gaze Behavior during rifle shooting. Journal of Sport & Exercise Psychology, 22(2) 167-182

Janis, I. (1973). Victims of Groupthink: A Psychological Study of Foreign Policy Decisions and Fiascos. Boston: Houghton-Mifflin.

Jany, E. personal communication, October, 2007.

Jacobson, E. (1974). Progressive Relaxation. Chicago: University of Chicago, Midway Reprint.

Johnson, A., & Proctor, R. (2004). Attention: Theory and Practice. Thousand Oaks, CA: Sage.

Kavanagh, J. (2005). Stress and Performance: A Review of the Literature and Its Applicability to the Military. Santa Monica, CA: Rand Corporation.

Keyes, M. (1996). Mental Training for Shotgun Sports. Auburn, Ca: Furthern Adventures, Inc.

Klinger, D. (2004). Into the Kill Zone: A Cop's Eye View of Deadly Force. San Francisco: Jossey-Bass.

Koster, O. (2007). 'Incredible Hulk' royal marine lifts two-ton truck off drowning comrade during gun battle in Afgahnistan. www.dailymail.co.uk.

Kubistant, T. (1988). Mind Pump: The Psychology of Body Building. Champaign, Il: Leisure Books/ Human Kinetics.

Krakow, B., et al. (2001). Imagery rehearsal therapy for chronic nightmares in sexual assault survivors with post-traumatic stress disorder: A randomized controlled trial. Journal of the American Medical Association, 286 (5), 537-545.

Landers, D. & Daniels, F. (1985). Psychophysiological assessment and biofeedback: Applications for athletes in closed skill sports. Chapter prepared for J. Sandweiss & S. Wolf (Eds.). Biofeedback and Sports Science, NY: Plenum.

Leach, J. (1994). Survival Psychology. Washington Square, NY: New York University Press.

Levitt, S. & Gutin, B. (1971). Multiple choice reaction time and movement during physical exertion. Research Quarterly, 42.

Levitt, S. (1972) The effects of exercise induced activation upon simple, two-choice and five-choice reaction time and movement time. Doctoral Dissertation.

Lepp, D. (2004). Combat psychology: An interview with Scott Sonnon. www.circularstrengthmag.com/28/sonnon3.html.

Lichtenstein, K. (1988). Clinical Relaxation Strategies. New York: John Wiley.

Lieberman, H., Bathalon, G., et al., (2005). The fog of war: Decrements in cognitive performance and mood associated with combat-like stress. Aviation, Space Environmental Med, Jul, 76 (7 suppl) C7-14.

Lindlaw, S., & Mendoza, M. (2006). Why Pat Tillman died remains unanswered. Associated Press, Harrisburg Patriot-News, 11-10-2006.

Lindlaw, S., & Mendoza, M. (2006). AP investigation into Pat Tillman's death in Afghanistan uncovers some startling findings. www.jacksonville.com.

Machowicz, R. (2002). Unleash the Warrior Within. New York: Marlowe.

Magill, R. (2007). Motor Learning and Control: Concepts and Applications. New York: McGraw-Hill.

Mansfield, S. (2005). The Faith of the American Soldier. New York: Jeremy Tarcher/Penguin.

Martin, J. (2006). Get Selected for Special Forces. Yuma, AZ: Warrior-Mentor Press.

Maurer, H., & Munzert, J. (2005). Can "choking under pressure" be explained by an internal focus of attention? A study with expert basketball players. NASPSPA Abstracts, Journal of Sport & Exercise Psychology, S14.

Maxwell, J. (2001). The 17 Indisputable Laws of Teamwork. Nashville: Thomas Nelson.

McClung, M. & Collins, D. (2007). "Because I know it will": Placebo effects of an ergogenic aid on athletic performance. Journal of Sport & Exercise Psychology, 29, 382-394.

McCraty, R., Tomasino, D., Atkinson, M., & Sundram, J. (1999). Impact of Heartmath self-management skills program on physiological and psychological stress in police officers. Boulder Creek, CO: Heartmath Research Center, Institute of Heartmath, Publication No. 99-075. www.heartmath.org/research/reasearch-papers/police/police-study.pdf.

McDonald, J. (2006). Gold Medal Policing. NY: Sloan Associates.

McMains, M., & Mullins, W. (2001). Crisis Negotiations: Managing Critical Incidents and Hostage Situations In Law Enforcement And Corrections, 2nd Ed., Cincinnati, Oh: Anderson Publishing Co.

Meichenbaum, D. (1985). Stress Inoculation Training. Elmsford, NY: Pergamon Press.

Meichenbaum, D. & Turk, D. (1976). The cognitive-behavioral management of anxiety, anger, pain. In P. Davidson (Ed.). The Behavioral Management of Anxiety, Depression and Pain. New York: Bruner-Mazel.

Miller, L. (2007). Mettle: Mental toughness training for law enforcement. Flushing, NY:Looseleaf Law Publications.

Mills, K. (2005). Disciplined Attention: How To Improve Your Visual Attention When You Drive. Chapel Hill, NC: Profile Press.

Mitchell, L., & Flin, R. (2007). Shooting decisions by police firearms officers. Journal of Cognitive Engineering and Decision Making, 1 (4), 375-390.

Moran, A. (1996). The Psychology of Concentration in Sport Performers: A Cognitive Analysis. East Sussex, UK: Psychology Pres, Taylor & Francis.

Morris, T., Spittle, M., & Watt, A. (2005). Imagery In Sport. Champaign, Ill: Human Kinetics.

Moseley, J., O'Malley, K., Petersen, N., et al (2002). A controlled trial of arthroscopic knee surgery for osteoarthritis of the knee. New England Journal of Medicine, 347 (2), 81-88.

Mullins, W. (2003). The effects of caffeine and caffeine withdrawal/deprivation on hostage negotiator performance. Journal of Police Crisis Negotiations, 3, (2), 39- 60.

Mummert, D., & Furley, P. (2007). "I spy with my little eye": Breadth of attention, inattentional blindness and tactical decision making in team sports. Journal of Sport and Exercise Psychology, 29, 365-381.

Murphy, S. (1996). The Achievement Zone. New York: Putnam.

Murphy, S. (2005). Imagery: Inner theater becomes reality. In S. Murphy (ed.) The Sport Psych Handbook. Champaign, Il: Human Kinetics.

Murray, K. (2004). Training at the Speed of Life: The Definitive Textbook for Military and Law Enforcement Reality Based Training. Gotha, Fl: Armiger Publications.

Muth, E., Kruse, A., Hoover, A., & Schmorrow, D. (2006). Augmented cognition: Aiding the soldier in high and low workload environments through closed loop human-machine interactions. In T. Britt, C. Castro, & A. Adler (Eds.). Military Life: The Psychology of Serving in Peace and Combat. Volume I: Military Performance, 108.

Nadelson, T. (2005). Trained to Kill: Soldiers at War. Baltimore, MD: The Johns Hopkins Press.

Nelson, M. (2006). Yoga trend catching on with soldiers. http://news.yahoo.com.

Nideffer, R. (1985). Athlete's Guide to Mental Training. Champaign, Il:
Human Kinetics.

Nideffer, R., & Sharpe, R. (1978). Attention Control Training: How to Get Control
of Your Mind Through Total Concentration. New York: WideView Books.

Nowicki, D. (1994). Gold Medal Mental Workout for Combat Sports.
Island Pond, VT: Stadion.

Oxendine, J. (1970). Emotional arousal and motor performance. Quest, 13, 23-32.
Perry, C. (2005). Concentration: Focus under pressure. In S. Murphy (Ed.).
Sport Psych Handbook. Champaign, Il: Human Kinetics.

Peynircioglu, Z. (2000). Improvement strategies in free-throw shooting and
grip-strength tasks. Journal of General Psychology, (Apr). www.findarticles.com.

Pinizzotto, A., Davis, E., & Miller, C. III. (2006). Violent Encounters: A Study of
Felonious Assaults on Our Nation's Law Officers. Washington, DC: U.S. Department
of Justice, FederalBureau of Investigation, Publication #0383.

Plunkett, M. (2008). Put your thoughts into words. www.policeone.com, 03-14-08

Pope, A., & Prinzel, L. (no date). Recreation Embedded State Tuning for Optimal
Readiness and Effectiveness (RESTORE). Hampton, VA: Research & Technology
Directorate, NASA Langley Research Center: MS152; D-318.

Price, M. (2008). Testing makes perfect, finds memory retrieval research.
APA Monitor on Psychology, 39, (6), 11.

Prinzel, L., Pope, A., & Freeman, F. (2001). Application of physiological self-
regulation and adaptive task allocation techniques for controlling operator
hazardous states of awareness. Hampton, VA: NASA TM 2001-211015.

Rachman, S. (1990). Fear and Courage. NY: WH Freeman.

Rahman, M. (2007a). A Discourse on Law Enforcement and Psychobehaviors:
Informing Design Displays from Displays in Ethology to High Velocity Human
Factors (Tech Report DHF-KFM-1) Plantation, Fl: Design International, Motorola.
(Copies may be obtained from the author at: moin.rahman@motorola.com.)

Rahman, M. (2007b). High velocity human factors: Human factors of mission critical domains in non-equilibrium. In Proceedings of the Human Factors and Ergonomics Society 51st Annual Meeting (pp.273-277), Santa Monica, CA: Human Factors and Ergonomics Society.

Rahman citing Orasanu, J., & Conolly, T. (1993). The reinvention of decision-making. In G. Klein, J. Orasanu, R. Calderwood, & C. Zsambok (Eds.). Decision making in Action: Models and Methods. Norwood, NJ: Ablex.

Rahman, M. (2007). Why do wars produce My Lai's and Hadithas? Unpublished paper and personal communication.

Ramsey, R. Cumming, J., et al., (2006). Mental imagery inflates performance expectations but not actual performance of a novel and challenging motor task. NASPSPA Abstracts 2006. Journal of Sport and Exercise and Psychology, 28, S148-149.

Reiter, B. (2007). Morten Andersen … still kicking. Sports Illustrated, October 1, 2007, 20-21.

Richardson,, F. (1978). Fighting Spirit: A Study of Psychological Factors in War. NY: Crane, Russak, & Company.

Rogers, T., & Landers, D. (2005). Mediating effects of peripheral vision in the life event stress/athletic injury relationship. Journal of Sport and Exercise Psychology, 27, 271-288.

Remsberg, C. (1986). The Tactical Edge. Northbrook, Ill: Calibre Press.

Rouse, E. www.psywarrior.com/quotes. Retrieved 04-2008.

Ruge, R. (2005) Preparing the mind for battle. American Police Beat. October, 26.

Ruge, R. (2005). The Warrior's Mantra. Fort Lee, NJ: Barricade Books.

Salas, E., Priest, H., Wilson, K., & Burke, S. (2006). Scenario-based training: Improving military mission performance and adaptability. In T. Britt, C. Castro, & A. Adler (Eds.). Military Life: The Psychology of Serving in Peace and Combat. Volume I: Military Performance, 33.

Sarason, I., Johnson, J., et al. (1979). Helping police officers to cope with stress: A cognitive-behavioral approach. *American Journal of Community Psychology*, 7, (6), 593-603.

Shalit, B. (1988). The Psychology of Conflict and Combat. NY: Praeger.

Shelton, T. & Mahoney, M. (1978). The content and effect of "psyching up" strategies in weight lifters. *Cognitive Therapy and Research*, 2, 275-284.

Shelyag, V., Glotochkin, A., & Platonov, K. (1972). Military Psychology: A Soviet View. Translated and published under the auspices of the United States Airforce; Washington, DC: US Government Printing Office, Document # 0870-00353.

Sherman, N. (2005). *Stoic Warriors.* New York: Oxford University Press.

Shipley, P., & Baranski, J., (2002). Police officer performance under stress: A pilot study on the effects of visuo-motor behavior rehearsal. International Journal of Stress Management, 9, (2), 71-80.

Siddle, B. (1995). Sharpening the Warrior's Edge. Belleville, Il: PPCT Research Publications.

Siddle, B. (2008). The stress paradox: Understanding how the body's innate programming can inhibit the performance of first responders. The War on Trauma. Supplement to Journal of Emergency Medical Services, October, 28-31.

Siebert, A. (1993). The Survivor Personality. Portland, OR: Practical Psychology Press.

Silbernagel, M., & Short, S. (2006). Athletes' use of imagery during weightlifting. NASPSPA Abstracts 2006, Journal of Sport and Exercise Psychology, 28, S165.

Slade, J., Landers. D., & Martin, P. (2002). Muscular activity during real and imagined movements: A test of inflow explanations. Journal of Sport & Exercise Psychology, 24, 151-167.

Smith, D. (2007). Heart Attacks on duty. Calibrepress.com Newsline, 01-16-07, www.policeone.com

Smith, D. (2006). Psychology and body building. In J. Dosil (Ed.). The Sport Psychologist's Handbook: A Guide for Sport-Specific Performance Enhancement. New York: John Wiley, 618-639.

Solomon, Roger (1990). The Dynamics of Fear in Critical Incidents. Training Key # 399. Alexandria, Virginia: IACP.

Sonnon, S. (2001). Keeping the Edge: Flow State Performance Spiral. Atlanta, GA: AARMACS.

Staal, M., Bolton, A., Yarowish, R. et al., (2008). Cognitive performance and resilience to stress. In Lukey, B., & Tepe, V. (eds.) Biobehavioral Resilience to Stress. Boca Raton, FL: CRC Press.

Starr, L. (1987). Stress inoculation training applied to cardiopulmonary resuscitation. Paper presented at the 95th Annual Convention of the American Psychological Association, New York, NY:

Steffan, G., Bluestein, B., Ogrisseg, J., Doran, A. & Morgan, C. (2006). Code of conduct and the psychology of captivity: Training, coping, and reintegration. In T. Britt, C. Castro, & A. Adler (Eds.). Military Life: The Psychology of Serving in Peace and Combat. Volume I: Military Performance, 83-119.

Stetson, C., Fiesta, M., Eagleman, D. (2007). Does time really slow down during a frightening event? PLoS One, www.plosone.org., December, 12, e1295.

Strozzi-Heckler, R. (2007). In Search of the Warrior Spirit: Teaching Awareness Disciplines to the Military. Berkeley, CA: Blue Snake Books.

Strentz, T. (2006). Psychological Aspects of Crisis Negotiation. Boca Raton, FL: CRC.

Suinn, R. (1985) Imagery rehearsal applications to performance enhancement. The Behavior Therapist, 8 (9), 179-183.

Suinn, R. (1984). Visual-motor behavior rehearsal: The basic technique. Scandinavian Journal of Behavior Therapy, 13, 131-142.

Suinn, R. (1980). Psychology and sport performance: Principles and applications. In R. Suinn (Ed.). Psychology in Sports: Methods and Applications. Minneapolis, Mn: Burgess.

Svoboda, E. (2009). Avoiding the big choke. Scientific American Mind, 20, (1), 36-41.

Sztajnkycer, M. (2008). Risk reduction in officer rescue: A scenario-based observational analysis of medical care. Unpublished paper.

Tennenbaum, G.,Edmonds, W., & Eccles, D. (2008). Emotions, coping strategies, and performance: A conceptual framework for defining affect-related performance zones. Military Psychology, 20, (Suppl. 1), S11-S37.

Tharion, W., Shukitt-Hale, B., et al., (2003). Caffeine effects on marksmanship during high stress military training with 72 hour sleep deprivation. Aviation, Space, & Environmental Medicine, 74 (4), 309-314,

Thomas, E., & Barry, J. (2008). The fight over how to fight. Newsweek, Mar 24, 38-39.

Thompson, M. (2008). America's medicated army. Time Magazine, June 16, 171, (24), 38-42.

Thompson, M., & McCreary, D. (2006). Enhancing mental readiness in military personnel. In T. Britt, C. Castro, & A. Adler (Eds.). Military Life: The Psychology of Serving in Peace and Combat. Volume I: Military Performance, 54-79.

Tremayne, P., & Barry, R. (2001). Elite pistol shooters: physiological patterning of best versus worst shots. International Journal of Psychophysiology, 41, (1), 19-29.

Trotter, J. (2007). High anxiety. Sports Illustrated. October 8, 93-95.

University of Michigan Health System, UMHS Health-E-News (2004). Steroid abuse not just an Olympic problem. www.med.umich.edu/health-e_news., September.

U.S. Army (2005) Recruiting advertisement: Every Position Counts. Special advertising section, ESPN, The Magazine, October 24, 2005.

U.S. Joint Chiefs of Staff (1997). Concept for Joint Operations. Washington, DC: Department of Defense, May.

Vernon, D. & Gruzelier, J. (2003). The effect of training distinct neurofeedback protocols on aspects of cognitive performance. International Journal of Psychophysiology, 47 (1), 75-85. (As cited in Researchers find link between improved memory and the use of neurofeedback. Imperial College London, www.ic.ac.uk.)

Vonk, K. (2007). Police officers and cardiovascular disease. PoliceOne.com.

Vonk, K. (2004). Heart Rate As It Relates to Police Performance Under Stress. Ann Arbor, MI: Ann Arbor Police Department.

Walsh, R. & Shapiro, S. (2006). The meeting of meditative disciplines and western psychology. American Psychologist, 61, (3), 227-239.

Ward, P., Farrow, D., Harris, K., Williams, A., Eccles, D., & Ericsson, K. (2008). Training perceptual-cognitive skills: Can sport psychology research inform military decision training? Military Psychology, 20 (Suppl. 1), S71-S102.

Webb, H., McMinn, D., et al. (2006). Stress hormone responses in firefighters during physical and psychological stress. NASPSPA Abstracts 2006. Journal of Sport and Exercise Psychology, 28, S190.

Wegner, D. (1989). White Bears and Other Unwanted Thoughts. New York: Penguin.

Wells, M. (1988). The human element and air combat. Aerospace Power Journal, (Spring). www.airpower.maxwell.af.mil/airchronicles/apj/apj/88/wells/html.

From Westmoreland, H. (1989). An Examination of Stress Shooting Stances, PPCT Research Publications, Millstadt, Il.

Whetstone, T. (1996). Mental practice enhances recruit police officers acquisition of crtitical psychomotor skills. Police Stress, 19, (1), 19-43.

Wilkison, S. (2005). Officer's winning mindset and calming self-talk saved his life after terrifying ambush. Newsline. Calibre Press, www.calibrepress.com.

Williams, A., Ericsson, K., Ward, P., & Eccles, D. (2008). Research on expertise in sport: Implications for the military. Military Psychology, 20 (Suppl. 1), S123-S145.

Williams, G. (2004). Real world tunnel vision and training.
The FireArms Instructor, 38, 6-9.

Williams, J. (2006). The psychology of combat. www.bugei.com/psychology.html.

Willis, B. (2004). Imagine vs. visualize: More than just semantics.
The FireArms Instructor, 38, 19-23.

Willis, B. (2005). The Power of Words. www.winningmindtraining.com

Wilson, T. (2002). Strangers to Ourselves: Discovering the Adaptive Unconscious.
Cambridge, MA: Belknap Press of Harvard University.

Wingert, P., & Thomas, E. (2006). On call in hell. Newsweek, March 20,
CXLVII, (12), 34-43.

Wisecarver, C., & Tucker, M. (2007). The force science reactionary gap.
Law and Order, 55 (9), 10-14.

Wulf, G. (2007). Attention and Motor Skill Learning. Champaign, Ill:
Human Kinetics Publishers.

Zimbardo, P. (2007) quoted in Out of the mouths of psychologists.
APA Monitor on Psychology, October, 38 (9), 10.

Zimmerman, L. (2008). Force decision-making.
ILEETA Use of Force Journal, 8, (1), 19-21

– Inducing Physiological Relaxation. www.stresseraser.com (2005)

– Time Magazine (2005), 165 (10), May 2.

– www.stresseraser.com

Zakaria, F. (2005). An imperial presidency. Newsweek, 12/19/05, 40.

Warrior Mindset

Photo Credits

Drill Sergeant:
Staff Sergeant William (Liam) O'Connor
Military Police Officer/Senior Drill Instructor
Kilo Company, 3dRTBn, MCRDSD
U.S. Marine Corps, May 1995 –May 2007

Dynamometer:
Tom Black; editor@bigsteel.iwarp.com

Female Medic:
Photo courtesy Law and Order

Matt Hing:
Photo courtesy Matt Hing, M.D.

Operators on platform:
Photo courtesy Patriot3, www.patriot3.com

Prone soldier:
Scottsdale Gun Club, Scottsdale Arizona

Ram Door Breach:
Louisiana State Police

Sighting Officer/Sight Picture:
Trijicon Products, Inc., www.trijicon.com.

SWAT Team on Ladder:
Photo courtesy Law and Order Magazine

Weapon Jam:
Photo courtesy Sergeant Dave Frisk

Epilogue

We close with some final thoughts about Warriors. First, a paraphrase of Kubistant's (1988) description of the Warrior. Then, a stirring poem that captures the nobility, selflessness and humility of our warriors.

From ancient Japan to the frontiers of the Wild West
    existed a type of person who was renowned for his ferocity
    and skill in fighting.
He was also feared and respected for his resourcefulness
    and ingenuity.
He would frequently overcome great odds and accomplish
    the tasks of four men.
He exhibited personal qualities that were envied by even his
    greatest adversaries.
This person was the WARRIOR.

The Warrior was revered for his single-mindedness of purpose
    and commitment to excellence.
Mastery and dedication were his trademarks.
He would endure great hardships to attain his goals and
    accomplish his mission.
However, the Warrior always put his achievements within
    a larger framework.
The Warrior also exhibited a wholeness of living, that at first glance,
    seemed so surprising for one so committed to duty
    and purpose.
The Warrior placed a great emphasis on advancing his culture,
    his family, his art, his spiritual pursuits, and his daily rituals.
The Warrior aimed at achieving a state of completeness from which
    he could contribute to a greater whole.
The ancient Warrior was purposeful, resourceful and even noble.

In many ways, the Warrior was an example of the highest levels
    of mastery and completeness that could be achieved by the
    human species.

The Christmas Poem of Now

The embers glowed softly, and in their dim light,
I gazed round the room and I cherished the sight.
My wife was asleep, her head on my chest,
My daughter beside me, angelic in rest.

Outside the snow fell, a blanket of white,
Transforming the yard to a winter delight.
The sparkling lights in the tree I believe,
Completed the magic that was Christmas Eve.

My eyelids were heavy, my breathing was deep,
Secure and surrounded by love I would sleep.
In perfect contentment, or so it would seem,
So I slumbered, perhaps I started to dream.

The sound wasn't loud, and it wasn't too near,
But I opened my eyes when it tickled my ear.
Perhaps just a cough, I didn't quite know, Then the
Sure sound of footsteps outside in the snow.

My soul gave a tremble, I struggled to hear,
And I crept to the door just to see who was near.
Standing out in the cold and the dark of the night,
A lone figure stood, his face weary and tight.

A soldier, I puzzled, some twenty years old,
Perhaps a Marine, huddled here in the cold.
Alone in the dark, he looked up and smiled,
Standing watch over me, and my wife and my child.

"What are you doing?" I asked without fear,
"Come in this moment, it's freezing out here!
Put down your pack, brush the snow from your sleeve,
You should be at home on a cold Christmas Eve!"

For barely a moment I saw his eyes shift,
Away from the cold and the snow blown in drifts..
To the window that danced with a warm fire's light
Then he sighed and he said "Its really all right,

I'm out here by choice. I'm here every night."

"It's my duty to stand at the front of the line,
That separates you from the darkest of times.
No one had to ask or beg or implore me,

I'm proud to stand here like my fathers before me.
My Gramps died at 'Pearl on a day in December,"
Then he sighed, "That's a Christmas 'Gram always remembers."

My dad stood his watch in the jungles of ' Nam ,'
And now it is my turn and so, here I am.
I've not seen my own son in more than a while,
But my wife sends me pictures, he's sure got her smile.

Then he bent and he carefully pulled from his bag,
The red, white, and blue ... An American flag.
I can live through the cold and the being alone,
Away from my family, my house and my home.

I can stand at my post through the rain and the sleet,
I can sleep in a foxhole with little to eat.
I can carry the weight of killing another,
Or lay down my life with my sister and brother..

Who stand at the front against any and all,
To ensure for all time that this flag will not fall."
"So go back inside," he said, "harbor no fright,
Your family is waiting and I'll be all right."

"But isn't there something I can do, at the least,
"Give you money," I asked, "or prepare you a feast?
It seems all too little for all that you've done,
For being away from your wife and your son."

Then his eye welled a tear that held no regret,
"Just tell us you love us, and never forget.
To fight for our rights back at home while we're gone,
To stand your own watch, no matter how long.

For when we come home, either standing or dead,
To know you remember we fought and we bled.
Is payment enough, and with that we will trust,
That we mattered to you as you mattered to us."

(author unknown)

About the Authors

Dr. Michael Asken

Dr. Michael Asken is the psychologist for the Pennsylvania State Police where he is involved with selection and training of Troopers. He functions as the psychologist for the PSP Special Emergency Response Team for both the tactical operators and crisis negotiators. He is involved with cadet performance issues at the Pennsylvania State Police Academy.

He is on the Editorial Board of the The FireArms Instructor. He has written articles for PoliceOne.com., SWAT Digest, The Crisis Negotiator, The Tactical Edge, Law Officer, The Bulletin of the Pennsylvania Chiefs of Police, and the FireArms Instructor.

Mike is an instructor for Top Gun undercover narcotics agent training. He has consulted with and/or provided training for the National Tactical Officers' Association, Eastern States Vice Investigators Association, the International Association of Law Enforcement Firearms Instructors, the New England Crisis Negotiator's Association, the International Association of Chiefs of Police, the Pennsylvania Attorney General's Agents, the Pennsylvania Tactical Officers' Association, the Naval ROTC Battalion at Villanova University, the United States Postal Inspection Service, the FBI, the United States Army War College and Naval Special Warfare Group.

Mike holds a B.A. degree in Social & Behavioral Sciences from the Johns Hopkins University. He completed his doctoral degree in Clinical Psychology with a minor in Medical Psychology at West Virginia University and served his internship at the East Orange (New Jersey) Veterans' Administration Hospital.

In relation to human performance, Mike is a Fellow of the Division of Sport and Exercise Psychology of the American Psychological Association. He taught the sport psychology course at Lebanon Valley College where he was awarded the Nevelyn Knisely Award for Inspired Teaching. He was involved in training physicians, intensive care nurses, neonatal intensive care nurses and nurse anesthetists for twenty-five years.

Mike has worked on maximizing performance with athletes at the youth, high school, collegiate and professional levels. He was the sport psychologist for two professional soccer teams, the Hershey Wildcats and the Harrisburg Heat, as well as the semi-pro football team, the Harrisburg Patriots. He is a co-editor of the book: *Sport Psychology: The Psychological Health of the Athlete* and wrote *Dying to Win: Preventing Drug Abuse in Sport*.

Mike was the psychologist consultant to the Camp Hill (Pa.) Fire Department and has worked with other local departments including Harrisburg City. He was an instructor at the Fire Training Academy at Harrisburg Area Community College. He was the Fire Psychology columnist for FireHouse magazine.

Loren W. Christensen

Loren W. Christensen is a Vietnam veteran, a retired police officer with 29 years of law enforcement experience, and a martial artist since 1965. His police experience includes working gang enforcement, street patrol, intelligence, the training division and dignitary protection.

As a martial artist, Loren has earned 11 black belts: 8th dan in karate, 2nd dan in jujitsu, and a 1st dan in arnis. He has starred in seven instructional DVDs.

As a writer, Loren has penned over 40 books and dozens of magazine articles on a variety of subjects. While his target audience is most often what he calls "the warrior community" — martial artists, cops, and soldiers — his writing includes a variety of other subjects for a broader audience, including fitness, nutrition, riots, street prostitution, street gangs, surviving workplace violence and surviving deadly school shootings.

Loren can be contacted through his website at www.lwcbooks.com.

Lt. Col. Dave Grossman

U.S. Army (Ret.) Director
Warrior Science Group
www.killology.com

Lt. Col. Dave Grossman is an internationally recognized scholar, author, soldier, and speaker who is one of the world's foremost experts in the field of human aggression and the roots of violence and violent crime.

Col. Grossman is a West Point psychology professor, Professor of Military Science, and an Army Ranger who has combined his experiences to become the founder of a new field of scientific endeavor, which has been termed "killology." In this new field Col. Grossman has made revolutionary new contributions to our understanding of killing in war, the psychological costs of war, the root causes of the current "virus" of violent crime that is raging around the world, and the process of healing the victims of violence, in war and peace.

He is the author of *On Killing*, which was nominated for a Pulitzer Prize; has been translated into Japanese, Korean, and German; is on the US Marine Corps' recommended reading list; and is required reading at the FBI academy and numerous other academies and colleges. Col. Grossman co-authored with Gloria DeGaetano *Stop Teaching Our Kids to Kill: A Call to Action Against TV, Movie and Video Game Violence*, which has been translated into Norwegian and German, and has received international acclaim. Col. Grossman's most recent book with Loren Christensen is *On Combat*, the highly acclaimed sequel to *On Killing*.

Col. Grossman has been called upon to write the entry on "Aggression and Violence" in the Oxford Companion to American Military History, three entries in the Academic Press Encyclopedia of Violence and numerous entries in scholarly journals, to include the Harvard Journal of Law and Public Policy.

He has presented papers before the national conventions of the American Medical Association, the American Psychiatric Association, the American Psychological Association, and the American Academy of Pediatrics.

He has presented to over 40 different colleges and universities world wide.

He has been an expert witness and consultant in state and Federal courts, to include serving on the prosecution team in UNITED STATES vs. TIMOTHY MCVEIGH.

He helped train mental health professionals after the Jonesboro school shootings, and he was also involved in counseling or court cases in the aftermath of the Paducah, Springfield, and Littleton school shootings.

He has testified before U.S. Senate and Congressional committees and numerous state legislatures, and he and his research have been cited in a national address by the President of the United States.

Col. Grossman is an Airborne Ranger infantry officer, and a prior-service sergeant and paratrooper, with a total of over 23 years experience in leading U.S. soldiers worldwide. He retired from the Army in February 1998 and has devoted himself full-time to teaching, writing, speaking, and research. Today he is the director of the Warrior Science Group, and in the wake of the 9/11 terrorist attacks he is on the road almost 300 days a year, training elite military and law enforcement organizations worldwide about the reality of combat.